Transcultural Research – Heidelberg Studies on Asia and Europe in a Global Context

Series Editors:

Madeleine Herren-Oesch
Axel Michaels
Rudolf G. Wagner

For further volumes:
http://www.springer.com/series/8753

Philipp Wolfgang Stockhammer
Editor

Conceptualizing Cultural Hybridization

A Transdisciplinary Approach

Editor
Dr. Philipp Wolfgang Stockhammer
Institut für Ur- und Frühgeschichte
und Vorderasiatische Archäologie
Marstallhof 4
69117 Heidelberg
Germany
stockhammer@asia-europe.uni-heidelberg.de

ISSN 2191-656X　　　　　　e-ISSN 2191-6578
ISBN 978-3-642-21845-3　　e-ISBN 978-3-642-21846-0
DOI 10.1007/978-3-642-21846-0
Springer Heidelberg Dordrecht London New York

Library of Congress Control Number: 2011937178

© Springer-Verlag Berlin Heidelberg 2012
This work is subject to copyright. All rights are reserved, whether the whole or part of the material is concerned, specifically the rights of translation, reprinting, reuse of illustrations, recitation, broadcasting, reproduction on microfilm or in any other way, and storage in data banks. Duplication of this publication or parts thereof is permitted only under the provisions of the German Copyright Law of September 9, 1965, in its current version, and permission for use must always be obtained from Springer. Violations are liable to prosecution under the German Copyright Law.
The use of general descriptive names, registered names, trademarks, etc. in this publication does not imply, even in the absence of a specific statement, that such names are exempt from the relevant protective laws and regulations and therefore free for general use.

Printed on acid-free paper

Springer is part of Springer Science+Business Media (www.springer.com)

Contents

1 **Questioning Hybridity** 1
  Philipp W. Stockhammer

2 **Cultural Hybridity: Between Metaphor and Empiricism** 5
  Andreas Ackermann
  2.1 Introduction 5
  2.2 Situating Hybridity 6
    2.2.1 Hybridity in Anthropology, Sociology and History 7
    2.2.2 Postcolonial Concepts of Hybridity 11
  2.3 Metaphors of Hybridity 14
    2.3.1 Borrowing 15
    2.3.2 Mixing 15
    2.3.3 Translating 16
  2.4 Researching Hybridity 17
    2.4.1 Varieties of Object 18
    2.4.2 Varieties of Situation 19
    2.4.3 Varieties of Response 20
  2.5 Concluding Remarks 22
  References 23

3 **Circulating Objects and the Power of Hybridization as a Localizing Strategy** 27
  Hans Peter Hahn
  3.1 Introduction 27
  3.2 The Ambivalence of Globalization Phenomena 29
  3.3 Hybridity and the Reformulation of the Concept of Culture
      in the Era of Globalization 34
  3.4 Hybrid Objects Reconsidered 37
  3.5 Conclusion 39
  References 39

4	**Conceptualizing Cultural Hybridization in Archaeology**	43
	Philipp W. Stockhammer	
	4.1 Introduction	43
	4.2 Potential and Limitations of Archaeological Sources	44
	4.3 "Hybridization" in Postcolonial Studies	45
	4.4 Terminological Preoccupations	46
	4.5 Developing a Concept of Cultural Entanglement	47
	4.6 Applying the Concept to the Archaeological Evidence	51
	References	56
5	**One World Is Not Enough: The Transformative Potential of Intercultural Exchange in Prehistoric Societies**	59
	Joseph Maran	
	5.1 The Long-Lasting Impact of Culture-Historical Ethnography	59
	5.2 Cultural Hybridity – A Useful Concept for Archaeology?	61
	5.3 Imagined Worlds	62
	References	64
6	**Adjusting the Image – Processes of Hybridization in Visual Culture: A Perspective from Early Christian and Byzantine Archaeology**	67
	Ute Verstegen	
	6.1 An Example of Iconophobic Activity Without Repair: The Church at Kursi (Palaestina Secunda, Today Israel)	69
	6.2 An Example of Iconophobic Activity of Damage and Repair: The Church of Saint Stephen at Umm er-Rasas (Arabia, Today Jordan)	72
	6.3 Early Christian Critique of Images	80
	6.4 Muslim Attitudes Towards Images	82
	6.5 The Emergence of a Hybrid Visual Culture	84
	6.6 Discussing Historical Visual Cultures in the Context of the Actual Discourse of Hybridity	88
	References	90
7	**Transfer of German Human Resource Management Practices: Replication, Localization, Hybridization**	95
	Torsten M. Kühlmann	
	7.1 Approaches to the Transfer of Management Practices to Foreign Subsidiaries	96
	7.2 Replication	96
	7.3 Localization	97
	7.4 Hybridization	97
	7.5 Transferring HRM Practices from German Headquarters to Chinese Subsidiaries	98

		7.6	Methods	100
			7.6.1 Data Collection and Sample	100
			7.6.2 Measures	100
		7.7	Results	101
		7.8	Discussion	102
		References		104

8 From Comparative Politics to Cultural Flow: The *Hybrid* State, and Resilience of the Political System in India 107
Subrata K. Mitra
  8.1 Introduction 107
  8.2 Comparative Politics of the Indian State: Analysing a Hybrid Reality Through Pure Categories 109
  8.3 The Post-colonial Condition and Hybrid State-Making 110
  8.4 Legitimising Power Through Accommodation and Hybridisation 113
  8.5 Genealogy of the Post-colonial State: The Conflation of Modernity and Tradition in Gandhi's *Satyagraha* 115
  8.6 The Hybrid Post-colonial State as Both Structure *and* Agency 117
    8.6.1 Ontology of the State: Individualist and Communitarian 118
    8.6.2 The Congress "System": Bridging Colonial Rule and Competitive Politics 119
    8.6.3 The Economy: Modern, Traditional, Liberal, Socialist and Gandhian, All at the Same Time 119
    8.6.4 Self Rule and Shared Rule: Combining Cultural Diversity and the Federal Structure 121
    8.6.5 Indian Personal Law: Conflating the Secular State and Sacred Beliefs 122
    8.6.6 The Modern State and Cultural Diversity: India's "Three Language Formula" 123
    8.6.7 Social Hierarchy and Rational Bureaucracy 123
    8.6.8 Public Buildings and Images of the Hybrid State 124
  8.7 Conclusion: Hybrid Modernity as a Solution to Post-colonial Legitimacy Deficit 126
  References 130

9 Hybridization in Language 133
Christina Sanchez-Stockhammer
  9.1 Is Hybridisation Hybrid? 133
  9.2 Hybridity and Hybridization in Language 135
    9.2.1 The Level of Speech Sounds 136
    9.2.2 The Level of Words: Morphemes and Words 137
    9.2.3 The Level of Fixed Constructions: Collocations and Idioms 143

	9.2.4 The Level of Syntax: Phrases, Clauses and Sentences	143
	9.2.5 The Level of Text: Texts, Text Types and Genres	144
	9.2.6 The Level of Individual Languages	145
	9.2.7 The Level of Communication	148
	9.2.8 The Level of Abstraction: Models of Language	152
9.3	Summary and Conclusion	152
	References	154

10 New Zealand English: A History of Hybridization 159
Daniela Wawra

10.1	Introduction	159
10.2	Methods	160
10.3	The Beginnings of New Zealand English as a Variety in Its Own Right	161
10.4	Special Features of the New Zealand Accent Today in Comparison to Received Pronunciation	161
10.5	Theories About the Development of the New Zealand Accent	163
	10.5.1 Lay Theories	163
	10.5.2 Single Origin Theories	163
	10.5.3 Multiple Origin Theories	166
10.6	Theories About the Development of Varieties	166
	10.6.1 Deterministic-Mechanistic Approach	167
	10.6.2 Sociolinguistic Approaches	170
	10.6.3 Cognitive-Biological Approach	170
10.7	Conclusion	171
	References	171

11 From Myths and Symbols to Culture as Text: Hybridity, Literature and American Studies 173
Carsten Schinko

11.1	Preliminary Remarks	173
11.2	American Studies, or the Roads to Hybridity	175
	11.2.1 Genealogies and Changing Self-descriptions	176
	11.2.2 Aesthetic Continuities	179
11.3	The Dislocation of Culture, or Acts of Reading	183
	11.3.1 The Politics of Poststructuralist Postcolonialism	183
	11.3.2 In-Between Politics and Aesthetics	185
	11.3.3 Cultural Difference and the Otherness of Literature	188
	References	193

12 The Agony of the Signified: Towards a Usage-Based Theory of Meaning and Society 195
Remigius Bunia

12.1	Towards a Theory of Communication	197
	12.1.1 Some Remarks on the History of Semiotics	197
	12.1.2 Words Are Things (Signs Versus Ordinary Things)	199

	12.1.3 Mental Signs	202
12.2	Social and Performative Signs	205
	12.2.1 Abstract Signs and Sentences	206
12.3	The Supremacy of Language	208
	12.3.1 Conditions and Modularization	208
	12.3.2 Two Digressive Remarks	211
12.4	Conclusions	212
References	213

Chapter 1
Questioning Hybridity

Philipp W. Stockhammer

Why should we question "hybridity" once again? This term that has been constantly debated since Homi Bhabha published his seminal work *The Location of Culture* in 1994. Especially within the context of globalization, cultural transformations are being increasingly analysed as hybridization processes. Hybridity itself, however, is often treated as a specifically postcolonial phenomenon and discussions have rarely overcome the narrow boundaries within this narrow field of study. In most other disciplines, the terms hybridity and hybridization are used to characterize phenomena which are easily detected as somehow "borderline" but not so easily explained.

The workshop "Conceptualizing Cultural Hybridization – A Transdisciplinary Approach" and its subsequent publication aim to go beyond the narrow realm of each discipline's focus. The contributors to this volume assume the historicity of transcultural flows and entanglements; they consider the resulting transformative forces to be a basic feature of cultural change. This broad, transdisciplinary perspective makes our approach unique, because many disciplines are represented in this volume that have just embarked on new theoretical and methodological approaches to analyse cultural hybridization. Apart from cultural and social anthropology, contributors come variously from archaeology, art history, linguistics, literature studies, political studies, philosophy, and business administration. Each discipline has its own perception of hybridization and related methodologies and each contributor to this volume presents his or her view of hybridization and shows how it operates in specific cases. The aim is to generate a multidisciplinary view of hybridity that paves the way for a wider application of this crucial concept within the social sciences.

During the workshop, crucial questions emerged about the phenomenon of "hybridity" and its conceptualization: Why do we need "hybridity"? Should we still use this term or do we have to find other terms for analyzing relevant phenomena? Can "hybridity" become a concept at all or should it only be used in a metaphorical way? Do we need a meta-theory of "hybridity"?

We are all aware that the possibilities offered by the concept of hybridity are deeply rooted in its even more problematic counterpart: purity. This has long been neglected in postcolonial studies, which have unconsciously re-introduced the notion of purity into cultural studies. Hybridity can only exist in opposition to purity; if we speak of hybridity, we must accept the existence of purity. Every aim to transcend borders starts with the acknowledgement of those borders, confirming the existence of what needs to be overcome. Every discipline which argues about hybridity has to define what it understands to be pure. If nothing can be designated as pure, everything is hybrid and hybridity becomes a redundant term which might then be used in a metaphorical way for stimulating discussion, but not as a conceptual tool. Without doubt, individuals or groups can perceive something as "pure" on ideological grounds. However, this perception of purity may not be useful for an epistemological approach, but deeply linked with xenophobia and racism. Purity has so often been invented by the powerful as a strategy of suppression that this term has to be handled with utmost caution. Therefore, it is important to acknowledge the existence of the three dimensions of hybridity: Firstly, the construction and perception of hybridity – and purity as its opposite – by different individuals or groups who have built structures and ideologies upon those two notions in order to maintain or enforce asymmetric power relations; secondly, hybridity as a metaphor for a scientific approach that aims at analyzing and deconstructing asymmetric power relations that result from assumptions of cultural purity; thirdly, hybridity as the basis of a methodological approach for the analysis of transcultural encounters.

On the basis of these three dimensions, our twofold interest in hybridity and thus also purity becomes obvious: within the broad framework of our research, we use hybridity in a metaphorical way to outline the scientific and, of course, political goal of our research. We are simultaneously scientists and contemporaries, and thus aware of the political routedness, dangers and opportunities of our approach. Within our particular realms of study, it is our goal to use "hybridity" in a methodological way, to operationalize the concept in a way that permits an analysis of each discipline's specific body of sources.

If "hybridity" is to develop into a useful concept, a plethora of questions need answering: what makes this phenomenon possible and how influential are factors such as power, market and space in bringing about hybridity? Can we distinguish different kinds of hybridization? How can we measure its various intensities and states? Some consider measurement theory to be a helpful tool, while others doubt the sense of measuring what might be defined as a political strategy. In order to recognize different manifestations of hybridization one has to divide its ongoing process into a consecutive series of arbitrary states and determine the factors triggering its start and development. One useful analytical tool might be agency theory, because hybridity is inseparably connected with creativity. However, creativity and agency are rooted in individual experiences and identities, which in turn explain the heterogeneity of hybridization processes. This heterogeneity is another obstacle in the search for structures underlying such processes. Thus, our analysis must start with individual processes of hybridization, within each of which the actor(s) in their context are examined first. Influential factors such as power, market, or space, which influence the actor's decisions, need to be evaluated in this initial analytical step. Secondly, we have to describe the evolution and subsequent outcomes of every individual process of hybridization. Thirdly, we must consider the dialectical relationship between the actor(s) and the outcomes of the ongoing process in which s/he participates creatively.

The workshop and its publication are part of Research Area D, "Historicities and Heritage", at the Heidelberg Cluster of Excellence "Asia and Europe in a Global Context". This research area's aim is to analyze different concepts of history as competing interpretations of time and space, the so-called historicities. The governing idea of historicity is deeply connected with hybridization in two ways. First, the use of the term "historicity" presupposes that history is always perceived and recorded locally and individually. This means that the so-called grand narratives or world histories are locally appropriated in a process which might, in many cases, be termed hybridization. Second, every historical perspective is diachronic and most diachronic developments are connected with change. Change, however, is often inseparably connected with phenomena of cultural hybridization.

Markus Hilgert, former head of Research Area D, has always been a supporter of my ideas and provided the necessary financial background for the workshop. I would like to express my deep gratitude to him and to all those people without whom the organization of this workshop and the subsequent publication of its results would not have been such an easy task. The Cluster's administration team, Brigitte Merz, Annette Kobler, Sabine Urbach, Petra Kourschil and Iris Mucha, supported the financial and administrative preparations as well as public relations in many ways. Andrea Hacker's help facilitated the fast publication of the workshop's results. Last but not least I would like to thank Joseph Maran and my wife Christina Sanchez-Stockhammer for invaluable discussions on the topic and their powerful and enduring support.

Chapter 2
Cultural Hybridity: Between Metaphor and Empiricism

Andreas Ackermann

Abstract Hybridity is becoming increasingly fashionable, most notably in the field of post-colonial literary studies, which focus, mainly through the analysis of texts, on the suppression and resistance of social as well as cultural minorities amid the present global condition. A brief outline of the history of the term shows, however, that for the most part of the twentieth century it was predominantly used in anthropology, sociology and history, until literary scholars took it up in the 1980s. Based first on a biological model focusing on the issue of miscegenation, the term shifted to a linguistic model stressing the subversive potential of a hybrid counter-culture. The essay then moves on to a discussion of the central metaphors of 'borrowing', 'mixing' and 'translating', underlying the concept of hybridity. After proposing to shift the perspective on hybridity from the text-based to a more empirically grounded analysis, potential areas of future research are discussed, such as hybrid objects, as well as situations of and responses to cultural contact.

2.1 Introduction

Hybridity is becoming increasingly fashionable, most notably in the field of post-colonial literary studies, which focus, mainly through the analysis of texts, on suppression and resistance of social as well as cultural minorities amid the global condition. In a way, it seems that hybridity and globalization always go together – and go together well. Both are slippery, ambiguous terms, at once literal and metaphorical, descriptive and explanatory. Both are in fashion – so much so, that serious definitional effort is needed to keep them as analytical tools. With globalization, the question is, what is not globalization, and when did it start? With hybridity, one has to ask, which culture is not hybrid – and have 'original' cultures ever existed? Although this essay cannot attempt to really answer these questions, it is more than obvious that cultural diversity and cultural borrowing are not exclusive phenomena of 'modernity'. Equating globalization with modernization and Westernization tends to overlook the influence of non-Western cultures on 'the West' and at the same time overrates the homogeneity of Western culture(s). Until the fourteenth century, Europe was an ardent recipient of cultural influences from the so-called 'Orient' and to speak of something like a Western hegemony makes sense only from the nineteenth century onwards. Ethnic as well as cultural diversity, on the other hand, are universal and diachronic phenomena, they can be found both in simple societies in pre-industrial times and in complex societies under late capitalism.

History provides us with many examples of plural societies such as the Roman Empire, Islamic Spain, the caste system in India, the Ottoman Empire, as well as the colonial societies of Southeast Asia. Recent examples of cultural pluralism are the USA, Canada and Australia, but also Singapore, Gibraltar and – increasingly so – Germany (cf. Ackermann and Müller 2002). Similarly, historians have discovered hybrid or syncretistic phenomena in many realms of supposedly homogeneous Western history, such as the interaction between Greeks and Romans in the process of 'Hellenization', in the Byzantine, Jewish and Muslim contributions to the Renaissance, in the cultural exchanges between Catholics and Protestants in the course of the Reformation, and also in the European missions to Asia, Africa and America.

The following essay intends to debate the analytic potential of the hybridity concept, by first outlining the history of the term, and then moving on to a discussion of the central metaphors underlying the concept of hybridity. In doing so, it is inspired to a large extent by the stimulating essay on cultural hybridity by the historian Peter Burke (b. 1937) (2009). Since it is written from an anthropological perspective, however, it will come as no surprise that the importance of empirically grounded analysis is stressed with regards to hybrid phenomena. Therefore, potential areas of future research are introduced, such as hybrid objects, as well as situations of and responses to cultural contact that are considered hybrid. However, a few opening remarks on the history of this concept seem appropriate.

2.2 Situating Hybridity

The word 'hybrid' has developed from biological and botanical origins: in Latin it meant the offspring of a tame sow and a wild boar, and hence, as the Oxford English Dictionary puts it, 'of human parents of different races, half-breed'. As a metaphor, the expression relates to linguistic compositions from different languages or, more generally, everything that is composed of different or incongruent elements. Until the nineteenth century the term was hardly used, and not with the racist undertone it accrued in the nineteenth century. Hybridity, according to the important scholar of hybridity Robert J. C. Young (b. 1950), was used to denote the crossing of people of different races only since the second half of the nineteenth century. By this time, it had received a wholly negative connotation, referring to the mixing of different species that would result in 'impurity'. However, the ambiguity of the term already surfaces when we consider that those of mixed race were often invoked as the most beautiful human beings of all (Young 1995, 16).

For a long time, hybridity, mixing and mutation were seen as degrading (that is, lowered by racial mixture from pure whiteness, the highest grade), harming a supposed purity in biology as well as in culture and society. The formulation of Mendel's Laws in 1865, however, as well as the developments in biology in the early twentieth century, resulted in a re-evaluation according to which cross-breeding and polygenetic material are seen as an enrichment of the gene pool. In nineteenth century conceptions of race the term changed from a biological to a cultural metaphor: various races were treated as biologically differing species, whose commingling was seen as problematic, dangerous and scandalous. As a result, aspects of 'fertility' and intermarriage determined discussions about hybridity. Hybridity as a sexual phantasm that is simultaneously feared and desired can be found in the debates about slavery and eugenics, as well as in anti-Semitic and Nazi texts.

2.2.1 Hybridity in Anthropology, Sociology and History

The concept of cultural hybridity started its academic career early in the twentieth century when it was taken up in various disciplines, particularly sociology, anthropology and history (even if the term was not always used). In anthropology and sociology, hybridity first played a part in the studies on migration in urban contexts. Robert Ezra Park (1864–1944), one of the founders of sociology in Chicago, used the term in the 1920s with reference to the massive influx of immigrants from Europe. Going back to depictions of the emancipated Jew and the stranger by Georg Simmel (1858–1918) and Alfred Schütz (1899–1959) respectively, he described migrants as 'marginal men' or 'cultural hybrids' living in two worlds, in both of which they would remain strangers, thus giving the term a rather negative connotation (Park 1974).

The anthropologist and sociologist Gilberto Freyre (1900–1987), by contrast, analysed the cultural hybridity of colonial society in Brazil in very positive terms. He described Brazil as a country where different racial and cultural contributions had met and generated a specific ethos and culture, full of harmonic and creative social relations (Freyre 1946). Although Freyre had no doubts about the existence of racial differences as regard habit, character, and attitudes to nature, he regarded these (after Franz Boas, under whom he had studied Anthropology in New York for 2 years) as the cultural product of long-term climatic, economic, and ecological adaptations. The type of social and psychological relations that were involved in colonial plantation society, according to Freyre, created the contradictory but dynamic system of social intimacy and violence, of negotiation and authority, of sexuality and reproduction between white masters and black slaves that was to constitute the true dynamics of Brazilian society. One of the reasons for this he saw in the fact that the Portuguese masters themselves had for a long time been the product of processes of cultural and racial miscegenation, particularly with their Arab and Jewish neighbours.

This 'miscibility', as Freyre called it, was responsible for the fact that the Portuguese easily mingled with 'women of color' and procreated *mestizo* sons. As a result, 'a few thousand daring males succeeded in establishing themselves firmly in possession of a vast territory and were able to compete with great and numerous peoples in the extension of their colonial domain and in the efficiency of their colonizing activity' (Freyre 1946, 11). A second factor contributing to the hybridity of Brazilian society was the 'mobility' of the Portuguese, as the colonial administration in Lisbon shifted warriors, administrators and technicians from Asia to America and from there to Africa. From the latter, whole communities were transported as slaves to Brazil. A little later, the sociologist Fernando Ortiz (1881–1969) and the novelist-musicologist Alejo Carpentier y Valmont (1904–1980) made similar points about Cuba (Ortiz 1947; Carpentier 2001).

At the same time, cultural anthropologist Melville Herskovits (1895–1963), working on Haiti, discussed what he called the 'syncretising' of African gods and Catholic saints into the religious practice of voodoo (Herskovits 1937a). The historical background of the phenomenon results from the efforts – made everywhere in the New World – to convert the African slaves to Christianity; in Haiti, baptism into the Catholic Church was required for all those who were unloaded from the holds of the slave ships. He described how followers of voodoo, descendents of the slaves brought to Haiti in the eighteenth century, professed nominal Catholicism, while at the same time belonging to so-called 'fetish cults' originating from Africa. These cults exhibit Catholic elements and specific identifications are made between African gods and Catholic Saints. St. Anthony, for example, corresponds with Legba, the widely worshipped god who in Dahomey guards crossroads and entrances to temples, compounds, and villages, for the reason that St. Anthony is represented on religious images as an old man, poorly dressed, carrying a wand which supports him as he walks. St. Patrick, on whose image serpents are depicted, is identified with Damballa, the Dahomean rainbow-serpent deity, one of the most widely worshipped and important Haitian voodoo gods. Following this logic further, Moses is held to be the 'father of Damballa', because of the miracle he performed before Pharaoh when he threw his staff to the ground and turned it into a serpent (Herskovits 1937b).

While not using the term explicitly, British social anthropologists associated with the Rhodes-Livingstone Institute in the 1940s and 1950s analysed hybrid phenomena occurring in the Copperbelt, an area of mining towns in British Central Africa (today Zambia). Designed after European models, rapidly-growing administrative and industrial centres develop in this region during the course of colonization. Since they attracted many people from the countryside looking for jobs, these towns constituted perfect fields of research for anthropologists interested in social and cultural change. The members of the Rhodes-Livingstone Institute thus moved away from descriptions of enclosed cultures to an open and explicit focus on colonial administration, race relations, urbanization, labour migration, 'tribalism', political ethnicity, and social movements. In this context two studies that focused on hybrid phenomena became prominent.

One is Max Gluckman's (1911–1975) study of the opening ceremony of a bridge in 1938, which he analyses as a hybrid mixture of Western technocrat-modernist and traditionalist Zulu symbolism (Gluckman 1958). The cutting of a tape stretched across the bridge by the car of the Chief Native Commissioner, which was preceded by Zulu warriors singing a traditional song, represented the key moment of the ceremony. Most of the important Zulu were dressed in European riding clothes, while the Zulu king wore a lounge suit; there were royal Zulu salutes and blessings and European clapping and hymns, as well as speeches in a mixture of English and Zulu. After the ceremony the whites retired to one side of the bridge for tea, while the Zulus had traditional beer and sacrificial meat on the other side. Finally, the Commissioner was sent some beer across the bridge, sending some tea back in the opposite direction. Gluckman describes in detail the spatial mixings and separations of the participants, in order to discuss their significance for an understanding of power and race relations in colonial Africa (cf. Werbner 2001, 134–135).

The *Kalela Dance* (1956) by J. Clyde Mitchell (1918–1995) provides the second example of a hybrid phenomenon, where a popular, supposedly 'tribal' dance is performed to emphasize the unity of the Bisa tribe against all others on the Copperbelt. Without using the term, Mitchell shows, however, the hybridity of the concept of 'tribe' in the colonial system. First of all, the twenty dancers, mostly men in their twenties, did not display any tribal insignia but wore European clothes instead: neat singlets, well-pressed grey slacks, and well-polished shoes. One member dressed as a 'doctor', in a white gown with a red cross at the front; he did not dance but urged the dancers on. A 'nursing sister', the only woman in the group and also in white, carried a mirror and a handkerchief around to the dancers so that they would keep neat. The inclusion of these offices marked the *kalela* as a type of dance inspired by the contact with Europeans, and it was widespread in East and Central Africa during the first half of the twentieth century. The *kalela*, according to Mitchell, originated from a kind of pantomime of the social structure of the local European community, at a time when Africans had no opportunity of appreciating the social pattern of the local community except through military rank and the clear evidence of uniforms and public ceremonies. In their general preoccupation with stylish appearances, the *kalela* dancers showed their adherence to European-oriented ideas of prestige and did not, Mitchell noted, express antagonism toward Europeans or ridicule them by mimicking their comportment. Apart from drumming, the dancing was accompanied by songs made up by the leader of the team. Similarly, these songs did not recount the exploits of traditional Bisa culture, but rather drew the attention of the audience to the attractive personalities of the dancers or described various characteristics of town life. Others were concerned with ethnic diversity, praising the virtues of the dancers' own tribe, but also ridiculing other groups and their customs. The language of the song, a so-called 'Copperbelt Bemba' and *lingua franca* of the town, was hybrid too, being admixed with English and Pidgin-Zulu words and phrases. Mitchell interpreted the *kalela* as a significant statement about the colonial, migratory and urban experience, which involved mingling with strangers of many ethnic backgrounds (including the whites), and finding ways of dealing with them (cf. Hannerz 1980, 131–135). (In addition, one could point to the several African possession cults, such as for instance the Haouka in West Africa, that evolved at the same time and likewise displayed predominantly military elements of Western colonial culture (cf. Jean Rouch's Maître fous).

Claude Lévi-Strauss (1908–2009) discussed hybridity on a more abstract level, with regard to mythology. Starting from an assumption about cosmic and social ordering he analysed the role of tricksters – gods, spirits or anthropomorphic animals who play tricks or otherwise disobey normal rules and conventional behaviour – and clowns as mediators of opposite terms in mythic thought. Both clown and trickster help to achieve the purpose of myth, which is to provide a logical model capable of overcoming contradiction. Lévi-Strauss noted that as mediators, tricksters must retain something of that duality – namely an ambiguous and equivocal character (Lévi-Strauss 1963). Elsewhere he talks about the specific quality of mythic thought, encompassing a double movement of de-contextualization and re-contextualization, whereby an item is lifted out of its original setting and modified to fit its new environment, an activity he refers to as 'bricolage' (Lévi-Strauss 1968).

The British anthropologist Victor Turner (1920–1983) devoted his attention to a particular hybrid phase in ritual he termed 'liminality'. Based on the model by van Gennep (2004), Turner distinguished three phases in *rites de passage* (such as, for example, birth, puberty, marriage and death): separation, margin and aggregation. Whereas the first phase of separation signifies the detachment of the individual or group either from an earlier fixed point in the social structure or a set of cultural conditions, the third phase concludes the passage, so that the ritual subject is in a stable state once more and has again rights and obligations of a clearly defined and structured type. The second phase Turner calls 'liminal', constituting a state of 'betwixt and between', where the ritual subject does not belong to the former state any more, but has not yet reached the new one. The position of the ritual subject is ambiguous; he passes through a realm that has few or none of the attributes of the past or coming state; he is alternately forced and encouraged to think about society, the cosmos, and the powers that generate and sustain them. "Liminality," writes Turner, "breaks, as it were, the cake of custom and enfranchises speculation, giving a 'certain freedom to juggle with the factors of existence' (Turner 1967, 106). Hybridity is thus both: threatening and creative.

Mary Douglas (1921–2007) was interested in the ambiguous powers of exchange inherent in anomalous conflations of otherwise distinct categories. Culture, following Douglas, is supposed to provide clear-cut categories, classifications and structured patterns that order the social life of a community. Hence, ambivalence, anomaly, and ambiguity, in short: hybridity is perceived as an abomination. 'Impurity' or 'pollution' usually pertain to substances, materials or qualities that are 'out of place', because they do not properly fit the categories provided by the respective culture. Douglas suggests, for example, that the only reason for the pig to be counted as 'unclean' in *Leviticus* is its failure to fit into the relevant class of clean animals that are both cloven-hoofed and ruminant (Douglas 1966, 56). Another example she gives is of the pangolin, a creature that conflates categories normally kept apart: it has scales like a fish, but climbs trees; it resembles rather an oviparous lizard than a mammal, but suckles its young. For the Lele, who live in the Congo and have built a cult around the animal, the pangolin invites its initiates to turn round and confront the categories on which their whole surrounding culture has been built up and to recognise them for the fictive, man-made, arbitrary creations that they are (thus paralleling Turners thoughts on liminality) (Douglas 1966, 169–170). Further, she concludes elsewhere that people who have nothing to lose by exchange and everything to gain will be predisposed towards the hybrid being, whereas people whose experience of foreigners has been disastrous will cherish perfect categories, reject exchange and refuse any doctrines of mediation (Douglas 1975, 307).

Starting with the 1960s, hybridity theory began to look to sites of resistance and exclusion in Europe, as in Michel Foucault's (1926–1984) analysis of *heterotopic* spaces, for example (Foucault 1986). The sociologists Roland Barthes (1915–1980) (Barthes 1972), and Pierre Bourdieu (1930–2002) (Bourdieu 1984), along with the linguist and philosopher Mikhail Bakhtin (Bakhtin 1984, see next section) analysed popular mass culture as subversive and revitalising inversions of official discourses, high-cultural aesthetic forms, or the exclusive lifestyles of dominant elites. Such popular mixings and inversions, such as the subversive *bricolages* of youth cultures analysed by media sociologist Dick Hebdige (b. 1951) (Hebdige 1979), are 'hybrid' in the sense that they juxtapose and fuse objects, languages and signifying practices from different and normally separated domains and, by glorifying natural carnality or 'matter out of place', challenge an official, puritanical public order (Werbner 1997, 2).

Europe likewise became the focus of historical studies dealing with hybrid phenomena. The English cultural historian Christopher Dawson (1889–1970) focussed on the period 500–1000, emphasizing the contributions by the Classical, Christian and 'Barbarian' traditions to 'the making of Europe' (Dawson 1932). Although Dawson did not use terms such as 'hybridity', the book may be viewed in retrospect as a study in cultural contact, interaction and hybridization. In 1948, the Spanish historian Américo Castro y Quesada (1885–1972) offered a then controversial interpretation of Spanish history that privileged the encounters and interactions between the Christian, Jewish and Muslim cultures, the so-called *convivencia* (Castro 1954). In the 1950s, the British historian Arnold Toynbee devoted two volumes of his multi-volume *A Study of History* to what he called 'contacts between civilizations' in space and time, 'colliding cultures', or the 'diffraction' of 'culture-rays' (Toynbee 1954; Burke 2009, 9).

2.2.2 Postcolonial Concepts of Hybridity

A strategic re-positioning of the term hybridity occurred during the 1980s, in the area of the so-called post-colonial studies. Scholars from the field of literary studies, most prominently Edward W. Said (1935–2003), Gayatri Chakravorty Spivak (b. 1942) and Homi K. Bhabha (b. 1949), were concerned with problems of representing 'the Other' in literature as well as in academia and thus developed a renewed interest in the hybrid. They argue that since no culture has been left untouched by the global circulation of people, artefacts, signs and information, culture these days is hybrid *per se*, constituting a locale of conflict between representations of identity and difference. Hence post-colonial theorists are interested more in transitions and disruptions than in origins and homogeneity, in difference more than in identity. This focus on the disruptive power of the 'Other' is the result not only of de-constructivist analyses and observations in the history of literature, but also of biographical aspects: whereas Said was born in Palestine but spent his life mostly in New York, Spivak moved from Calcutta to New York and Bhabha from Bombay via Oxford to Chicago. Their personal histories exemplify the fact that national cultures in the global condition are co-produced increasingly from the perspective of minorities.

Post-colonial theory relies heavily on the ideas of the Russian linguist and philosopher Mikhail Bakhtin (1895–1975) who used 'hybridity' in its philological sense in order to describe something particular in his own theory. For him, hybridity delineates the way in which language, even within a single sentence, can be double-voiced – one voice ironising and unmasking the other within the same utterance. Bakhtin gave the sixteenth-century theological satire *The Letters of Obscure Men* with its complex linguistic hybrid of Latin and German as one example, illustrating what he called the 'inter-illumination' of languages. This inter-illumination, according to Bakhtin, reached its highest point during the Renaissance and helped stimulate literary innovation and creativity, most obviously in the works of François Rabelais, to whom Bakhtin devoted a whole book (Bakhtin 1984). The idea of the hybrid was linked to two concepts that were central to his thought, 'heteroglossia' and 'polyphony'. While 'heteroglossia' refers to the diversity of language within a single text, 'polyphony' is used to refer to the different voices adopted by novelists such as Dostoyevsky (Burke 2009, 50–51).

However, it is Bakhtin's distinction between *intentional* and *organic* hybridity that appears to be most relevant for the phenomena discussed in this essay, because it helps not only to avoid the postmodern paradox of celebrating hybridity 'as powerfully interruptive' while at the same time theorizing it 'as commonplace and pervasive' (Werbner 1997, 1), but also to account for the simultaneous coexistence of both cultural change and resistance to change in groups. With *organic* hybridization Bakhtin refers to the unintentional, unconscious, everyday mixing and fusing of diverse cultural elements, as for example in language. This can have culturally productive effects, because unconscious hybrids 'are pregnant with potential for new world views, with new internal forms for perceiving the world in words' (Bakhtin 1981, 360). Applying this to culture and society more generally, one can say that 'despite the illusion of boundedness, cultures evolve historically through unreflective borrowings, mimetic appropriations, exchanges and inventions', as Pnina Werbner puts it, concluding that there 'is no culture in and of itself' (Werbner 1997, 4–5).

In contrast, *intentional* hybridity is the result of using conscious contrasts and oppositions in an antithetical movement where, within a single discourse, one voice is able to unmask authoritative discourse. With intentional hybridity two points of view are not mixed, but set against each other dialogically. This can be used, for example in the aesthetic domain, 'to shock, change, challenge, revitalise or disrupt through deliberate, intended fusions of unlike social languages and images' (Werbner 1997, 5), thus creating an ironic double consciousness, a collision between differing points of view on the world. In organic hybridity, the mixture merges and is fused into a new language, world view or object; but intentional hybridity sets different points of view against each other in a conflictual structure. As Young has pointed out, Bakhtin's doubled form of hybridity offers a particularly significant dialectical model for cultural interaction: organic hybridity that tends towards fusion, conflicting with intentional hybridity that enables a contestatory activity, a politicised setting of cultural differences against each other in a dialogical mode (Young 1995, 22). This deliberate, provocative aesthetic challenge to an implicit aesthetic, social or political order and identity, is felt to be most threatening by those responsible for safeguarding the *status quo*. From a different aesthetic, social or political position, however, this intentional hybridity can be seen as liberating, revitalising, or simply 'fun' (Werbner 1997, 5).

Bhabha took up Bakhtin's concept of intentional hybridity, shifting it as a means of subverting authority to the colonial situation. In his interpretation of colonial texts, hybridity reveals 'the ambivalence at the source of traditional discourses of authority', where the discourse of colonial authority loses its univocal grip on meaning and finds itself open to traces of the language of the Other, enabling the critic to chart complex movements of disarming alterity. One example is Bhabha's reading of a report by Anund Messeh, one of the first indigenous catechists in India (Bhabha 1994). In the year of 1817, Messeh meets a group of about 500 Indian men, women and children in a grove of trees outside the city of Delhi. It turns out that they are reading the Bible in a translation which they claim has been given them by an angel (who, as Messeh knows, must have been a missionary). When the catechist points out to them that this is the religious book of the white man, translated so that they could also use it, he is confronted with disbelief. For the Indians this is inconceivable because the white man eats meat, which is also the reason why they would not partake of the Christian sacrament. Bhabha finds hybridity in the fact that–contrary to the original purpose of the missionaries–the translated Bibles did not help to depose the Indian gods, but inspired them rather to question the authority of the colonisers. The book, intended to demonstrate the superiority of English civilisation, becomes the starting-point for questioning this very superiority. Thus colonialism, according to Bhabha, produces hybridity as the starting-point for resistance against its authority (cf. Ackermann 2004, 148f.).

With *Orientalism* (1978), Edward Said already focused the study of colonialism on its discursive operations, showing the intimate connection between the language and forms of knowledge developed for the study of cultures and the history of colonialism and imperialism. The book analysed the kinds of concepts and representations of 'the Orient' as well as of 'the Oriental' used in literary texts, travel writings, memoirs and academic studies as a means to grasp the diverse ideological practices of colonialism. In charting 'the complicity of Western literary and academic knowledge with the history of colonialism' (Young), Said emphasized the ways in which seemingly impartial, objective academic disciplines had in fact colluded with, and indeed been instrumental in, the production of actual forms of colonial subjugation and administration. *Orientalism* thus provided powerful evidence of the complicity between politics and knowledge. Orientalism, Said argued, is simply 'a kind of Western projection onto and will to govern over the orient' (Young 1995, 159–160). Regarding hybridity, Said argued that since all cultures are involved in one another, none could be understood as single and pure, because all are heterogeneous (Said 1993, xxix).

The work of Spivak focuses on the complex mechanisms of subjugation not only of the colonial subject, but of the female subject in particular. Her most famous essay 'Can the Subaltern Speak?' (1988) discusses the position of women in colonial discourse, taking as an example the ban on the practice of burning or burying alive widows along with the body of their deceased husband ('sati') by the colonial authorities in India. Spivak finds that the women concerned have no voice in the discourse of 'sati', being neither represented adequately by the indigenous elite nor by the English. Both sides claim to speak for and at the same time in place of the women, the colonial administration depicting them as passive victims that have to be protected from their own culture, Brahmin ideology suggesting their deliberate choice of death. Thus the women are not only oppressed, but are in a subaltern position where they cannot speak, because they are not listened to. Spivak points to the fact that this is the case not only in colonial discourse, but also in many ongoing, supposedly intellectual-critical discourses. Hence she cautions 'our enthusiasm for migrant hybridity', lest 'the subaltern is once again silent for us' (Spivak 1993, 255).

This short outline of the use of the term hybridity in the humanities has revealed two paths in its transformation. On the one hand, it has moved from a biological conceptualization that extends the problems of miscegenation to embrace a more culturo-political meaning, which has been mediated by the linguistic model of Bakhtin. On the other hand, the originally rather negative connotations of the concept make way for a much more positive understanding of mixing and fusion that would lead to a challenging counter-culture. At the same time, the perspective on hybridity shifts from the (colonial) periphery, of for instance Brazil (Freyre), Haiti (Herskovits) or Africa (Gluckmann, Mitchell, Turner, Douglas) to the post-colonial centre (at least in the perspective of those involved, although Park already did his research in the Metropolis). So we now have a background against which the various metaphors pertaining to hybridity can be discussed in order to reveal their potential for new insight.

2.3 Metaphors of Hybridity

Of course, hybridity is but one in a sea of metaphors attempting to come to terms with processes of cultural transformation. Roughly three metaphorical fields can, following Burke, be distinguished as dominating the discourse on phenomena regarded as 'hybrid': borrowing, mixing, and translating.

2.3.1 Borrowing

First, there is the field of 'borrowing', a term referring to economics and in which several metaphors can be found. Cultural interaction has often been discussed in terms of *imitation* – sometimes with a positive connotation (as in classical and renaissance literary theory), sometimes with negative connotations, as for instance when people following foreign models are denounced as 'aping' or imitating in a slavish manner. The idea of *appropriation* stems from the context of theological discussions about the uses early Christians were allowed to make of pagan culture. Interestingly enough, the French Catholics Michel de Certeau (1926–86) and Paul Ricoeur (1913–2005) both have drawn on this tradition (Burke 2009, 36; 38).

Cultural *borrowing* is often a pejorative term, indicating that the borrowers' culture is not sufficiently original. Both the French historian Fernand Braudel (1902–1985) and Edward Said, however, were convinced that the history of all cultures is the history of cultural borrowing. *Acculturation*, on the other hand, is a more technical term, suggesting a subordinate culture adopting traits from the dominant culture. Thus it can be equated with *assimilation*, a word frequently used in discussions about the processes of cultural transformation in the course of migration. More interesting with regards to hybridity is the concept of *transculturation* attributed to Freyre (1986) and Ortiz (1947) and now advocated by media studies scholar Marwan Kraidy, because is implies not merely a one-way, but rather a two-way process (Kraidy 2005, 51ff.).

Finally, there are the concepts of *accommodation* and *negotiation*. While Cicero referred to *accommodation* by stressing the need for orators to adapt their style to their respective audience, Pope Gregory used the term to point out the necessity to make the Christian message acceptable to pagans. The concept of *negotiation* is frequently employed in analyses of ethnic identity, aimed at expressing the multiplicity and fluidity of identification, which can be modified in different ways according to different situations (Burke 2009, 42–45).

2.3.2 Mixing

As we have already seen with the concept of hybridity, mixture, 'hotchpotch' or 'mishmash' was for a long time viewed mainly as a kind of disorder. *Fusion* is a 'metallic' metaphor, first used by German explorer and botanist Karl von Martius (1794–1868) to imply that the history of Brazil might be written in terms of the fusion of the three races, the Portuguese, the Indians and the Africans (Martius 2003). Today the concept of fusion has become widespread in contexts ranging from music to cuisine. The idea of 'the melting pot' is, of course, not very far removed. The Jewish writer Israel Zangwill (1864–1926) was the author of the eponymous drama, where he envisaged the acceptance of immigrants as 'Americans' in 'God's crucible, the great Melting Pot where all the races of Europe are melting and refining' (Zangwill 1925). Plutarch (c. 46–120) was the first to use the term *syncretism*, in the sense of a political alliance. In the seventeenth century the term railed against efforts to unite different groups of Protestants, evoking a kind of religious chaos. Two centuries later the word had acquired a positive meaning in the context of studies of religion in classical antiquity, as for example with the Belgian scholar Franz Cumont (1868–1947), who used it to discuss the identification between gods or goddesses from different cultures. The aforementioned anthropologist Herskovits applied the concept in his study of Afro-American religion in Haiti, discussing the equation between Christian saints and African deities. The term of *mestizaje*, a kind of Spanish-American conceptualization of hybridity, is simultaneously used in the literal sense of 'interbreeding' and the metaphorical sense of the 'intermingling of cultures'. It has been a term of abuse and praise as well as of academic analysis, as employed for example by Freyre and the sociologist Roger Bastide (1898–1974) (the latter using its French version, *metissage*).

2.3.3 Translating

The idea of cultural *translation* has been quite successful in the humanities, a fact that may be linked to the so-called 'linguistic turn' and in particular to the idea of 'culture as text', which has been championed most prominently by the cultural anthropologist Clifford Geertz (1926–2006). The concept of anthropology as 'the art of translation' (Crick 1976, 164), however, is older than that. British social anthropologists Bronislaw Malinowski (1884–1942) and Edward Evans-Pritchard (1902–73) both used the term in describing the methods of their discipline. Malinowski claimed that 'the learning of a foreign culture is like the learning of a foreign tongue' and that, through his books, he was attempting to translate Melanesian conditions into our own (Malinowski 1929, 25–26). Similarly, Evans-Pritchard in 1951 wrote about 'translation from one culture to another' and the skill necessary 'to translate a foreign culture into the language of one's own' (Evans-Pritchard 1951, 81–82). His student Godfrey Lienhardt (1921–1993) described translation as a central task of social anthropology: 'The problem of describing to others how members of a remote tribe think then begins to appear largely one of translation, of making the coherence primitive thought has in the languages it really lives in, as clear as possible in our own' (Lienhardt et al. 1954, 97).

The term 'creole' has been employed for centuries in Spanish, Portuguese, French and English to describe people born in the Americas whose ancestors came from other continents. Generalizing from studies of the Caribbean, linguists have come to employ the term *creolization* to describe the situation in which a former *lingua franca* or pidgin develops a more complex structure as people begin to use it for general purposes, or even to learn it as their first language. Building on their affinities or congruence, two languages in contact change to become like one another and thus 'converge' to create a third, which often takes most of its vocabulary from one of the parent languages and its structure or syntax from the other (Burke 2009, 61–62). The anthropologist Ulf Hannerz (b. 1942) has transferred the creole concept to the post-colonial cultures of the global condition, which he describes as a 'world in creolisation'. Thus he speaks of 'creole cultures' that draw in some way on two or more historical sources, often originally widely different (Hannerz 1987, 552).

After this brief *tour d'horizon* through a sea of metaphors and concepts it might look as though there are too many terms in circulation to describe and analyse the processes of cultural transformation that interest this essay. However, although concepts are supposed to help solve intellectual problems, they often create problems themselves. So a plurality of concepts should not confuse but rather help us to come to terms with the discussed phenomena, because 'each concept encourages its users to become aware of problems that alternative concepts obscure' (Burke 2009, 54).

In the case of 'appropriation', for example, we have to ask who appropriates what and for what purposes, and what is the logic of a choice that selects some items from a repertoire and rejects others. The concept of 'syncretism', on the other hand, asks for an investigation into the extent to which the different elements have blended. Hybridity, like 'mixing', seems to exclude individual agency, evoking the outside observer that studies culture as if it were nature, and the products of individuals and groups as if they were botanical specimens. By contrast, concepts such as 'appropriation' 'accommodation' and 'cultural translation' throw more light on human agency and creativity (Burke 2009, 54–55).

The notion of translation, again, has the further advantage of emphasizing the work that needs to be done in order to domesticate the alien, as well as the strategies and tactics employed. In addition, it is a fairly neutral term with associations of cultural relativism. However, when employing the metaphor of translation one also has to pay attention to what in a given culture resists translation, as well as to what is lost in the process of translation from one culture to another (Burke 2009, 58–61). Finally, it should not be forgotten that Geertz' idea of 'culture as text' has sparked a long and intense debate about the limits of the metaphor and the ways cultures do differ from texts (e.g. Clifford and Marcus 1986).

2.4 Researching Hybridity

Discussing the post-colonial analyses of hybrid texts, where 'hybridity' to a large extent seems to depend on the interpretative efforts of the sympathetic intellectual, as well as navigating through the sea of metaphors, it will probably have become more than obvious that the concept of hybridity needs some empirical grounding if it is to reveal its analytical usefulness. Thus we need to move ahead (rather than going back to concepts of race or an essentialized notion of culture) from the analysis of texts to the observation of tangible objects, situations and responses.

The following section provides an outline of hybridity regarding these three aspects suggested by Burke.

2.4.1 Varieties of Object

With regard to varieties of object, three kinds of hybridity can be distinguished: Firstly, hybridity can be found regarding *artefacts*: Architecture, for example, very often combines elements of different traditions, as in the case of Spanish churches or synagogues with Islamic geometrical decorations and even Arabic descriptions, which were probably done by Muslim craftsmen. Similarly the employment of local craftsmen by Jesuit missionaries in India and Latin America led to various combinations of Italian Renaissance or baroque structures with decorative details deriving from local Hindu, Islamic or Inca traditions (Burke 2009, 14). The same can be said about furniture, sculpture, images and, of course, texts and literary genres. *Practices* can be hybrid, too. Syncretism has been mentioned several times now, in particular with reference to religious practices, such as the Caribbean Voodoo, Candomblé and Umbanda. The same can be said of music. In times of globalization with its omnipresent label of "World Music" and thinking of musical styles such as Bossa Nova, Salsa and Reggae, this might appear obvious. However, the mixing of different musical traditions has also been attributed to classical composers such as Claude Debussy, who is supposed to have been inspired by the gamelan music of Java (Burke 2009, 23). The term *creolization*, referring to the hybrid elements of language, has already been mentioned. Even in sport hybrid practices can be found, the most striking example probably being 'Trobriand Cricket'. The inhabitants of the Melanesian Trobriand islands took the very controlled game of British cricket, first introduced to them some 70 years earlier by Methodist missionaries, and changed it into an outlet for mock warfare and inter-village competition, political reputation-building among leaders, dancing and chanting, and wild entertainment (cf. *Trobiand Cricket* 1976).

Hybridity regarding *people* includes groups as well as individuals. Many hybrid groups develop within the context of migration and colonialism, such as the Anglo-Irish, Anglo-Indian and African-Americans or the Chinese-Malay communities of Southeast-Asia called *Peranakans* or *Babas* (cf. Rudolph 1998). Individuals can likewise present interesting cases for the analysis of hybridization processes. People like Hasan al-Wazzân (c. 1494–1554), the sixteenth-century geographer known in the West as 'Leo Africanus', Samuel Pallache (d. 1616), a Moroccan Jew who was active in both Catholic and Protestant Europe, Edward Said, the already mentioned US-Palestinian literary theorist, or the Chinese-Australian cultural theorist Ien Ang (b. 1954) have either been praised as translators between cultures or been condemned as renegades. The latter has been the case with the Portuguese *Lançados* of the fifteenth and sixteenth century on the West African coast, Christians who turned Muslim in the Ottoman Empire, the Canadian *Coureur de bois* of the seventeenth century, as well as the eighteenth- and nineteenth-century beachcombers of the South Pacific islands or the explorers and early anthropologists 'going native' (Kohl 1987).

2.4.2 Varieties of Situation

When analysing hybridity, it is important to take into account the differences of situation, context and locale in which cultural encounters occur. Therefore, one has to look at not only a geography and a chronology, but also a sociology of hybridization, because 'when cultures meet, some individuals and groups participate in the process more than others' (Burke 2009, 67). Of course, this concerns aspects of power, as in the *encounters of equals and unequals*. The strategies employed by Catholic missionaries, for example, have differed greatly, depending on their position in the societies they had been sent to. Being in a position of a strong 'lender' against a weak 'borrower' (as in Mexico, Peru or Brazil), they were able to use force to impose Christianity on the Indians. In China, on the other hand, the Jesuits were in such a weak position that they had to adapt to their environment to such a degree that they were sometimes accused of having been converted by the Chinese, instead of converting them. In Africa, on the other hand, there often seems to have been a 'working misunderstanding' between Christianity and local religions, where missionaries believed that they had achieved conversions when the local rulers simply wished to incorporate new and powerful practices into their religious traditions. In the New World, by contrast, many African slaves conformed outwardly to Christianity, while retaining their traditional beliefs. As we have already seen, Christian saints such as St. Anthony or St. Patrick, as well as liturgical practices such as prayers and hymns, were taken up through an act of 'cultural mimicry', only to begin a life of their own during their course of transformation into the practices of Voodoo, Candomblé and Umbanda.

Prominent among *locales of encounter* particularly favourable to cultural exchange are the metropolis, the port and the frontier. Big cities like New York, London, Lagos, Los Angeles, Mumbai or São Paulo constitute crossroads of both trade and culture. It is particularly the presence of different groups of immigrants that makes the metropolis an important site of cultural exchange. In this way, Hannerz has argued, 'London, Paris, Brussels and Miami are among the major Third World cities, and a varied cultural flow passes from them through the networks of migrant workers, students, exiles, international petty entrepreneurs and tourists' (Hannerz 1987, 50). This development has led researchers to speak, for example, of 'the Caribbeanization of New York City', or to refer to Los Angeles as 'the capital of Latin America' (Kearney 1995, 554). However, despite the attempts of some groups to keep to themselves and marry within the group, most migrants are usually gradually assimilated into the local urban culture, each of them adding something new to the mix. For this reason, some scholars also speak of 'mestizo cities' (Burke 2009, 74). Burke also lists a number of European ports that served as important sites of encounter: Fifteenth-century Venice, sixteenth-century

Lisbon and Seville, seventeenth-century Amsterdam. Nagasaki and Canton (Guangzhou) were key locations of cultural exchange between Europe and Asia in the seventeenth and eighteenth centuries (Burke 2009, 73).

The *frontier* and its surrounding *borderlands* represent another area that favours exchange and hybridization, on the metaphorical level as well as in a geopolitical sense. One example would be the cultural frontier between Islam and Christianity in Eastern Europe. Polish and Hungarian nobles in the sixteenth and seventeenth century, according to Burke, regularly fought the Turks on the grounds of religion, while at the same time using Turkish clothing and weaponry. On both sides of the Ottoman-Habsburg frontier existed a common tradition of epic and ballad, including the same heroes and battles (although victory was accorded depending on the identification of the respective narrator) (Burke 2009, 75–76). Another example of such a frontier area can be found in medieval Spain, where cultural exchanges between Christians, Jews and Muslims were frequent and long-lasting, particularly in the area of architecture and literature.

In recent years, anthropologists have been attracted to such frontier areas, and an 'anthropology of borderlands' is slowly being established within the discipline (cf. Alvarez 1995). While the concept was originally limited to the Mexican-US border, its scope in the meantime has been substantially broadened in a geographical as well as a structural sense (Donnan and Haller 2000; Donnan and Wilson 2001; Rösler and Wendl 1999). This is a consequence of the insight that borders are of an ambivalent nature, encompassing dividing lines as well as passageways, which means that they not only separate but also connect people. Borderlands are locales of complexity, creating translocal cultures characterized by liminality, hybridity and ambiguity. The emphasis is usually more on contact, mixing and exchange than separation, demarcation and isolation, as borders cannot be controlled in an absolute sense.

2.4.3 Varieties of Response

The current discourse on the global and the local, reflecting the fears of globalization as 'Westernization', has renewed the interest in traditions of *appropriation* and *resistance*. The sociologist Roland Robertson was one of the first to point out, however, that globalization has involved and increasingly involves the creation and the incorporation of locality. Homogenization and heterogenization are only *seemingly* opposing trends: they are simultaneous, complementary and interpenetrative, even though they certainly can and do collide in concrete situations. In order to transcend the tendency to cast the idea of globalization as inevitably at variance with the idea of localization, Robertson suggests the term 'glocalization', which previously was used largely in marketing (Robertson 1995). Glocalization thus directs the perspective towards hybrid phenomena and strategies of local responses to global developments.

Following Burke, four local responses to cultural exchange can be distinguished. The first is *acceptance*, as exemplified by the fashion for the foreign, which can be found throughout history. Prominent European examples would be the Italophilia of the Renaissance, seventeenth-century Francophilia, and the Anglomania of the eighteenth and nineteenth century. Since cultural identities are often defined by opposition, a second response would be outright *rejection*, either in the form of resistance or of purification. A prominent example for the former would be the Japanese policy of *sakoku* from the 1630s to the 1860s, when the government attempted to cut the country off from foreign influences. Instances for cultural purification or 'dehybridization' can be found particularly in the realm of language. Already in the late classical period, one finds a movement to return to pure 'Attic' Greek, in response to what was perceived as an invasion of the language by foreign words. A third possible strategy to respond to foreign influences from outside is that of *segregation*, where the line is drawn not between the self and the other, but inside the home culture. Not the culture as a whole, but certain 'essential' parts should remain free from 'contamination'. A well-known example of this would be the attempts of the advocates of many non-Western societies to appropriate 'Western' technology while retaining their supposedly Islamic, Confucian or Asian values. Finally, there is the strategy of *adaptation*, probably the most common local response to an encounter with another culture. This strategy entails a double movement of de-contextualization and re-contextualization, whereby an item is lifted out of its original setting and modified to fit its new environment, something that Lévi-Strauss has called 'bricolage'. More recently, this process of appropriation and re-employment has been described by de Certeau in his study on the practice of everyday life (1984) or in the process of 'Tropicalization' discussed by Freyre (Burke 2009, 79–94).

Sometimes, adaptations of foreign items of culture are so thorough-going that the result can sometimes be successfully 're-exported' to the place from which the item originated, a process Burke refers to as *circularity* (Burke 2009, 96). Two examples should suffice here: If musicians in the Congo or in Lagos are inspired by colleagues in Cuba or Brazil, then Africa adapts to Africa via America, 'making a circular tour, and yet one that does not end in the place that it started, since every imitation is also an adaptation' (Burke 2009, 26). The second example of circularity concerns 'chicken tikka masala', a supposedly typical Indian curry dish. Already 10 years ago the BBC had reported that chicken tikka masala had achieved the status of a 'national dish' in the United Kingdom, whereas it seems to have been unknown in India. However, because an increasing number of British tourists demanded what they deem to be a typically Indian dish, chicken tikka masala is now imported from England (cf. Ackermann 2002). In 2009, the Scottish Member of Parliament Mohammed Sarwar started a campaign with the European Union to recognize the 'Protected Designation of Origin' for chicken tikka masala to the city of Glasgow, which claims to have invented the dish. This claim is vigorously disputed by Indian chefs who variously assert that it is an 'authentic Mughlai recipe', 'basically a Punjabi dish not more than fifty years old' or 'has been prepared in India for generations' (*Daily Telegraph*, August 4, 2009). It will be interesting to follow the vagaries of this hybrid dish and to see if one day it will be considered 'authentic' in some way or other.

2.5 Concluding Remarks

This essay set out to debate the analytic potential of the hybridity concept. It did so by first outlining the history of the idea, and pin-pointing two shifts in perspective. The first shift concerned academic disciplines: the term was used for the greater part of the twentieth century, mainly in anthropology, sociology and history, until literary scholars took it up in the 1980s. The second shift concerned the underlying ideas of hybridity, which were initially based on a biological model focusing on the issue of miscegenation. Postcolonial scholars then applied a linguistic model after Bakhtin, stressing the subversive potential of a hybrid counter-culture. One question we started with was, which culture is not hybrid – and have 'original' cultures ever existed? Using the distinction established by Bakhtin, we can now say that 'original' cultures did exist in a way, since their hybridity was an 'organic' one, where unintentional, unconscious, everyday mixing and fusing of diverse cultural elements took place more or less unnoticed, thus allowing for an imagined homogeneity. On the other hand, theorists of post-colonialism in particular are interested in examples of 'intentional' hybridity, in the deliberate, provocative juxtaposition and fusion of objects, languages and signifying practices from different and normally separated domains, that threaten an implicit – in the sense of 'original' – social order and identity.

Next, the central metaphors pertaining to the concept of hybridity were placed under closer inspection, emphasizing the need for an empirically grounded analysis regarding hybrid phenomena. Finally, potential areas of future research were introduced, for example hybrid objects, as well as hybrid situations of and hybrid responses to cultural contact. In this perspective, the following questions might seem helpful: (a) Biological or linguistic hybridity? When researching hybrid phenomena, we should always enquire into whether the underlying model of the applied concept is more a biological or rather a linguistic one. As a result, we might ask if we are confronted with fears or celebrations of miscegenation or rather with the search for the subversive potential of an ostensible counter-culture. Whereas the biological model results in either the fear or the celebration of miscegenation, the linguistic model leads to a search for the subversive potential of a counter-culture. (b) Organic or intentional hybridity? The next important distinction concerns the problem of whether we are witnessing organic or intentional hybridity. This distinction by Bakhtin is most important in deciding whether the phenomena in question have to be interpreted as everyday unconscious fusion, or rather as deliberate, provocative aesthetic challenge to an implicit aesthetic, social or political order and identity. (c) Which metaphor? A sensible choice of metaphor – e.g. borrowing, mixing or translating – will raise the researcher's awareness of hybridity, regarding who appropriates what and for what purposes, according to which logic of choice, as well as regarding cultural elements that resist translation. (d) Which research area? Finally, we have to consider whether we are looking at hybridity regarding objects, situations or responses, so as to account for instance for aspects of power, as in the encounters of equals and unequals or in conflicting claims of authenticity. Empirically grounded in such a way, the concept of hybridity could stimulate further fruitful and necessary research into the dynamics of cultural contact–an area that continues to grow in importance in the present context of globalization.

References

Ackermann, Andreas. 2002. "Wechselwirkung – Komplexität: Einleitende Bemerkungen zum Kulturbegriff von Pluralismus und Multikulturalismus." In *Patchwork: Geschichte, Problematik und Chancen multikultureller Gesellschaften*, edited by Andreas Ackermann and Klaus E. Müller, 9–29. Bielefeld: transcript Verlag.
Ackermann, Andreas. 2004. "Das Eigene und das Fremde: Hybridität, Vielfalt und Kulturtransfers." In *Handbuch der Kulturwissenschaften, Band III: Themen und Tendenzen*, edited by Friedrich Jäger and Jörn Rüsen, 139–154. Stuttgart: J.B. Metzler.
Ackermann, Andreas, and Klaus E. Müller. 2002. *Patchwork: Dimensionen multikultureller Gesellschaften*. Bielefeld: transcript Verlag.
Alvarez, Jr., Robert. 1995. "The Mexican-US border: the making of an anthropology of borderlands." *Annual Review of Anthropology* 24: 447–470.
Bakhtin, Mikhail (1941) 1984. *Rabelais and his world*. Bloomington: Indiana University Press.
Bakhtin, Mikhail 1981. *The dialogic imagination: four essays*. Austin: University of Texas Press.
Barthes, Roland. (1957) 1972. *Mythologies*. London: Paladin.
Bhabha, Homi. 1994. "Signs taken for wonders: questions of ambivalence and authority under a tree outside Delhi, May 1817". In *The location of culture*, edited by Homi Bhabha, 132–144. Milton Park: Routledge.
Bourdieu, Pierre. (1979) 1984. *Distinction: a social critique of the judgement of taste*. Harvard: Harvard University Press.
Burke, Peter. 2009. *Cultural Hybridity*. Cambridge: Polity Press.
Carpentier, Alejo. (1946) 2001. *Music in Cuba*. Minneapolis.
Castro, Américo. (1948) 1954. *The structure of Spanish history*. Princeton: Princeton University Press.
Clifford, James, and George E. Marcus, eds. 1986. Introduction, In *Writing culture: The poetics and politics of ethnography*. Berkeley: University of California Press.
Crick, Malcolm. 1976. *Explorations in Language and Meaning*. London: Malaby Press.
Dawson, Christopher. 1932. *The making of Europe*. London: Sheed and Ward.
De Certeau, Michel. (1980) 1984. *The Practice of Everyday Life*. Berkeley: University of California Press.
Donnan, Hastings, and Dieter Haller. 2000. "Liminal no more: the relevance of borderland studies." *Ethnologia Europaea* 30/2: 7–22.
Donnan, Hastings, and Thomas M. Wilson. 2001. *Borders: Frontiers of Identity, Nation and State*. Oxford: Berg.
Douglas, Mary. 1966. *Purity and Danger: an analysis of concepts of pollution and taboo*. London: Routledge.
Douglas, Mary. 1975. *Implicit Meanings: selected essays in anthropology*. London: Routlegde.
Evans-Pritchard, Edward Evan. 1951. *Social Anthropology*. London: Routledge.

Foucault, Michel. 1986. Of other spaces. *Diacritics* 16/1: 22–27.
Freyre, Gilberto. (1933) 1946. *The Master and the Slaves.* New York.
Freyre, Gilberto. (1936) 1986. *The Mansions and the Shanties.* Berkeley: University of California Press.
Gluckman, Max. (1940) 1958. *Analysis of a Social Situation in Modern Zululand.* Rhodes-Livingstone Papers 28. Manchester: University Press for the Rhodes-Livingstone Institute.
Hannerz, Ulf. 1980. *Exploring the City: inquiries toward an urban anthropology.* New York: Columbia University Press.
Hannerz, Ulf. 1987. "The world in Creolisation." *Africa* 57/4: 546–559.
Hebdige, Dick. 1979. *Subculture: the meaning of style.* London: Methuen.
Herskovits, Melville. 1937a. *Life in a Haitian Valley.* New York: Alfred A. Knopf.
Herskovits, Melville. 1937b. "African Gods and Catholic Saints in New World Negro Belief." *American Anthropologist* 39/4, 1: 635–643.
Kearney, Michael. 1995. "The local and the global: the anthropology of globalization and transnationalism." *Annual Review of Anthropology* 25: 547–565.
Kohl, Karl-Heinz. 1987. "Travestie der Lebensformen" oder "kulturelle Konversion"? Zur Geschichte des kulturellen Überläufertums." In *Abwehr und Verlangen: Zur Geschichte der Ethnologie*, edited by Karl-Heinz Kohl, 7–38. Frankfurt am Main: Campus.
Kraidy, Marwan M. 2005. *Hybridity, or the cultural logic of globalization.* Philadelphia: Temple University Press.
Leach, Jerry and Gary Kildea. 1976. *Trobriand cricket: an ingenious response to colonialism.* 54 mins.
Lévi-Strauss, Claude. (1958) 1963. *Structural Anthropology.* Basic Books.
Lévi-Strauss, Claude. (1962) 1968. *The Savage Mind.* Chicago: University of Chicago Press.
Lienhardt, Godfrey. 1954. "Modes of thought." In *The Institutions of Primitive Society*, edited by Edward E. Evans-Pritchard et al., 95–107. Oxford: Basil Blackwell.
Malinowski, Bronislaw. 1929. "The Sexual Life of Savages in North-Western Melanesia." London.
Martius, Carl Friedrich Philipp von. (1845) 2003. "Bemerkungen über die Verfassung einer Geschichte Brasiliens." *Institut Martius-Staden Jahrbuch* 50: 189–213.
Mitchell, J. Clyde. 1956. *The Kalela Dance: aspects of social relationships among urban Africans in Northern Rhodesia.* The Rhodes-Livingstone Papers 27. Manchester: University Press for the Rhodes-Livingstone Institute.
Nelson, Dean, and Jalees Andrabi. 2009 . "Chicken tikka masala row grows as Indian chefs reprimand Scottish MP over culinary origins." *Daily Telegraph*, August 4. http://www.telegraph.co.uk/foodanddrink/5972643/Chicken-tikka-masala-row-grows-as-Indian-chefs-reprimand-Scottish-MPs-over-culinary-origins.html.
Ortiz, Fernando. (1940) 1947. *Cuban Counterpoint: Tobacco and Sugar.* Park, Robert Ezra. (1928) 1974. "Human Migration and the Marginal Man." In *The Collected Papers, Vol. 1.*, ed. Robert Ezra Park, 345–356. New York.
Park, Robert Ezra. (1928) 1974. "Human migration and the marginal man." In *The collected papers, vol. 1.*, 345–356. New York: Arno Press
Robertson, Roland. 1995. "Glocalization: time-space and homogeneity-heterogeneity." In *Global modernities*, edited by Mike Featherstone, Scott Lash, and Roland Robertson, 25–44. London: Sage.
Rösler, Michael, and Tobias Wendl. 1999. *Frontiers and Borderlands: anthropological perspectives.* Frankfurt am Main: Peter Lang.
Rouch, Jean. 1956. *Les Maîtres fous.* (28 mins.)
Rudolph, Jürgen. 1998. Reconstructing identities: a social history of the Babas in Singapore. Aldershot: Ashgate.
Said, Edward W. 1978. *Orientalism.* London: Routledge & Kegan Paul.
Said, Edward W. 1993. *Culture and Imperialism.* London: Chatto & Windus.

Spivak, Gayatri Chakravorti. 1988. "Can the subaltern speak? Speculations on widow sacrifice." In *Marxism and the Interpretation of Culture*, edited by Cary Nelson and Lawrence Grossberg, 271–313. London: Macmillan.

Spivak, Gayatri Chakravorti. 1993. *Outside in the Teaching Machine*. New York: Routledge.

Toynbee, Arnold J. 1954. *A Study of History, vol. VIII*. 495 ff. London: Oxford University Press.

Turner, Victor. 1967. *The Forest of Symbols: aspects of Ndembu ritual*. Ithaca: Cornell University Press.

Van Gennep, Arnold. (1909) 2004. *The Rites of Passage*. New York: Routledge.

Werbner, Pnina. 2001. "The limits of cultural hybridity: on ritual monsters, poetic licence and contested postcolonial purifications." *The Journal of the Royal Anthropological Institute* 7/1: 133–152.

Werbner, Pnina. 1997. "The dialectics of cultural hybridity." In *Debating Cultural Hybridity: multi-cultural identities and the politics of anti-racism*, edited by Pnina Werbner and Tariq Modood, 1–26. London: Zed Books.

Young, Robert J.C. 1995. *Colonial Desire: Hybridity in theory, culture and race*. New York: Routledge.

Zangwill, Israel. (1909) 1925. *The Melting Pot: a drama in four acts*. London.

Chapter 3
Circulating Objects and the Power of Hybridization as a Localizing Strategy

Hans Peter Hahn

Abstract The worldwide circulation of goods is one of the driving forces of globalization. This statement holds true in particular for the early globalizing phenomena like the widespread adoption of clothing, weapons and alcohol, whereas nowadays, electronic devices like mobile phones are perceived as having higher relevancy. Modifications of these and many other objects and the constitution of new contexts are at the core of the new cultural concept of hybridization. Rejecting the notion of purity, hybridity contributes to the understanding of mixing cultural phenomena, regardless of their origins, and refers to the transformation of objects, values and cultural institutions, but also to the unequal power relations in many cultural contacts. Historical and ethnographical examples show how hybridity helps to explain the subversive character of many of these changes. As indicated fifty years ago by Arnold Toynbee, Western culture in non-Western contexts undergoes a process of fragmentation. Although Toynbee did not use the term of hybridity, he was the first to hint at the sometimes problematic entanglements that are highlighted by this concept.

3.1 Introduction

All the world over, societies justify their existence by the notion of recognizable and distinguishable roots. According to this logic, cultural diversity is embedded in an ideology of purity which bestows the character of uniqueness of the selected roots (Friedman 2002). Such societies are built around primordial concepts of culture; they defend the unity of a given culture by referring to the distinct identity of their traditions. During the second half of the 20th century, the increasing awareness of globalization was accompanied by the growing popularity of new cultural concepts that differed fundamentally from such ideas. Thus, the notion of the "purity" of a culture was replaced by the idea of the worldwide circulation of goods, institutions and norms. The intensification of global communication, the increase in mobility, and the ever-growing exposure of individuals to global influences seemed to lead to new dimensions of cultural exchange, which ultimately contributed to the emergence of a "world society" in which cosmopolitanism is the norm. These few lines give a rough sketch of globalization up until around the turn of the millennium. From the present point of view, it is more accurate to describe this as an affirmative ideology of "Globalism" (Tsing 2000). It is not the concern, however, of this essay to follow the lines of such a globalistic ideology. Instead, this article will deal with the contradictions of this ideology and with the global influences, which have shifted in focus over about the last 10 years.

Obviously there is no way back to the primordialist ideas. Cultures are not pure, no culture can boast unique roots and the history of human societies was always a story of intermixing and mutual influences (Schulte 1997; Nederveen Pieterse 1995). As a consequence, the debate on globalization has directed itself in recent years to the question on how global influences are adopted, modified, transformed or, by contrast, rejected. Today, globalization is no longer understood as a trend to convergence or a unidirectional process. As a consequence of this, current research questions have to focus on new struggles, ambiguities and contradictions on the social and political level (Wagner 2001, 25). The challenge for research today is to explain the role of global influences in conflicts and possibly in violent encounters. This surprising turn in the globalization debate, which scarcely anyone could have foreseen 15 years ago, leads to the examination of global influences on the grassroots level. It may well be that the earlier affirmative attitude towards globalization has led us to neglect the actors' perspective, and most especially that of the actors struggling for most humble level of daily survival (Burawoy 2000; Stewart 1999).

With these considerations in mind, the relevance of the ideas of cultural appropriation and hybridization becomes clearer. Both concepts were already on their way in the globalization debate over twenty years ago. Even at that time, its propagators used these terms to criticize some of the commonsense assumptions about globalization. The power of both terms derives from their focus on the agency of local actors, without denying the relevance of globalization (Nederveen Pieterse 2001a, b).

In the following, we shall look at the contradictory assessments ascribed to global influences. The classification of globally circulating goods illustrates these contradictions best of all, so a description and assessment of some of these will serve as the starting point of the article. On the one hand such goods are generally seen as important factors in globalization as such (Elwert 2000; Applbaum 2000). On the other hand, they already sparked debates very early on about the open and unpredictable character of their global diffusion (Kohl 2001).

In order to understand the consequences of globalization for cultural images of self and other, the foregoing will be followed by a discussion of the implications of the new concepts of culture. Cultural appropriation and hybridization cannot be adequately explained in a simple framework of cultural mixtures, diversity or "global melange" (Nederveen Pieterse 2003). Against the backdrop of historical case studies and ethnographic evidence, it will be argued that differences in power relations are an important aspect of these new concepts of culture. As will be shown, hybridity has the peculiar capacity to focus on the phenomenon of inequality and multivocality in the context of cultural mixing (Weißköppel 2005). Thus the conclusion will address the political import of the concept of hybridity. Hybridity sheds light on conflicting systems of values and on the logics of exclusion in the context of the intermixing of cultural influences. A deepened understanding of hybridity will reveal some ambivalent states of intermingling which are often overlooked in the popular and mostly affirmative perspective on hybrid objects (Ha 2004).

3.2 The Ambivalence of Globalization Phenomena

Changes in material culture and new patterns of mass consumption constitute crucial phenomena in contemporary globalization (Wallerstein 1974; Trentmann 2009). Consumption may even be one of the future core issues of cultural anthropology – in particular when it comes to understanding the way that different identities and social structures are generated. This is the view held by of a wide range of culture theorists dealing with economic, social and cultural changes in the emerging global situation (Amselle 2002; Jackson 2004). Although there is no consensus on the question as to when globalization started and who are the main actors, most observers agree that it is possible to identify a set of items that were among the first trading goods, and have achieved a somehow iconic status for globalization as such (Kraidy 2003; Wimmer 2003).

While the early phases of globalization were dominated by the circulation of weapons, textiles and alcoholic beverages (Ertl 2008), the range of globally circulating goods has expanded considerably up to the present: today, media and communication technologies like television and mobile phones count among the most important phenomena of globalization (Castells 2007). Globalization is not only a question of the distribution of these commodities and the accompanying techniques, but also about the benefit for the societies that adopt such things (Carlsson 2009; Kaplan 2006). It is a commonly accepted assumption that free media can contribute to the democratic development of many nations. For example, the unhindered reporting of violations against human rights is a valuable tool for the promotion of democraty (Wittmann 2005). Furthermore, there are strong indicators pointing to the contribution of mobile phones to the development in some of the poorest countries (Scott 2004). Thus, it has been shown how the lack of basic infrastructure can be redeemed by the new communication technologies (Petersdorff 2007). As development agents recently claimed, people in remote areas have access to markets, and thus millions of smallholders in Africa may benefit from mobile phones because these makeit possible to get information about the prices of their agricultural products (Goergen and Krause 2006; Cronin 2004). Another example comes from Nepal. Development expert Kamal Raj Dhungel reports how people in remote villages use mobile communication devices to access medical advice if the nearest doctor is at an unattainable distance. Is it possible to imagine something more hybrid than a household without running water and electricity, but with a mobile that serves as a telemedical device?

But this affirmative or even euphoric perspective needs to be tempered in order to open up space for a closer understanding of the ambiguity of the globally circulating material culture. For goods like weapons and alcohol, their questionable value is obvious. Goods of this kind have not always contributed to the development of the receiving societies. Reflecting further on the consequences, it is clear that these things have triggered completely different and very often totally unforeseeable patterns of social change. In contrast to those historical examples, the present phenomena of globalization are accompanied by an overwhelming optimism: globalization seems in this perspective to be a "win-win" situation. Whoever participates in globalization trends may count on a better future, regardless of whether this leads to a new cosmopolitan world society or to a more complex and culturally diverse future. In the context of these visions, the circulating objects will have an important role. Their worldwide usage appears to be a safe base by which the social and political entanglements of their owners can be evaluated (Benhabib 2006). By using the new technologies, like mobile phones, internet or TV, people – at least implicitly – show an affirmative attitude to globalization. Most people around the world, however critical to globalization they might position themselves, undeniably show a considerable "greed for western technologies". Even the Islamic terrorists, who were setting a sign against globalization with the events of 9/11, used Western techniques without questioning them. They are part of globalization and there is no reason to assume that they will turn back the clock by rescinding globalization (Appadurai 2006).

The appeal of Western goods is a driving force for the accelerating impact of globalization (Orlove 1997). This assumption summarizes the current perspective on the reasons for the ever-increasing global influences on many societies worldwide. A similar point of view was already expressed well over fifty years ago by Arnold Toynbee. In his work *The Present-Day Experiment in Western Civilization*, first published in 1958, he describes three important areas of cultural exchange between the Western and non-Western cultures: (1) science and modernity (2) democracy, and (3) religion. Still following Toynbee's train of thought, there is also a clear hierarchy: while the first of these domains attracts the greatest interest, the desire for democracy and religion is comparatively lower. Half a century later we can acknowledge that Toynbee was quite correct in his considerations. As a matter of fact, consumption, technologies and material goods, being the outcome of modernity and science, are highly appreciated worldwide. They even achieved the status of symbols of globalization.

Without using the term of "globalization", Toynbee, however, refers to "cultural refraction", stating that cultural elements transferred by this process of cultural exchange are no longer what they were in their original context. Not only do these elements undergo a profound transformation, but they simultaneously contribute to a change of the societies themselves. The term "refraction" is associated with the metaphor of the prism as an optical device that irreversibly transforms white light into the colours of the spectrum. As will be shown, the idea of "refraction" as the destruction of origins and transformation of properties is easily recognizable in many current usages of the term of hybridization.

Considering today's debate about cultural diversity in the context of globalization, Toynbee's insights are surprisingly apt. At the time of publication his arguments meant a radical break with the ideology of colonialism, which considered the "civilizing mission" to be a core feature of the Western self-image. His remarks on cultural "refraction" as transformation and fragmentation (or even destruction) were highly provocative. To declare that the colonised people, who at that time had been excluded from any kind of political participation for almost a century, might be capable of shaping their future themselves was a threatening perspective for Western decision-makers who firmly believed in their culture's superiority.

The dispute of the last 15 years concerning the cultural consequences of globalization presents at least in some cases positions that are not far from Toynbee's ideas. Some authors have even taken a step back and argued in favour of the expansion of Western culture. A point in case is Thomas L. Friedman, the U.S. journalist, government adviser and author of the book *The Lexus and The Olive Tree* (1999). In this book he uses the metaphor of the "golden horde"; this refers to the global elite (obviously dominated by Western-style protagonists) permanently looking for the optimal economic conditions and bringing prosperity to those places in the world where such conditions are favourable. George Ritzer is another case in point, being one of the most prominent representatives of the homogenization theory. Ritzer, famous for his book on "McDonaldization" (1993), more recently expanded his theory by stressing that the real issues of globalization are not any kind of given objects, topics or ideas. As he explains in another essay, *The Globalization of Nothing* (Ritzer 2003), globalization concerns the way how things are done. The expansion of and domination by norms and the standardization of procedures are the true phenomena of globalization, leaving their impact in the most diverse contexts all over the globe.

However, current research in anthropology and sociology provides relevant criticism against the image of the powerful "golden horde" and against the compulsion to standardization. Ethnographic studies highlight enduring if not increasing diversity. One of the popular new strategies of identification refers to the underscoring of cultural differences. These findings demonstrate how cultural difference is maintained despite of global influences, even when the related phenomena often remain unnoticed. Cultural anthropology has a particular capacity to promote this criticism, since the diversity of cultural phenomena has always been a key element of its research (Hahn 2008). Twenty years ago, cultural anthropology reached a critical point in its own academic history; it had to decide whether to come to the discipline's end because of the rise of a cosmopolitan society, or to take the new forms of intentionally expressed difference for serious. In order to describe these cultural processes which make diversity possible in spite of the dominance of globalization, anthropologists have created a range of catchwords and theoretical approaches. These concepts include the terms creolization, syncretization, cultural appropriation, as well as hybridization (Hannerz 2002).

In spite of pertinent differences, these concepts have some important points in common: they all focus on the perception of the particular agency of groups or individuals who do not consider themselves to be part of the "West" (adopting for a moment the terminology of Toynbee). The concepts imply that these protagonists do actually have their own norms and values.

By speaking about "our and other cosmologies", Marshall Sahlins (1996) aptly demonstrated some dangerous shortcomings in older anthropological concepts. As he explains, the appropriate basis for thinking about cultural difference requires to refer not only to the observable phenomena, but also to the societal images of the world. Western societies have availed themselves of such images of non-Western societies since the days of Greek philosophy. In contrast to the Western historians' sensitivity to Western history, little effort has been spent on understanding images of non-Western societies about the West (Burke 1999). It is obvious that the creation of images about the West historically precedes the adoption of Western goods. The acceptance of things is not the origin, but merely a consequence of an already established idea about the place of the foreign culture in the local set of values and norms (Prestholdt 2008). This insight is the basis from which Sahlins starts his criticism of earlier anthropological work. Even today, many anthropologists wrongly subdivide the history of non-Western societies into two phases, namely before and after the contact with European cultures.

An increased sensitivity to the local, non-Western cosmologies is required in order to overcome the inherent Eurocentrism of this mode of categorizing non-Western history. Popular images of the European's arrival are often caricatures. An example for this is the picturesque image of the Spanish soldiers on horses who were taken for gods. In reality most of the "first contacts" were much less spectacular. The members of other cultures certainly did not immediately lose their agency in cause of the "sudden" presence of the Europeans. They were not - from one moment to the other - convinced of the superiority of the Europeans, if ever they were. The fact that, following the first contact, merchants and missionaries were successfully trading in clothes, alcohol or weapons, does not mean an unquestioned acceptance of Western culture. The relevance of these considerations for the notion of hybridity and the related new concepts of culture is the following: they point to the agency of those who were marginalized as colonial subjects throughout most of the 20th century. Accepting the agency of these people puts the process of mixing into a quite different framework.

As a matter of fact, the continuity between pre-contact and post-contact phases or pre-colonial and colonial times is much more important than historians have suggested so far. This continuity has a direct impact on the way people act when assigning norms and meanings to Western goods. This shift in perspective reveals the hybrid character of societies, even in pre-colonial contexts. A historically authentic example is the case of Westerwälder stoneware which had been brought to Africa since the 17th century (Reineking von Bock 1980; Zeischka 2003). In Central Europe these ceramic household items hat the role of everyday dishes, in Africa they were sacralized after purchase. They achieved the status of ancestor vessels and were kept in sacred places (Fig. 3.1).

3 Circulating Objects and the Power of Hybridization as a Localizing Strategy

Fig. 3.1 Stoneware from Westerwald (Germany) was imported to West Africa from the seventeenth to the nineteenth century. Today these pots are regarded as ancestor vessels and are used for specific rituals (Photo before 1974 by L. Meurer, published in Zeischka (2003))

The driving motive of this particular instance of local "refraction" (or re-contextualizing) is the desire to express cultural continuity, and - simultaneously - a mixing of cultures. Through the power of the local cosmology, Western norms are rejected and replaced by local concepts. The stoneware as such remains unchanged, but it has become a hybrid object by being transferred into another context. Among the consequences is not only a common misunderstanding (stoneware was not acquired as something "superior" to local ceramics, but rather as something "different"), but also a different kind of usage which resulted in its exceptional longevity and in the practice of copying at least some of the ornaments and ceramic forms by local potters.

As this example shows, cultural difference in the context of increasing cultural exchanges can only be explained by emphasizing local cosmologies and local agency. This is the common starting point of the new culture concepts. People act with these objects and draw thereby on the power of local sets of norms and values. And they do so with the intention of localising global goods and other cultural phenomena (Hahn 2004).

Very often, the power of cultural appropriation can be recognized only via the slightest modifications in the objects or in the arrangement of things. A superficial look gives the impression of an imitation or the copying of Western objects and attitudes. But a closer look reveals the cultural strategy of mimicry, which can thwart Western logic and ridicule Western power claims (Taussig 1993). Mimicry in the sense of the Lacanian "mimétisme" does not mean adaptation, but creating a homogenous surface that conceals the differences. Hybridity can thus be an intentional strategy (Toro 2002). The creation of such hybrid objects produces a "scary similarity" and a criticism of the superior (Western) power, without openly offensing the powerful (Bhabha 1985).

Another illustrating example for this has been documented by Jean and John Comaroff (1991) while studying the clothing habits of proselytised men and women in South Africa in the 19th century. The correct wearing of shirts, trousers and robes was the key for testing adherence and good behaviour in public. The missionaries required of a good Christian to respect the Victorian rules of clothing (at least on Sundays) and the African parishioners seemed to subject themselves to this rule without any hesitance. They appropriated these clothes, however, by practicing some minor changes, i.e. by not wearing the shirts in the prescribed manner. Thus, the actors formally accepted the norm of the powerful (the missionaries) and subsequently, by the smallest changes, demonstrated difference. In this way, they were able to show their agency and their ability to articulate their own position (Fig. 3.2). Similar observations have been made in different parts of Africa, very often in colonial contexts. The Africans' copying of Western clothing habits has regularly been suspected by the colonists as a subversive act (Prein 1994). As the example shows, cultural diversity cannot be quantitatively measured; cultural difference is a consequence of a local cosmology and the intention to express difference. Hybrid contexts may be a result of compulsion and even suppression, and they are articulated in spite of the very limited amount of space for agency.

3.3 Hybridity and the Reformulation of the Concept of Culture in the Era of Globalization

The examples given so far (mobile phones, but also stoneware and clothing in colonial contexts) are sufficient to address some shortcomings in commonsense notions of culture. Hybridity as a new concept of culture sensitizes for the antagonistic powers within cultural contexts. Culture can no longer be conceived of as one single system of meanings in the Geertzian sense, but rather as a patchwork and a process of negotiating differences (Zapf 2002). Culture is not a structure (or a "web of meaning"), but a movement. As historians know very well, cultures may blossom, they may vanish, or they may diffuse through time and space. Going beyond the old Geertzian model of culture as text, it is more correct to speak of culture as intertextuality. The concept of cultural hybridity suggests the co-presence of unequal sets of norms and values which struggle for domination or survival.

Hybridity as a concept within *cultural studies* has been fundamentally shaped by the Indian cultural theorist Homi Bhabha (1994). He based his important contributions on findings from what came to be known as *postcolonial studies*, which are a branch of *cultural studies,* focusing on contemporary Indian societies (Nanda 2001). Taking his prior research on the colonial and ex-colonial societies in India as a starting point, Bhabha emphasizes that neither of the two cultures constituting this society (British and Indian) are represented in their integrity in the colonial society.

Fig. 3.2 Local chief in Lesotho, dressed up as a Western gentleman. This fashion was a kind of mimicry. Simultaneously, minor changes made clear that it also served to articulate self-conscious resistance against Western domination (Picture from Schapera (1934))

For this historical context, Bhabha has coined the term "third space". "Third space" designates a societal frame that compels the actors to create new cultural forms under the impact of colonial power. In this new space two cultures join under the auspices of violence and force. The subaltern actors as well as the colonizing actors are cut off from the means to consolidate and legitimise their actions by tradition, because the old cultures no longer have any validity (Dougan 2004). In this emphasis on the novelty of cultural forms, hybridity reveals an astonishing similarity with Claude Lévi-Strauss's notion of "bricolage" (Saalmann et al. 2006).

Hybrid societies and hybrid cultural phenomena deny the authority of tradition; they can be only indirectly explained by the differences in cultural roots. Tensions, violence and unequal power conditions are constitutive of cultural hybridity. The new cultural traits are not intended for permanence, because the inherent tensions render sustainable innovations impossible. Hybrid societies live for the moment and try to make it from one day to the next tackling uneven power relations. As the example of the Christian converts in South Africa makes clear, the domination of Western cultural traits is just a superficial description. A closer look and a deeper understanding bring us to the strategy of mimicry, to a cunning imitation that has arisen under pressure and appears only temporarily.

Cultures marked by hybridity can also be a battleground (Said 1993), and, as the examples from the context of colonialism have made clear, culture can even be a nightmare. Taking these conditions seriously means furthermore that culture is not spatially contained. As Bhabha (1994) has shown in the introduction to his seminal book, *Loctions of Culture*, there is no longer just "one location" for a culture, and even the colonists are unable to delimit the mixing of cultures to the colony. Indian postcolonial cultures undeniably exist in India, as well as in Great Britain and elsewhere. It has become impossible to control who is part of the hybrid culture and who has the option to stay out. Hybrid phenomena spread throughout the globe and engulf any kind of previously existing competing cultural form (Kruse 2006).

Quite possibly, multiculturalism was the last tentative attempt to integrate the ideology of globalism into the observations of persisting diversity. But multiculturalism structured the relations between cultures as a simple apposition, which means adding one culture to another on an equal level (Lenz 1996). As the examples indicate, the history is much more complicated, and cultures intermingle and mix on uneven terms. Multiculturalism is linked to the idea that several cultures coexist at one place; it fails to explain how cultures mesh, intertwine and interlock. The discernible distance between cultures in one society is never just the outcome of diversity, but rather the result of powerful strategic acting, when people aim at making differences visible. Hybridity is, still following Bhabha (1988), not about diversity but about difference.

Generally speaking, notions of culture have frequently borrowed from biology, and in particular such notions metaphorized the process of growing and blossoming (or even dying) plants (Böhme 1996). Hybridity is based on this tradition of metaphors while introducing some new properties. Culture in the context of hybridity does not simply refer to the plant that grows according to the cultivator's capacity to take care of it. Hybridity can also be the super phenotype, as it is in the case of a hybrid plant. Moreover, hybridity may become the "bastard", which is its invective (Kruse 2006). Thus, the biological metaphor associated with the term hybridity reveals a particular ambivalence, which I perceive as the strength of this concept. Whereas pure forms, i.e. distinctive species, live together without mixing, every bastard is a danger for the pure "natural" form of a species, because it can mix up and bring purity to an end. But this bastard can also be the result of a scientific breeding strategy which leads to the combination of properties that have never been united in one plant before. Furthermore, the "hybrid" as a biological category is not intended to produce offspring showing the same phenotype. Hybrids are powerful and unique; permanence is not a relevant characteristic. More often than not they are isolated. Therefore it is legitimate to claim that hybridity is a kind of disruption, creating new kinds of phenomena and making it impossible to turn back to the older forms, which are misleadingly labelled as "pure" forms. In spite of the continuing usage of "purity" as a discursive topic (Friedman 1997), the permanently irreversible transformations are a basic condition of cultures. Cultural renaissances, integralism and fundamentalism are no exception of this, as they are the results of cultural relations and the desire to dissociate once own culture from others. Like the hybrids in biology, colonial societies are a short-term phenomenon with highly specific qualities; they are not capable of becoming durable.

There is a current trend to treat hybrid technologies as something fashionable. This image is rooted in the new functionality of objects that combine quite different devices in one technical unit of complexity (Ha 2005). This much-admired hybrid technology promises seamless functioning and makes the user forget the different principles of operation. It is even possible to say that in this sense, colonialism was affirmative to hybridization insofar as the subaltern was associated with quite particular new "functions". As Robert Young (1994) emphasises, functional differentiation was an integral part of the colonial dream, and it was accepted as a rule for all domains of social life, not only for work. The introduction of new technologies, including those of hybrid character was highly appreciated.

Two questions result from these reflections. The first is: who benefits in a particular historical context from hybridity? And the second: how stable are hybrid societies over time? The shift from the colonial to the postcolonial context means that hybrid societies are rapidly changing and transgressing spatial boundaries. The postcolony is no longer a phenomenon related to the former colonies, but also concerns particular contexts of cultural hybridity in all societies worldwide.

3.4 Hybrid Objects Reconsidered

Returning to the beginning of the paper, it becomes clear that mobile phones, the ultimate hybrid objects and most emblematic gadgets of globalization, must be something more than just the fulfilment of dreams of boundless communication. In the light of the hybridization concepts, the assumption that mobile phones might have a similar role in non-Western societies as they do have in Europe becomes untenable. Ethnographic studies confirm this scepticism: in contrast to widespread expectations, mobile phones are not simply a means of accessing information in the least developed countries. As recent research in Tanzania (Mercer 2005), Ghana (Slater and Kwami 2005) and Burkina Faso (Hahn and Kibora 2008) has shown, people use mobile phones quite differently in geographically scattered places. The purpose for acquiring these devices and using them has little to do with global connections, but much more with re-establishing family networks, thereby contributing to the strengthening of local ties. Mobile phones do not give access to economically relevant information, as international development agents suggest. Instead, mobiles are crucial for the vitality of family relations and the functioning of the kinship network as a specific feature of society in the countries concerned. Nobody in such places would assume that mobile phones are less relevant or inferior to mobile phones in developed countries.

Thus, the notion of "bricolage" previously mentioned is closely connected to hybridity and takes into account the improvised character of the intentional changes in contexts and usages. There is a new use of the mobile phone which gives even stronger evidence of its provocative character. Currently mobile phones are used as remote control units and triggers for improvised explosive devices in Iraq and Afghanistan (Freudenrich 2010). Obviously the lifespan of objects in this kind of usage is just a few minutes, and the communication aspect is highly debatable. These technically modified mobiles, however, are truly hybrid phenomena. They constitute perfectly matching examples for the notions of Toynbee and Bhabha. They are hybrid not only in the technical sense (combining GSM technology with IED triggering functionality), but also in a strict sense of the concept, because their functional efficiency is far beyond the ordinary function of the "pure" mobiles. Last but not least, they demonstrate interaction in a society without a consensus about how this object should be used. These objects do not have any location. The hybrid technology may be assembled anywhere in the world, there is no way of restricting the use of these objects, once the combatants appreciate that the technology suits their intentions.

To be sure, this example of hybrid objects is shocking. It is obvious that for ethical reasons no ethnographic research can be done to find out more about this object. Certainly, it serves its purpose here because it makes the political dimension quite clear. This last example gives evidence to a hybridity that is not only relevant to literature and popular culture, but for understanding what Toynbee called the "Present-Day Experiment of the West" (Toynbee 1962) (Fig. 3.3).

Fig. 3.3 Mobile phone modified to act as a trigger for an improvised explosive device. This truly hybrid object not only shows the material inventiveness, but also represents the violence of cultural contacts in the context of unequal power relations. Photo from URL: http://science.howstuffworks.com /ied.htm

3.5 Conclusion

In conclusion it might be useful to add some further remarks to the question of how the new concept of culture is characterized by hybridity. As has become clear, hybridity can be an explicit statement by those who actually introduce, invent or use a hybrid object. It always draws its power from the combination of cultural traits originating at different sources. This combination is not a simple apposition, but a kind of functional differentiation or intermingling. Those who act in a hybrid way, by generating hybrid objects or using them, have no interest in cultural purity. "Distinguishable roots" are not an issue any more. This refusal to identify origins can be considered a consequence of unequal power relations. In this context "purity" may even be regarded as a sign of weakness. (Imagine the perspective of the combatants using mobile phones as triggers for explosive devices.) From the point of view of hybridity, "pure objects" cannot have the same power as objects that have been captured, modified and thus transformed. Following Gérard Genette's reflections about palimpsests as a mode of "over writing", Robert Stam (1999) has coined the term "Palimpsestic Aesthetics" for the specific appreciation of hybrid objects. The greatest appeal is evinced by cultural phenomena which do not have unique roots, or whose properties have been modified without considering at all what might be the "roots" of the object.

In the wake of these thoughts, hybridity has taken on quite a political message. Possibly Toynbee was the first precursor of the inadvertent entanglements between Western and non-Western ideas, institutions and structures. Although a categorical distinction between Western and non-Western cultural phenomena is untenable today, and in spite of the fact that Toynbee himself never used the term of hybridity, his untimely work foreshadows the provocative and sometimes dangerous entanglements between cultures with uneven statuses of power, which later on were conceptualised by the term of hybridity. Toynbee was one of the first cultural theorists to understand that there is no such thing as the superiority of the "pure" and that the idea of colonialism (to civilize the rest of the world) is an unacceptable ideology. Today it is evident that hybrid cultural phenomena are not only articulations made within a particular historical and regional context, but also a political statement for any future society, because all societies have mixed roots and live under conditions of uneven power relations.

References

Amselle, Jean-Loup. 2002. "Globalization and the Future of Anthropology." *African Affairs* 101: 213–229.

Appadurai, Arjun. 2006. *Fear of Small Numbers. An Essay on the Geography of Anger*. Durham: Duke University Press.

Applbaum, Kalman. 2000. "Crossing Borders: Globalization as Myth and Charter in American Transnational Consumer Marketing". *American Ethnologist* 27/2: 257–282.

Benhabib, Seyla. 2006. *Another Cosmopolitanism*. Oxford: Oxford University Press.
Bhabha, Homi K. 1985. "Signs Taken for Wonders: Questions of Ambivalence and Authority under a Tree Outside Delhi, May 1817." In *'Race', Writing and Difference*, edited by Henry L. Gates, 163–185. Chicago: University of Chicago Press.
Bhabha, Homi K. 1988. "The Commitment to Theory." *New formations* 5: 5–23.
Bhabha Homi K. 1994. *The Location of Culture*. Oxford: Oxford University Press.
Böhme, Hartmut. 1996. "Vom Cultus zur Kulturwissenschaft. Zur historischen Semantik des Kulturbegriffs." In *Literaturwissenschaft – Kulturwissenschaft. Positionen, Themen, Perspektiven*, edited by Renate Glaser and Matthias Luserke, 48–68. Opladen: Westdeutscher Verlag.
Burawoy, Michael. 2000. "Grounding Globalization." In *Global Ethnography. Forces, Connections, and Imaginations in a Postmodern World*, edited by Michael Burawoy, 337–350. Berkeley: University of California Press.
Burke, Peter. 1999. "Westliches historisches Denken in globaler Perspektive - 10 Thesen." In *Westliches Geschichtsdenken. Eine interkulturelle Debatte*, edited by Jörn Rüsen, 31–52. Göttingen: Vandenhoeck und Ruprecht.
Carlsson, Ulla. 2009. "Media and Global Divides. IAMCR World Congress, Stockholm 20–25 July 2008." Jubilee issue of the *Nordicom Review* 30. Stockholm: University of Gothenburg Press.
Castells, Manuel. 2007. *Mobile Communication and Society. A Global Perspective*. A Project of the Annenberg Research Network on International Communication. Cambridge: MIT Press.
Comaroff, Jean, and John L. Comaroff. 1991. *Of Revelation and Revolution: Christianity, Colonialism, and Consciousness in South Africa*. Volume One. Chicago: University of Chicago Press.
Cronin, Jon. 2004. "Rural Africa joins mobile revolution" (from BBC -News).
Dougan, Henry. 2004. "Hybridization: Its Promise and Lack of Promise." *CODESRIA Bulletin* 1&2: 33–38.
Elwert, Georg. 2000. "Globalisierung als Phänomen der sozialen und kulturellen Entwicklung." In *Die Bedeutung des Ethnischen im Zeitalter der Globalisierung. Einbindungen, Ausgrenzungen, Säuberungen*, edited by Rupert Moder, 1–16. Bern: Paul Haupt.
Ertl, Thomas. 2008. *Seide, Pfeffer und Kanonen. Globalisierung im Mittelalter*. Darmstadt: Primus.
Freudenrich, Craig. 2010. "How IEDs work." Last visited November 8, 2010, http//science.howstuffworks.com/ied1.htm.
Friedman, Jonathan. 1997. "Global Crises, the Struggle for Cultural Identity and Intellectual Porkbarreling: Cosmopolitans versus Locals, Ethnics and Nationals in an Era of De-Hegemonisation." In *Debating Cultural Hybridity*, edited by Pnina Werbner and Tariq Modood, 70–89. London: ZED Books.
Friedman, Jonathan. 2002. "From Roots to Routes. Tropes for Trippers." *Anthropological Theory* 2/1: 21–36.
Friedman, Thomas L. 1999. *The Lexus and the Olive Tree*. New York: Anchor Books.
Goergen M., and Axel Krause. 2006. "Jetzt funkt's auch in Afrika." *Stern* 2006/22:16–22.
Ha, Kien Nghi. 2004. "Kolonial-rassistisch - subversiv - postmodern: Hybridität bei Homi Bhabha und in der deutschsprachigen Rezeption." In *Interkultureller Transfer und nationaler Eigensinn*. Edited by Rebekka Habermas and Rebekka von Mallinckrodt, 53–69. Göttingen: Wallenstein.
Ha, Kien Nghi. 2005. *Hype um Hybridität. Kultureller Differenzkonsum und postmoderne Verwertungstechniken im Spätkapitalismus*. Bielefeld: Transcript Verlag.
Hahn, Hans Peter. 2004. "Global Goods and the Process of Appropriation." In *Between Resistance and Expansion. Explorations of Local Vitality in Africa*. Beiträge zur Afrikaforschung, 18, edited by Peter Probst and Gerd Spittler, 211–230. Münster: Lit Verlag.
Hahn, Hans Peter. 2008. "Diffusionism, Appropriation, and Globalization. Some Remarks on Current Debates in Anthropology." *Anthropos* 103: 191–202.

Hahn, Hans Peter and Ludovic Kibora. 2008. "The Domestication of the Mobile Phone Oral Society and New ICT in Burkina Faso." *Journal of Modern African Studies* 46: 87–109.
Hannerz, Ulf. 2002. *Flows, Boundaries and Hybrids: Keywords in Transnational Anthropology.* Stockholm: Stockholm University Press.
Jackson, Peter. 2004. "Local Consumption Cultures in a Globalizing World." *Transactions of the Institute of British Geographers (N.S.)* 29: 165–178.
Kaplan, Warren. 2006. "Can the Ubiquitous Power of Mobile Phones be Used to Improve Health Outcomes in Developing Countries?" *Globalization and Health* 2: 1–14.
Kohl, Karl-Heinz. 2001. "Sakralisierung, Demonetarisierung, Zerstörung. Über den Umgang mit europäischen Warenimplantaten in außereuropäischen Kulturen." In *Begegnung und Konflikt - eine kulturanthropologische Bestandsaufnahme*, edited by Wolfgang Fikentscher, 63–73. Munich: Bayerische Akademie der Wissenschaften.
Kraidy, Marwan M. 2003. "Globalization avant la lettre? Cultural Hybridity and Media Power in India." In *Global Media Studies. Ethnographic Perspectives*, edited by Patrick D. Murphy and Marwan M. Kraidy, 276–298. London: Routledge.
Kruse, Jan. 2006. "Hybridisation: The Agenda of a Paradigm Shift in Cultural Theory - or: How St Nicholas the Bastard Became a Discoursive Figurehead." In *Hybridising East and West. Tales beyond Westernisation*, edited by Dominique Schirmer, Gernot Saalmann and Christl Kessler, 35–54. Münster: Lit Verlag.
Lenz, Günter H. 1996. "Transnational American Studies: Conceptualizing Multicultural Identities and Communities." In *Fremde Texte verstehen. Festschrift für Lothar Bredella zum 60. Geburtstag*, edited by Herbert Christ and Lothar Bredella, 191–202. Tübingen: Narr.
Mercer, Claire. 2005. "Telecentres and Transformations: Modernizing Tanzania through the Internet." *African Affairs* 105: 243–264.
Nanda, Meera. 2001. "We are All Hybrids Now: The Dangerous Epistemology of Post-Colonial Populism" (Review Article). *Journal of Peasant Studies* 28/2: 162–186.
Nederveen Pieterse, Jan. 1995. "Globalization as Hybridization." In *Global Modernities*, edited by Mike Featherstone et al., 45–68. London: Sage.
Nederveen Pieterse, Jan. 2001a. *Development Theory: Deconstructions / Reconstructions.* London: Sage.
Nederveen Pieterse, Jan. 2001b. "Hybridity, So What? The Anti-Hybrity Backlash and the Riddles of Recognition." *Theory, Culture and Society* 18 (2–3): 219–245.
Nederveen Pieterse, Jan. 2003. *Globalization and Culture: Global Melange.* Lanham: Rowman & Littlefield.
Orlove, Benjamin S.1997. *The Allure of the Foreign. Imported Goods in Postcolonial Latin America.* Ann Arbor: University of Michigan Press.
Prein, Philipp. 1994. "Guns and Top-Hats: African Resistance in German South West Africa." *Journal of Southern African Studies* 20/1: 99–121.
Prestholdt, Jeremy. 2008. "Domesticating the World. African Consumerism and the Genealogies of Globalization." Oakland: University of California Press.
Reineking von Bock, Gisela. 1980. "Verarbeitung von rheinischem Steinzeug." *Keramos* 87: 11–50.
Ritzer, George. 1993. *The McDonaldization of Society: An Investigation into the Changing Character of Contemporary Social Life.* (Revised Edition). Thousand Oaks: Pine Forge Press.
Ritzer. George. 2003. *The Globalization of Nothing.* Thousand Oaks: Pine Forge Press.
Sahlins, Marshall D. 1996. "The Sadness of Sweetness: The Native Anthropology of Western Cosmology." *Current Anthropology* 37: 395–428.
Saalmann, Gernot, Dominique Schirmer and Christl Kessler. 2006. "Introduction: Hybridity and Hybridisation." In *Hybridising East and West. Tales beyond Westernisation*, edited by Dominique Schirmer, Gernot Saalmann and Christl Kessler. Münster: Lit Verlag.
Said, Edward W. 1993. *Culture and Imperialism.* New York: Knopf.

Schulte, Bernd. 1997. "Kulturelle Hybridität. Kulturanthropologische Anmerkungen zu einem 'Normalzustand'." In *Hybridkultur. Medien - Netze – Künste*, edited by Irmela Schneider and Christian W. Thomsen, 245–263. Cologne: Wienand.

Scott, Nigel. 2004. "The Impact of Mobile Phones in Africa." Background paper, Contract ref: CNTR 02. London: Commission for Africa.

Slater, Don and Janet Kwami. 2005. "Embeddedness and Escape: Internet and Mobile Use as Poverty Reduction Strategies in Ghana." Information Society Research Group (ISRG) Working Paper. London: University College Press.

Stam, Robert. 1999. "Palimpsestic Aesthetics." In *Performing Hybridity*, edited by May Joseph and Jennifer Fink, 59–78. Minneapolis: University of Minnesota Press.

Stewart, Charles. 1999. "Syncretism and its Synonyms. Reflections on Cultural Mixture." *Diacritics: A Review of Contemporary Criticism* 29 (3): 40–62.

Taussig, Michael T. 1993. *Mimesis and Alterity. A Particular History of the Senses*. London: Routledge.

Toro, Alfonso de 2002. "Jenseits von Postmoderne und Postkolonialität. Materialien zu einem Modell der Hybridität und des Körpers als transrelationalem, transversalem und transmedialem Wissenschaftskonzept. " In *Räume der Hybridität. Postkoloniale Konzepte in Theorie u. Literatur*, edited by Christoph Hamann, 15–52. Hildesheim: Olms.

Toynbee, Arnold J. 1962. *The Present-Day Experiment in Western Civilization*. Oxford: Oxford University.

Trentmann, Frank. 2009. "Consumption and Globalization in History." *Journal Consumer Culture* 9 (2): 187–220.

Tsing, Anna L. 2000. "The Global Situation." *Cultural Anthropology* 15: 327–360.

Von Petersdorff, Winand. 2007. "Tüchtige Unternehmer entwickeln Afrika." *Frankfurter Allgemeine Sonntagszeitung*, June 3.

Wagner, Bernd. 2001. "Kulturelle Globalisierung: Weltkultur, Lokalität und Hybridisierung." In *Kulturelle Globalisierung. Zwischen Weltkultur und kultureller Fragmentierung*. Schriftenreihe der HDGÖ, 13, edited by Bernd Wagner, 9–38. Essen: Klartext.

Wallerstein, Immanuel M. 1974. *The Modern World System*. New York: Academic Press.

Weißköppel, Cordula. 2005. "'Hybridität' - die ethnografische Annäherung an ein theoretisches Konzept." In *Globalisierung im lokalen Kontext. Perspektiven und Konzepte von Handeln in Afrika*. Beiträge zur Afrikaforschung 20, edited by Roman Loimeier, Dieter Neubert, and Cordula Weißköppel, 311–347. Münster: LIT.

Wimmer, Andreas. 2003. "Globalisierungen Avant la Lettre: Isomorphisierung und Heteromorphisierung in einer vernetzten Welt." *Sociologus (N.F.)* 53: 1–41.

Wittmann, Frank. 2005. "Medienpluralismus in einem semiautoritären System. Die Grenzen öffentlicher Kommunikation in Burkina Faso." *Medienheft, edited by Katholischer Mediendienst Züric*h, March 29: unpag.

Young, Robert. 1994. *Colonial Desire. Hybridity in Theory, Culture and Race*. London: Routledge.

Zapf, Harald. 2002. *Dekonstruktion des Reinen: Hybridität und ihre Manifestationen im Werk von Ishmael Reed*. Würzburg: Königshauen & Neumann.

Zeischka, Annette. 2003. *Westerwälder Keramik in Afrika*. Höhr-Grenzhausen: Helmuth Ecker.

Chapter 4
Conceptualizing Cultural Hybridization in Archaeology

Philipp W. Stockhammer

Abstract Today, there continues to be an enormous epistemological gap between the lively discussion on the phenomenon of cultural hybridization in cultural anthropology and the reality of methodological approaches in archaeological interpretation. The diversity of human interaction and the hybridization processes connected therewith, on the one hand, and the fragmentary and silent character of archaeological source material on the other have been seen as insuperable obstacles to the translation of this concept into a practical method for archaeology. In my contribution, I shall attempt to overcome these barriers by breaking down a complex anthropological discourse into components that may be useful for archaeological sources. My aim is to unravel hybridization processes, which I call processes of entanglement, into distinct stages and consider the potential of each stage to be materialized in the archaeological record. I shall further attempt to distinguish between the entanglement of objects and the entanglement of social practices, because foreign, but in their materiality still unchanged, objects can be used in already entangled social practices. Subsequently, I shall examine what stage of the process of entanglement has given rise to an entangled object or social practice. Finally, the application of the concept of hybridization in recent studies on the Late Bronze Age Eastern Mediterranean will be reviewed and my own approach demonstrated on the basis of a case study.

4.1 Introduction

Hybridization – many archaeologists consider this term either to be unnecessary, or a concept that will be helpful at any conceivable occasion. Beyond the still existing lack of interest towards theoretical issues on the part of many Central European archaeologists, one can identify an increase in the use of the term hybridity in current archaeological publications. However, the theoretical debates in many of these writings are mostly limited to a quotation of *The Location of Culture* by Homi Bhabha (2007) and the other major contributors to this topic, and generally show that little thought has been given to the use of this term. In this paper, I shall attempt to go beyond the current usage in the relevant discourse in archaeology. I would like to take a step back and ask whether hybridization can be transformed from a metaphor into a concept, whether it should be called "hybridization" at all, whether this concept has indeed any validity in archaeology, and if so, how we can adapt it to the needs of the discipline.

Before trying to conceptualise hybridization for archaeology, we have to be aware of the character of archaeological sources and outline their potential and limitations. Following that, we can examine Homi Bhabha's definition of "hybridity" and how material cultural studies try to harness this theoretical concept for their material evidence. As a third step, I will discuss the term "hybridity" in the light of its inherent terminological difficulties and argue for a term less coloured by biological or postcolonial backgrounds. Furthermore, I will contrast my analysis of the postcolonial concept of "hybridity" with the epistemological potential of archaeological sources and propose a methodology that will allow past cultural transformation processes to be analysed. Finally, I shall illustrate this methodological approach by analysing archaeological evidence from the Late Bronze Age Eastern Mediterranean of the 2nd millennium BC.

4.2 Potential and Limitations of Archaeological Sources

Before employing concepts from other disciplines for one's own subject, i.e. prehistoric archaeology in the present case, one must look at the potential and the limitations of the sources used by archaeologists. Prehistoric archaeology analyses material objects and materialized social practices from periods and regions for which literary sources are either very rare or completely missing. This lack of literary sources, together with the scarcity of pictorial depictions on prehistoric objects, makes it impossible to go far beyond a merely etic perspective. Any reconstructions of emic perspectives remain hypothetical, although a systematic comparative approach based on ethnographic analogies might enable us to get an idea of what kinds of prehistoric emic perspectives could have existed (Furholt and Stockhammer 2007). Moreover, we have to be aware that the surviving archaeological record from prehistoric times must not be interpreted as a mirror of past life. Only a small part of the artefacts used by prehistoric man can survive the millennia of decay. Primarily, these are stone tools, bones and pottery. Wood, textiles and other organic materials are only very rarely preserved. Metals have always been recycled and are usually only found when they were intentionally deposited in the ground – e.g. as a hoard or as burial goods. Moreover, prehistoric artefacts are very often separated from their past functional context. Only in rare instances are artefacts excavated at their place of prehistoric use, which we call "in situ". In most cases, archaeologists are limited to analysing what was left behind, overlooked or forgotten by prehistoric man and which has been re-deposited many times. Therefore, prehistoric archaeology deals with the surviving fragments of prehistoric artefacts, which are mostly deprived of their past functional contexts, in a situation where there are no literary sources to tell us about the perception of these objects. And obviously we are also unable to observe or talk with the people who used them. This particular characteristic of archaeological sources must be kept in mind when we are trying to conceptualize cultural hybridization for archaeology.

4.3 "Hybridization" in Postcolonial Studies

Since I have just used the term "cultural hybridization", it is necessary to take a close look at the concept as defined by Homi Bhabha, to whom it is mostly referred to in archaeology. A close reading of Bhabha's *The Location of Culture* reveals an interesting development in its definition throughout the volume. In his introduction he gives a surprisingly clearly written definition of "cultural hybridization", where he compares it with a stairwell: "The stairwell as liminal space, in-between the designations of identity, becomes the process of symbolic interaction, the connective tissue that constructs the difference between upper and lower, black and white. The hither and thither of the stairwell, the temporal movement and passage that it allows, prevents identities at either end of it from settling into primordial polarities. This interstitial passage between fixed identifications opens up the possibility of a cultural hybridity that entertains difference without an assumed or imposed hierarchy" (Bhabha 2007, 5). This means that cultural hybridity can emerge from the liminal space, where two different identities – i.e. two different cultural entities – overlap, and that this space is free from the structural hierarchies of the entities themselves. However, in the course of his book Bhabha politicises his concept of hybridity (Bhabha 2007, 19, 35, 37, 83–84, 143–144, 153, 158–172, 292, 358–360), until it becomes the symbol of the strategies that the subaltern and migrants develop in colonial and postcolonial contexts to deal with their particular situations: "Hybridity is the sign of the productivity of colonial power, its shifting forces and fixities; it is the name for the strategic reversal of the process of domination through disavowal (that is, the production of discriminatory identities that secure the "pure" and original identity of the authority). Hybridity is the revaluation of the assumption of colonial identity through the repetition of discriminatory identity effects. It displays the necessary deformation and displacement of all sites of discrimination and domination" (Bhabha 2007, 159). Consequently, "hybridity" loses the adjective "cultural" (Bhabha 2007, 5) within the book, which is replaced by the adjective "colonial" (Bhabha 2007, 160–161). This is based on Bhabha's equating of "the theoretical" with "the political" (Bhabha 2007, 45). Reading through his book, one might therefore distinguish between two kinds of definition for hybridity: a cultural-theoretical one and a political-theoretical one. This is not a distinction made by Bhabha, for whom the political connotation is central, but this is the beginning and the end of the development of his concept of hybridity. In Bhabha's view, hybridity cannot be conceptualized without a political dimension. His political definition of hybridity was highly influential in postcolonial studies.

However, if we stick to this political definition, the concept can hardly go beyond the narrow realm of postcolonial studies and cannot be used beyond any colonial or post-colonial context. Looking at my archaeological source material, I have to decide whether I refrain completely from using the term hybridity (acknowledging its political dimension) or whether I further explore the applicability of Bhabha's initial, less political definition of "cultural hybridity".

4.4 Terminological Preoccupations

Depriving Bhabha's terminology of its political dimension brings us back to the biological connotations of the term "hybridity". There is no doubt that hybridity as a biological metaphor is highly problematic (cf. Papastergiadis 1997; Stewart 1999, 45; Weißköppel 2005, 317–319) and its translation into an apolitical concept for the cultural sciences is questionable. Recently, Peter Burke (2009, 34–65) has taken a deep look at the different terms which might be used instead of "hybridity". He refers to terms like "borrowing", "melting pot", "stew", "creolization",[1] "syncretism",[2] "cultural mixing", "glocalization"[3] and "cultural translation": "As for 'hybridity', it is a slippery, ambiguous term, at once literal and metaphorical, descriptive and explanatory. The concepts of mixing and hybridity also suffer from the disadvantage of appearing to exclude individual agency. 'Mixing' sounds too mechanical. 'Hybridity' evokes the outside observer studying culture as if it were nature, and the products of individuals and groups as if they were botanical specimens." (Burke 2009, 54–55). He concludes: "Although there are still too many terms and concepts in circulation to describe and analyse the processes that are the subject of this volume, we do need a number of them to do justice both to human agency (as in the case of 'appropriation' or 'cultural translation') and to changes of which the agents are unaware (as in the case of 'hybridization' or 'creolization'). An awareness of alternative concepts offers a defence against the confusion of concepts with the world they are used to analyse" (Burke 2009, 65).

In my view, however, a multitude of terminologies and concepts is more of a hindrance than a help when it comes to developing the "hybridity" metaphor into a concept useful for archaeology. Moreover, it seems to me that in modern academic

---

[1] Stewart 2007a presents a broad range of perspectives on "creolization". However, the editor himself refrains from any distinct definition of the term, which he sees exemplified by processes of restructuring in contexts of migration and adaptation to new environments under the experience of disease and deprivation (Stewart 2007b, 18).

[2] cf. Stewart 1999 for an intense discussion of the problems connected with the term "syncretism".

[3] The term "glocalization" originates from Japanese business practices and was popularised by Robertson (1992, 173–174; 1995) in order to accentuate a spatial perspective (cf. Wicker 2000, 208–209). However, the interconnectedness of the local and the global does not permit a clear distinction in most contexts (Loimeier et al. 2005).

discourse "hybridity" is either perceived as untenably laden with a pejorative biological background, or as purely politically postcolonial. So, on my way towards devising a concept based on a depoliticised version of Bhabha's cultural hybridity, I first wish to change my terminology. In order to avoid the preoccupations of a biological metaphor I would like to switch to a different term, which is "entanglement" in English and "Geflecht" and "Verflechtung" in German. Both terms comprise the aspects of agency, processuality and the creation of something new which is more than just an addition of its origins. "Entanglement" and "Geflecht/Verflechtung" avoid the notion of text – and therefore culture as a text – which is connected with terms like "texture" or "Gewebe", and point rather to the unstructuredness of human creativity. The term "entanglement" is also favoured by Nicholas Thomas in his influential study on exchange, material culture and colonialism in the Pacific (Thomas 1991) regardless of the negative connotations the term may have in everyday use. Moreover, the term "entangled history" is widely acknowledged in the scientific community and emphasizes transcultural interaction in historical processes (Conrad and Randeria 2002; Kaelble 2005) and is also increasingly used in archaeology (e.g. Dietler 1998). In the following, I will develop a concept of what could be called "cultural hybridization", but which I would like to call "entanglement" and which is based on a depoliticized version of the postcolonial concept, as I do not believe it is helpful to stop using the concept beyond the fields of postcolonial studies.

4.5 Developing a Concept of Cultural Entanglement

One has to admit that not much is left when Bhabha's concept is deprived of its political character, but it is the core from which he created his political theory: i.e. the creative potential of liminal spaces, the border regions of entities which he calls identities or identifications. Of course, to speak of entities evokes the idea of essentialism, of superseded assumptions of cultural purity.[4] In my view, however, material culture studies cannot exist without creating entities from an etic perspective for their analytical approaches. But we should regard them only as "crutches for understanding (cf. Geiger 1964, 126–127: "Definitionen sind Krücken der Erkenntnis. Krücken aber sollen vor allem handlich sein."), not as static and historically existing structures. I would like to focus on the liminal spaces of our etic entities and, therefore, etically defined liminal spaces which were probably

---

[4] In Ackermann's (2004, 152) view, the differentiation between "hybrid" and "original" cultures has led to a new and unjustified essentialisation of the concept of "culture". It is, therefore, a fallback to the nineteenth century's construction of cultures as pure and homogenous political entities (cf. Wagner 2001, 22–25).

never perceived as being liminal by prehistoric man.[5] The creative potential of these liminal spaces can result in what I would like to call "entanglement" and which Bhabha calls "hybridity", which in his own words is "at once a mode of appropriation and of resistance" (Bhabha 2007, 172).

However, even if I refrain from using the term "hybridity", I am still confronted with the problem that "hybridity" and related terms are dominantly used in a metaphorical way (Ackermann 2004, 140), e. g. when Claude Lévi-Strauss (1994, 424) postulates: "All cultures are the result of a mishmash" or in Edward W. Said's (1993, xxv) words: "All cultures are involved in one another; none is single and pure, all are hybrid". As a result of his terminological comparisons Peter Burke (2009, 34–65) gives different names for what he calls a "concept", but does not elaborate on the analytical procedure connected therewith. Similar to Burke, Nicolas Thomas calls "hybridity" a concept but considers it to be "too general and reactive to contribute to either the understanding or the political critique of cultural forms" (Thomas 1996, 9). But even if the world seems to be completely entangled, I consider it possible to develop the metaphor into an epistemologically useful concept by restricting the use of the term "entanglement" and connected terms like "liminal spaces" and "in-between" to the analysis of distinct processes of appropriation.

If one wishes to transfer the concept of cultural entanglement to archaeological sources, the analysis thereof requires a methodological approach to processes of appropriation that emerge from the dialectical relationship of acceptance and resistance – or as Igor Kopytoff (1986, 67) has already stated: "What is significant about the adoption of alien objects – as of alien ideas – is not the fact that they are adopted, but the way they are culturally redefined and put to use". Although appropriation is a crucial concept, only Hans Peter Hahn (2004a) has attempted to develop the theoretical discussion into a methodological approach for the analysis of material culture. Hahn (2004a, 64–67; 2004b, 218–220; 2005, 102–104; 2007, 209–210) defines four different aspects of what he calls the process of appropriation: i.e. appropriation, objectivization, incorporation and transformation. All four aspects are entangled and occur simultaneously.

1. The first aspect, appropriation, refers to the transition of objects from wares to goods by becoming personal possessions. This may be connected with formal changes in the objects e.g. by decoration.
2. Second, objectivization, comprises the attribution of an object to an existing category of one's own objects. This classification goes together with the attribution of a certain meaning to the object.
3. Incorporation as the third aspect refers to the competence to deal with the object in a "right" way.
4. Lastly, transformation means the attribution of new meanings to objects, which very much depends on the local context where an object is used.

---

[5] This etical perspective is also enforced by Thomas 1998, 109: "Hybridity may be an appearance salient to an outside viewer rather than a condition that is in any way significant to local people engaging in a particular practice or producing a particular form."

All of these aspects can also be discerned in well preserved and meaningful archaeological contexts, which most frequently result from natural disasters or other catastrophes and thus conserve snapshots of past realities. Whereas appropriation and incorporation can often be identified in a well-preserved context of finding, objectivization and transformation are very difficult to reconstruct, as they refer to the perception of artefacts and, therefore, require rather an emic perspective. However, the context of an object within a find may give us some hint for both, e.g. foreign drinking vessels found together with local drinking vessels indicate past systems of classification, foreign drinking vessels in local burial contexts suppose the attribution of a new meaning. Moreover, Hahn's four aspects mix two different elements which have to be distinguished in archaeological analysis: the objects and the social practices connected therewith. Hahn's appropriation and objectivization refer to the object, the incorporation and transformation to the social practices. While the objects are easily found – if they are preserved at all – it is often difficult to detect past social practices in the archaeological evidence. Whereas the ethnologist can observe such practices, the archaeologist is lucky to get even an idea of what practices might have been connected with a certain object. Consequently, I would like to distinguish between the appropriation of objects and the appropriation of social practices and meanings (i.e. symbols, traditions etc.) as this makes a huge epistemological difference for archaeological sources.

For the sake of archaeological analysis, it is necessary to structure these processes of transformation into several stages in order to check their potential for visibility in the archaeological evidence:

The process starts with the "encounter" of at least two different etically defined entities. These entities are, for example, different archaeological cultures as defined by present-day archaeology (e. g. the Mycenaeans, the Minoans, the Canaanites, etc.). The definition of such entities always poses the risk of falling back on ideas of essentialism and purity. We have to be aware of the etic character of these entities and of the fact that our analytical categorizations differ from past systems of classification (e. g. archaeological cultures vs. past ethnic groups). These entities are mental templates only created for analytical purposes. Therefore, I do not mind if the two entities interacted before. However, the etic recognition of difference supposes that this difference might also have been perceived by past individuals– perhaps only in the short moment of the first encounter. This moment of encounter, the construction and perception of otherness and difference, is the central trigger, taking place in liminal spaces, which I visualize as situations and spaces which are not limited to a certain geographical area. I define liminal space as space of encounter, irrespective where this encounter happens, and I want to release it from the political dimension assigned by Bhabha.[6] If this encounter does not result in further actions, the process of appropriation never begins. However, if the

---

[6] Bhabha (2007, 212) states that a liminal space "is internally marked by the discourses of minorities, the heterogeneous histories of contending peoples, antagonistic authorities and tense locations of cultural difference".

process is triggered, it results in what I would like to call the state of "relational entanglement". This transition from encounter to relational entanglement is characterized by Hahn's four aspects, i.e. appropriation, incorporation, objectivization and transformation: the object becomes a personal possession, is classified within local classification systems, is connected with certain practices and is attributed with a new meaning. Nevertheless, it is important to acknowledge that an appropriated artefact is not an entangled artefact. If one would excavate a foreign object in a local context, the evidence may clearly show that the foreign ware had become a personal possession, classified, used and attached with a certain meaning. But the object in its sheer materiality is most often unchanged. It is only the context which has changed, the social practices, meanings and traditions connected with the object or, as Hahn (2005, 101; cf. also Hahn 2004b, 226) states: there has been a "transformation of the relation between humans and objects".[7] All the creative powers of liminal spaces are first invested in creating new practices connected with the object. The context is created and not the object. In the moment of encounter we do not trigger a change in the object, but the object changes us. Merely its material presence changes perceptions of social space and of movements. Therefore, the state of relational entanglement is not a state of entanglement of the object, but a state of entanglement of social practices and meanings, as these are newly created, whereas the object is, at most, only manipulated. So it is important to distinguish between "relational entanglement" and "materiality". However, we have to bear in mind that "the 'work of appropriation' is in this very sense never completely finished, and its results are called into question time and again" (Hahn 2004b, 220; cf. also Hahn 2005, 106–107). Since appropriation never ends, "relational entanglement" can only be a momentary and unstable state.

It has also to be kept in mind, that the processes leading to the state of relational entanglement were most probably not only guided by individual choices, but also by rules and rituals of a society. These rules and rituals were created to deal with otherness and newness, as these attributes were certainly not perceived as neutral or meaningless (cf. Helms 1988).

It is only the second step that leads to the development of entangled objects. I would like to call this second step "material entanglement", which is attained by the process of "material creation". Now, the creative energies originally released by the encounter and broadened within the process of appropriation result in the creation of a new object that combines the familiar with the previously foreign. This entangled object is produced at some place (which does not have to be the place where the object is found), but its materiality shows that it is not the result of

---

[7] Hahn (2005, 107) further states: "The object is invested with meanings and contexts, it is transformed in order to be newly invented as part of the appropriating society" (translation by P. W. Stockhammer). Although appropriation cannot exist without creativity, I consider it necessary to distinguish between the invention of a context and the creation of a new object, because it makes a huge epistemological difference in archaeology whether one is dealing with the object or with social practices and meanings possibly materialized in the object's context of finding.

local continuities, but of changes triggered by encounters with otherness. It is more than just a sum of the entities from which it originated. It is an indissoluble combination of all of them – a cultural "Geflecht" – and might be seen as a new entity.

Even if such an object has lost its functional context over time – which means that we have hardly any idea of social practices and meanings connected with the object – we can still identify it as an entangled artefact in the archaeological evidence from an etic perspective. This kind of decontextualized material entanglement is the dominant evidence of entanglement in archaeology. We excavate the final embodiment or result of a multitude of process of appropriation and creation without being able to document the specific process of material entanglement. We are confronted with the material uniqueness of an entangled object and are unable to explain how and why it was created, because the social practices and meanings are hardly materialized. And most frequently we are unable to understand if and how this object was perceived (e.g. local vs. foreign) or even if there was one overriding perception at all.

One has to take into consideration that it is impossible to determine the end of such processes of appropriation and creation. These processes can result in continuous re-interpretations, incorporations, manipulations and creations (Hahn 2005, 106–107). But for the sake of analysis, I would like to fix the end of a certain process of entanglement to the creation of an entangled object. This entangled object may be a unique specimen and forgotten after its deposition, but it may happen that a flourishing local production of entangled objects is triggered. It is possible that these products were never perceived as being the product of a former process of entanglement by prehistoric man, but only by us archaeologists.

4.6 Applying the Concept to the Archaeological Evidence

After elaborating my methodological approach, I would now like to shift the focus to archaeological evidence from the East Mediterranean Late Bronze Age roughly between the fifteenth and thirteenth century BC. This area of research comprises the Levantine coast with its so-called Canaanite culture, Cyprus, Crete (Minoan culture) and Southern Greece (Mycenaean culture).[8] "Hybridization" and kindred

---

[8] I am totally aware that my concentration on the Eastern Mediterranean Late Bronze Age can do no justice to the discussion on issues of "hybridity" in archaeology as a whole. There are vivid discussions on this topic with relation to the Phoenician and Greek expansion in the first half of the first millennium BC in the Western and Central Mediterranean (e.g. Antonaccio 2003; 2010; Vives-Ferrándiz Sánchez 2005; 2007; 2008; van Dommelen 2006) and in the field of Romanization studies that Peter van Dommelen kindly pointed out to me (e.g. Webster 2001; Hodos 2006; van Dommelen and Terrenato 2007). For reflections on "colonialism" and its different realizations from a comparative archaeological perspective cf. Gosden 2004.

terms have already been introduced to this field of research. However, before applying my methodological approach to archaeological source material, I would like to start with an overview of current archaeological studies dealing with phenomena of "hybridity" and "hybridization" in the Eastern Mediterranean Late Bronze Age.

The prominence of the term "hybridization" in this field of study is at least partly due to Marian H. Feldman's (2006) seminal work on *"Diplomacy by Design"*. In her analysis of the so-called "international style" of Late Bronze Age pieces of art, she argues "that the application of the term international be restricted to only those pieces that exhibit complete hybridization such that no one "foreign" culture can be said to predominate" (Feldman 2006, 30). "The cultural intermixture characterizing the international artistic *koiné* occurs at the thematic level, where many of the primary motifs are literally hybrid entities, composites of typically disassociated elements" (Feldman 2006, 59), i.e. "visually hybrid elements" (Feldman 2006, 58). Her understanding of hybridity is based on the biological definition which in her view "carries a basically value-neutral connotation" (Feldman 2006, 60). She is aware of the postcolonial re-definition, but does not consider it helpful for her analysis, as this discourse led "to a solidly negative valence for the term" (Feldman 2006, 60). Feldman's perception of the biological and postcolonial definition is therefore contrary to the dominating one in the humanities which celebrated the postcolonial studies' positive revaluation of the biological term hitherto loaded with negative connotations. One may ask, however, if the definition of a highly problematic term like "international" should draw on the use of a similarly problematic term – which "hybridization" assuredly is. Indeed, both terms convey a number of similar obstacles, such as the pre-existence of unmixed entities (international vs. national, hybrid vs. pure) and their dominant metaphorical use. Feldman is well aware of the notions of essentialism connected with "hybridity". Therefore, she proposes to "examine and define the specific form of visual hybridity exhibited on the *koiné* works" (Feldman 2006, 59). Her approach can be considered quite close to my emphasis on an etic approach, as etically defined categories are pure by definition. In Feldman's view, the negative or positive perception of "hybridity" depends on the perception of borders and border crossing. If borders are considered to be "ideally fixed and impermeable, then their crossing by the hybrid form will be viewed as transgressive and the hybrid self will be considered dangerous or degenerative" (Feldman 2006, 61). In her field of study of the Late Bronze Age, Feldman points to indications (e. g. international greeting letters) of positive evaluated border crossing and associated material culture. Therefore, she concludes emphasizing the positive aspects of "hybridity": "Hybridity can denote strength and vitality as a way to constitute and facilitate channels of interaction. Furthermore, the state of being hybrid is relative to time and place, never constant, and always determined by the various participants in any exchange – just as the cultures from which hybridity derives are likewise always in flux, always in the state of becoming. Hybridity can be thought of as the process of interaction .... It is in this positive and active light that I view the visual hybridity of the international *koiné*" (Feldman 2006, 61).

In her analysis of Canaanite culture, Kristina Josephson Hesse (2008, 48) speaks of "hybridization" and considers it to be "a Canaanite cultural feature", because "Canaanite art did not develop any great general style like the art in Mesopotamia and Egypt". Egyptian and Mesopotamian art are, therefore, seen as pure styles more or less untouched by transcultural interaction. Josephson Hesse neither discusses this problematic notion of purity nor the fact that her broad use of the term should consequently lead to the awareness that all cultures are "hybrid" in some way – at least in a metaphorical sense. As has been discussed above, this broad understanding of what I would like to call "entanglement" as a constituting feature of all cultures is undoubtedly justifiable, but it deprives the concept of its heuristic value and reduces it to a metaphor.

In their study on phenomena of hybridization in Late Bronze and Early Iron Age Cyprus, Iannis Voskos and A. Bernard Knapp explicitly root their terminology in the postcolonial discourse on hybridity. However, they state that: "Hybridization neither presupposes the dominance of colonial cultures over indigenous ones nor maintains any sociocultural divisions. All groups engaged in such entanglements contribute to the shaping of hybridized cultures through interaction and negotiation" (Voskos and Knapp 2008, 661). This statement stands in clear opposition to Bhabha's definition of hybridity as a strategy of the subaltern in contexts of colonial oppression which informs postcolonial studies. Therefore, their definition seemingly relies on the postcolonial discourse, but actually fits into the biological definition of hybridity. Voskos and Knapp recognise the dominating metaphorical use of the term "hybridization", which they designate a concept suited to analysing "ancient contact and colonizing situations" (Voskos and Knapp 2008, 661). In their study on the developments in Cyprus in the twelfth century BC, they wanted to show with the help of this concept that no Hellenic colonization took place on the island – in contrast to the dominating view in Cypriot Bronze Age archaeology (Voskos and Knapp 2008, 661). Although the concept of hybridization is a useful tool to analyse the processes triggered by the encounter with otherness, I do not see its use for distinguishing colonization from other processes of socio-cultural interaction. On the contrary, it analyses processes of intercultural interaction which may equally take place in migrant or colonial contexts. The encounter is not the analytic focus, but the prerequisite for the process which should be analysed by the concept.

In his book on prehistoric and protohistoric Cyprus, Knapp (2008, esp. 57–61) further elaborates on the topic that has already been addressed by him and Voskos and emphasizes that "the concept of hybridity – as a social, material, or cultural mixture – has the potential to refine the understanding of any contact situation involving colonization, migration, or acculturation" (Knapp 2008, 59). He therefore does not go beyond the notion of hybridity and the methodological approach connected with it, which was already applied in his article with Voskos.

Contrary to the current trend of applying "hybridization" and other related terms to the Late Bronze Age Eastern Mediterranean, Reinhard Jung (2009, 82) considers the use of this concept to be "premature". He states: "'Hybridisation' describes a phenomenon, but does not give the answer whether or not a certain mixture of cultures was the outcome of colonisation, immigration or of radical changes in the relations of production and in the realm of goods exchange" (Jung 2009, 82). This criticism seems to be based on the acknowledgement of the work of Voskos and Knapp only, and still misunderstands the explanatory value of the concept. The analytical value of the concept starts with the encounter with otherness, but does not focus on the processes which lead to this encounter. Migrant communities and colonial contexts are simply examples of creative liminal spaces where processes of entanglement are often triggered. In Jung's view (2009, 82), it is also a problem that not every instance of colonization resulted in clear phenomena of hybridization. Even though this scenario is quite improbable, its possible existence is still no obstacle for the concept because hybridity has never been defined as a *conditio sine qua non* for colonial contexts in postcolonial studies. Moreover, Jung (2009, 82) criticises the identification of the state of hybridity, whereby he does not recognise the necessary distinction between a relational and a material aspect: "There are no clear criteria for identifying when this point is reached". This lack of clear criteria can easily be explained by the fact that the processes of appropriation and creation connected with relational and material entanglement are never-ending and continuously produce entangled practices and objects.

On the basis of the methodological approach developed in this contribution, I would like to focus on processes of appropriation and/or creation which took place in the Levantine region during the Late Bronze Age. The starting point of these processes was the transport of pottery from what is nowadays called Southern Greece and Crete to the Levant. This pottery repertoire comprises mainly small transport vessels and feasting dishes, i.e. cups and high-stemmed bowls as drinking vessels and kraters for mixing water and wine. There must have been a multitude of liminal spaces where Levantine people came across these dishes for the first time, e.g. harbour sites, markets etc. Indeed, the excavation of eminent harbour sites on the Levant (e.g. Ugarit, Sarepta, Sidon, Tell Abu Hawam) have brought to light a broad range of imported Aegean type pottery (cf. Bell 2006). As we can see from the material evidence, only a small part of the broad range of Aegean type pottery that reached the harbours and markets was actually acquired by the Levantine people beyond these maritime gateways, because only a small selection of shapes reached the towns and settlements in the hinterland.

I would like to illustrate two examples of processes of appropriation, one resulting in relational entanglement and the other one in material entanglement. The first one refers to the imported feasting dishes. In the Aegean, a set of feasting dishes quite regularly consisted of around 10 drinking vessels and one very large krater for mixing water and wine (Stockhammer 2008, 135). Since Aegean type drinking vessels and kraters have been found at a great number of Levantine sites, current research is dominated by the view that Aegean feasting practices were taken up in the Levant. However, an analysis of contexts in which these vessels were found shows that at the Levant, Aegean type drinking vessels and kraters are hardly ever found together in the same architectural context. Moreover, the proportions of the two vessel types is very different to that found in Greece, with the share of kraters being much higher. Although these kraters remained unchanged in their physical materiality, the social practices connected with them had obviously changed. One possible explanation is that Levantine people continued to use kraters as mixing vessels for water and wine, but combined them with local drinking vessels. There is pictorial evidence from two carved ivory objects from the site of Megiddo showing the use of mixing vessels together with drinking vessels (Loud 1939, pl. 4, 2; 32, 160; Yasur-Landau 2005, 173 fig. 1, 1–2). On the other hand, other depictions show Levantine people drinking beer with straws from huge collective vessels, e.g. on the grave stele of a Syrian mercenary found in Egypt. Therefore, it is also possible that they used the Aegean type kraters to drink beer through straws. Both possible ways of using the foreign kraters show a process of appropriation. They became personal possessions, were probably classified, used in possibly two different ways and probably invested with a Levantine meaning. But these vessels as such never became entangled in their materiality.

However, we also have evidence that the encounter with Aegean type pottery at the Levant also triggered processes of creation leading to material entanglement. One of the pieces of evidence for such a process was found among the burial goods in the cave tomb of Nahalat Ahim in the area of present-day Jerusalem, which was used in the fourteenth and probably also early thirteenth century BC (Amiran 1960). As well as many other finds, the tomb contained imported pottery from Cyprus and the Aegean and several local imitations of Aegean type vessels. Whereas contemporaneous grave contexts from the Southern Levant frequently include small containers – so-called stirrup jars, alabastra, piriform jars etc. (e.g. Hazor, Burial 8144–8145: Yadin et al. 1960, 140–141, 145–153) – imported from the Aegean, the burial cave of Nahalat Ahim only contained an Aegean stemmed drinking cup (a so-called kylix) (Amiran 1960, 35 fig. 1, 1). In the chronology of Mycenaean decorated pottery, this kylix dates to the pottery phase LH III A2 Early (mid fourteenth century BC), which means that it reached the Levant before most of the other Mycenaean pottery which left Greece in the late fourteenth and thirteenth century BC. Small Aegean type container vessels were also found in this burial context, i.e. two piriform jars and one alabastron (Amiran 1960, 37 fig. 3, 53–55). However, all three vessels are local imitations of their late fourteenth century BC. Aegean counterparts. The imported kylix was obviously appropriated and documents the state of relational entanglement. The local imitations of Aegean type vessels go one step further, because those are not just imitations of imported vessels but show the creative dialogue triggered by the encounter of the potter with a foreign vessel. The most noticeable evidence for this creative potential among local potters is one of the piriform jars (Amiran 1960, 37 fig. 3, 53), which copies the imported Aegean piriform jars in its size and upper part. However, the lower part does not show the typical flat base for this form, but a rounded base which is typical of local Levantine storage vessels and is totally unusual for such vessels in the Aegean. Why a local potter created this new vessel shape by the combination of an Aegean type upper part with a Levantine lower part remains unclear. This vessel can doubtlessly be considered as entangled in its materiality and presents a singular ceramic creation.

To sum up: as demonstrated by the piriform jar from Nahalat Ahim, archaeologists are regularly confronted with objects in their material entanglement. They are neither able to observe how these objects were used and perceived nor able to ask the producer why he decided to create them in this specific way. However, a systematic methodological approach for the analysis of appropriation and creation processes gives us an idea of what processes could have taken place and what we should look for in the material record when we are excavating. It should make us sensitive to the context of an object, if it is preserved, and look at the interrelations between an object and other objects as well as the materialized fragments of past social practices.

Acknowledgments This article is part of my current research project on the entanglement of materiality and practice in the Late Bronze Age Eastern Mediterranean which is part of the Heidelberg Cluster of Excellence "Asia and Europe in a Global Context". I would like to thank Hans P. Hahn, Markus Hilgert, Susan Sherratt, Peter van Dommelen, Joseph Maran and Christina Sanchez-Stockhammer for intensively discussing the topic with me. Carol Bell and Andrea Hacker kindly helped me to improve my English.

References

Ackermann, Andreas. 2004. "Das Eigene und das Fremde: Hybridität, Vielfalt und Kulturtransfers." In *Handbuch der Kulturwissenschaften III, Themen und Tendenzen*, edited by Friedrich Jäger and Jörn Rüsen, 139–154. Stuttgart: Metzler.
Amiran, Ruth. 1960. "A Late Bronze Age II Pottery Group from a Tomb in Jerusalem." *Eretz-Israel* 6: 25–37. (in Hebrew)
Antonaccio, Carla M. 2003. "Hybridity and the Cultures within Greek Culture." In *The Cultures within Ancient Greek Culture. Contact, Conflict, Collaboration*, edited by Carol Dougherty and Leslie Kurke, 57–74. Cambridge: Cambridge University Press.
Antonaccio, Carla M. 2010. "(Re)defining Ethnicity: Culture, Material Culture, and Identity." In *Local and Global Identities: Rethinking Identity and Material Culture in the Ancient Mediterranean*, edited by Shelley Hales and Tamar Hodos, 32–53. Cambridge: Cambridge University Press.
Bell, Carol. 2006. *The Evolution of Long Distance Trading Relationships across the LBA/Iron Age Transition on the Northern Levantine Coast: Crisis, Continuity and Change, BAR International Series 1574*. Oxford: Archaeopress.
Bhabha, Homi K. 2007. *The Location of Culture*. London: Routledge.
Burke, Peter. 2009. *Cultural Hybridity*. Cambridge and Malden: Polity Press.
Conrad, Sebastian, and Shalini Randeria. 2002. "Einleitung. Geteilte Geschichten – Europa in einer postkolonialen Welt." In *Jenseits des Eurozentrismus. Postkoloniale Perspektiven in den Geschichts- und Kulturwissenschaften*, edited by Sebastian Conrad and Shalini Randeria, 9–49. Frankfurt a. Main: Campus.
Dietler, Michael. 1998. "Consumption, Agency, and Cultural Entaglement: Theoretical Implications of a Mediterranean Colonial Encounter." In *Studies in Culture Contact. Interaction, Culture Change, and Archaeology*, edited by James G. Cusick, 288–315. Carbondale: Center for Archaeological Investigations, Southern Illinois University.
Feldman, Marian H. 2006. *Diplomacy by Design. Luxury Arts and an 'International Style' in the Ancient Near East, 1400–1200 B.C.E.* Chicago: University of Chicago Press.
Furholt, Martin, and Philipp W. Stockhammer. 2007. "Wenn stumme Dinge sprechen sollen: Gedanken zu semiotischen Ansätzen in der Prähistorischen Archäologie." In *Transcriptions. Cultures Concepts Controversies – Kulturen Konzepte Kontroversen*, edited by Michael Butter, Regina Grundmann, and Christina Sanchez, 59–71. Berlin: Peter Lang Verlag.

Geiger, Theodor. (1947)1964. *Vorstudien zu einer Soziologie des Recht*, Soziologische Texte 20. Neuwied: Luchterhand.
Gosden, Chris. 2004. *Archaeology and Colonialism: Culture Contact from 5000 BC to the Present*. Cambridge: Cambridge University Press.
Hahn, Hans P. 2004a. "Globale Güter und lokales Handeln in Afrika. Einige methodische Vorbemerkungen." *Sociologus* 53: 51–77.
Hahn, Hans P. 2004b. "Global Goods and the Process of Appropriation." In *Between Resistance and Expansion. Explorations of Local Vitality in Africa*, Beiträge zur Afrikaforschung 18, edited by Peter Probst and Gerd Spittler, 211–229. Münster: LIT Verlag.
Hahn, Hans P. 2005. *Materielle Kultur. Eine Einführung*. Berlin: Reimer.
Hahn, Hans P. 2007. "Zur Ethnologie des Konsums in Afrika." Paideuma 53:199–220.
Helms, Mary W. 1988. *Ulysses' Sail. An Ethnographic Odyssey of Power, Knowledge, and Geographical Distance*. Princeton: Princeton University Press.
Hodos, Tamar. 2006. *Local Responses to Colonization in the Iron Age Mediterranean*. London: Routledge.
Josephson Hesse, Kristina. 2008. *Contacts and Trade at Late Bronze Age Hazor: Aspects of Intercultural Relationships and Identity in the Eastern Mediterranean*. Accessed 4 October 2009, http://urn.kb.se/resolve?urn=urn:nbn:se:umu:diva-1816.
Jung, Reinhard. 2009. "Pirates of the Aegean: Italy – the East Aegean – Cyprus at the End of the Second Millennium BC." In *Cyprus and the East Aegean. Intercultural Contacts from 3000 to 500 BC. An International Archaeological Symposium Held at Pythagoreion, Samos, 17th–18th Oktober 2008*, edited by Vassos Karageorghis and Ourania Kouka, 72–93. Nicosia: A. G. Leventis Foundation.
Kaelble, Hartmut. 2005. "Die Debatte über Vergleich und Transfer und was jetzt?" *H-Soz-u-Kult*, August 2, http://hsozkult.geschichte.hu-berlin.de/forum/id=574&type=artikel.
Knapp, A. Bernard 2008. *Prehistoric and Protohistoric Cyprus. Identity, Insularity, and Connectivity*. Oxford: Oxford University Press.
Kopytoff, Igor. 1986. "The Cultural Biography of Things." In *The Social Life of Things. Commodities in Cultural Perspective*, edited by Arjun Appadurai, 64–91. Cambridge: Cambridge University Press.
Lévi-Strauss, Claude. 1994. "Anthropology, Race, and Politics: A Conversation with Didier Eribon." In *Assessing Cultural Anthropology*, ed. Robert Borofski, 420–429. New York: McGraw-Hill.
Loimeier, Roman, Dieter Neubert, and Cordula Weißköppel. 2005. "Einleitung: Globalisierung im lokalen Kontext – Perspektiven und Konzepte von Handeln in Afrika." In *Globalisierung im lokalen Kontext – Perspektiven und Konzepte von Handeln in Afrika*, Beiträge zur Afrikaforschung 20, edited by Roman Loimeier, Dieter Neubert, and Cordula Weißköppel, 1–30. Münster: LIT Verlag.
Loud, Gordon. 1939. *The Megiddo Ivories, The University of Chicago Oriental Institute Publications 52*. Chicago: University of Chicago Press.
Papastergiadis, Nikos. 1997. "Tracing Hybridity in Theory." In *Debating Cultural Hybridity. Multi-Cultural Identities and the Politics of Anti-Racism*, edited by Pnina Werbner and Tariq Modood, 257–281. London: Zed Books.
Robertson, Roland. 1992. *Globalization. Social Theory and Global Culture*. London: Sage Publications.
Robertson, Robert. 1995. "Glocalization: Time-Space and Homogenity-Heterogeneity." In *Global Modernities*, edited by Mike Featherstone, Scott Lash, and Roland Robertson, 25–44. London: Sage Publications.
Said, Edward W. 1993. *Culture and Imperialism*. New York: Chatto & Windus.
Stewart, Charles. 1999. "Syncretism and its Synonyms. Reflections on Cultural Mixture." *Diacritics* 29(3): 40–62.
Stewart, Charles. 2007a. *Creolization: History, Ethnography, Theory*. Walnut Creek: Left Coast Press.

Stewart, Charles. 2007b. "Creolization: History, Ethnography, Theory." In *Creolization: History, Ethnography, Theory*, edited by Charles Stewart, 1–25. Walnut Creek: Left Coast Press.

Stockhammer, Philipp W. 2008. *Kontinuitäät und Wandel – Die Keramik der Nachpalastzeit aus der Unterstadt von Tiryns*. Accessed August 29, 2009. http://www.ub.uni-heidelberg.de/archiv/8612/.

Thomas, Nicholas. 1991. *Entangled Objects: Exchange, Material Culture, and Colonialism in the Pacific*. Cambridge/Massachusetts: Harvard University Press.

Thomas, Nicholas. 1996. "Cold Fusion." *American Anthropology (N. S.)* 98, 1:9–16.

Thomas, Nicholas. 1998. "Hybrid Histories: Gordon Bennett's Critique of Purity." *Communal/Plural* 6, 1: 107–116.

van Dommelen, Peter. 2006. "The Orientalizing Phenomenon: Hybridity and Material Culture in the Western Mediterranean." In *Debating Orientalization. Multidisciplinary Approaches to Processes of Change in the Ancient Mediterranean, Monographs in Mediterranean Archaeology 10*, edited by Corinna Riva and Nichoals C. Vella 135– 152. London: Equinox.

van Dommelen, Peter, and Nicola Terrenato. 2007. "Local Cultures and the Expanding Roman Republic." In *Articulating Local Cultures: Power and Identity under the Expanding Roman Republic*. Journal of Roman Archaeology Supplementary Series 63, edited by Peter van Dommelen and Nicola Terrenato, 7–12. Portsmouth.

Vives-Ferrándiz Sánchez, Jaime. 2005. *Negociando encuentros. Situaciones coloniales e intercambios en la costa oriental de la península Ibérica (ss. VIII–VI a.C.)*. Cuadernos de Arqueología Mediterránea 12. Barcelona: Bellaterra.

Vives-Ferrándiz Sánchez, Jaime. 2007. "Colonial Encounters and the Negotiation of Identities in South-East Iberia." In *Mediterranean Crossroads*, edited by Sophia Antoniadou and Anthony Pace, 537–562. Athens: Pierides Foundation.

Vives-Ferrándiz Sánchez, Jaime. 2008. "Negotiating Colonial Encounters: Hybrid Practices and Consumption in Eastern Iberia (8th–6th centuries BC)." *Journal of Mediterranean Archaeology* 21(2): 241–272.

Voskos, Ioannis, and A. Bernard Knapp. 2008. "Cyprus at the End of the Late Bronze Age: Crisis and Colonization or Continuity and Hybridization?" *American Journal of Archaeology* 112: 659–684.

Wagner, Bernd. 2001. "Kulturelle Globalisierung: Weltkultur, Glokalität und Hybridisierung." In *Kulturelle Globalisierung – Zwischen Weltkultur und kultureller Fragmentierung*, edited by Bernd Wagner, 9–38. Essen: Klartext Verlag.

Webster, Jane. 2001. "Creolizing the Roman Provinces." *American Journal of Archaeology* 105: 209–225.

Weißköppel, Cordula. 2005. "'Hybridität' – die ethnografische Annäherung an ein theoretisches Konzept. " In *Globalisierung im lokalen Kontext – Perspektiven und Konzepte von Handeln in Afrika*. Beiträge zur Afrikaforschung 20, edited by Roman Loimeier, Dieter Neubert, and Cordula Weißköppel, 311–347. Münster: LIT Verlag.

Wicker, Hans-Rudolf. 2000. "Globalisierung, Hybridisierung und die neue Authentizität." In *Die Bedeutung des Ethnischen im Zeitalter der Globalisierung. Einbindungen, Ausgrenzungen, Säuberungen*, edited by Rupert Moser, 201–217. Bern, Stuttgart, Wien: Haupt Verlag.

Yadin, Yigael, Yohanan Aharoni, Ruth Amiran, Trude Dothan, Immanuel Dunayevsky, and Jean Perrot, 1960. *Hazor 2: An Account of the Second Season of Excavations, 1956*. Jerusalem: Magnes Press.

Yasur-Landau, Assaf. 2005. "Old Wine in New Vessels: Intercultural Contact, Innovation and Aegean, Canaanite and Philistine Foodways." *Journal of the Institute of Archaeology of Tel Aviv University* 32, 2: 168–191.

Chapter 5
One World Is Not Enough: The Transformative Potential of Intercultural Exchange in Prehistoric Societies

Joseph Maran

Abstract The field of prehistory and early history has an extraordinary potential for widening the scope of our understanding of the effects of interculturality, since it deals with the material remains of societies that were characterized by a true universe of differing systems of value and forms of social space. It is argued that the concept of cultural hybridity raises too many problems to be useful for a better understanding of interculturality, since, in spite of its promise to overcome outdated obsessions with purity and origins, the application of this concept bears the danger of these very aspects sneaking in through the back door. Moreover, if the concept of cultural hybridity is thought to be generally applicable, it is far too unspecific to be of any explanatory value. In dealing with the appearance of foreign traits, the focus of attention must be placed on clarifying the ways of appropriation on a local level and on how, in the course of their integration into existing practices, new cultural forms were created. Such an investigation of the appropriation of objects coming from the outside necessitates, however, radically questioning our presuppositions about the factors guiding pre-modern intercultural exchange. While this is quite clear in the case of the assumption of a general applicability of "rational" economic behaviour, it is much less obvious that our concept of the "world" cannot be assumed to apply universally. Based on differing social imaginaries, societies have conceived the shape of the surrounding world in very different ways, which in turn must have had an immediate bearing on the changing attitudes towards goods and ideas coming from the outside.

5.1 The Long-Lasting Impact of Culture-Historical Ethnography

The field of prehistory and early history deals with the material remains of such societies of the past in which systems of writing were either unknown or only used to a very limited degree. In the light of this it is no wonder that material features are decisive for the prevalent definition of archaeological cultures as constantly recurring groupings of structures and artefacts that are thought to be separable in space and time (Childe 1929, VI). This definition, however, did not derive from within the field, but was adopted from what was later called the "Kulturkreislehre" (Bernbeck 1997, 27–28),[1] which in the beginning of the twentieth century was the most influential current of culture-historical ethnography in German-speaking academia (Schmitz 1967b; Harris 1968, 382–392; Rössler 2007, 8–15). Its proponents aimed at differentiating cultural circles by charting the distribution of certain aspects of the social structure, material culture, language, religion, music, myths and what was regarded as "race" (cf. Ratzel 1967; Graebner 1967). The special relevance of culture-historical ethnography for prehistory and early history was rooted in a common interest in material culture, diffusion and origins. The cultural circles were believed to be so conclusive that similarities in the form of specific cultural traits even between far-removed regions were regarded as meaningful and were used to reconstruct cultural origins by disentangling sequences of diffusion or migration in space and time. The definitions of culture used in culture-historical ethnography and the field of prehistory and early history share the tendency to treat culture in an object-like way. The appearance of the same form is taken to represent the same origin and the same meaning, or, as Jonathan Friedman (1997, 82) has put it "...culture was contained in its embodiment rather than its generativity". It goes without saying that such a static definition makes it extremely difficult to explain cultural change from within a given society. Instead, change is attributed to outside factors, such as migration, diffusion of novelties, or acculturation.

While in the decades after the Second World War the culture-historical approach rather quickly lost its importance in cultural and social anthropology, some of its methodology and way of reasoning still lingers on in the field of prehistory and early history. In my opinion, it is insufficient to ascribe the often deplored theoretical abstinence of German prehistory and early history in the post-war period solely to the sinister role of the discipline during National Socialism and the experience with unfounded theories of ethnic and racial origins (Veit 1989, 48–49; Bernbeck 1997, 30–31). Instead, the reasons for the reluctance to engage with theory should be sought in the very low degree of theoretical reflection in the field already before the Second World War as well as in the fact that in post-war Germany, ethnology for good reasons turned away from the ideas and methods of culture-history, which led to a severing of ties with prehistory and early history. In this way, the latter field became detached from the theoretical discourses within contemporary cultural studies and carried on a methodological framework that had long been abandoned in the discipline in which it had originated. On the other hand, in Great Britain and the USA, where the culture-historical method never had many followers, the close academic ties archaeology had to cultural and social anthropology were not disrupted after the war and further developed on the basis of common theoretical

---

[1] I am indebted to Hans-Peter Hahn for pointing-out that the proponents of culture-historical ethnography did not use the term "Kulturkreislehre" to designate this school of ethnography.

paradigms like functionalism, historical-particularism and later structuralism and neo-evolutionism. For differing reasons, however, these theoretical currents were not as interested in either material culture or intercultural contacts as culture-historical ethnography (Streck 2000; Hahn 2008a, 89–92; 2008b, 191–194). This, in turn, led to the under-representation of such subjects in Processual Archaeology, Social Archaeology and other approaches in theoretical archaeology until the 1980s. For archaeology the post-structuralist re-discovery of the significance of materiality and interculturality has opened up new perspectives for dealing with such issues, although this requires a careful reflection on the shortcomings of the culture-historical approach, unless one wants to run the risk of repeating earlier mistakes and end-up creating a kind of neo-diffusionism (Streck 2000). The flaws of culture-history consisted, above all, in the object-like approach towards culture, the concentration on abstract "flows" of cultural traits, the lack of concepts of agency and of practice, as well as the obsession with origins and the disinterest in the contextualization of cultural forms and possible shifts in meaning (Streck 2000; Hahn 2008b, 199). For a reassessment of the significance of subjects related to materiality and interculturality, archaeology can draw on a variety of new theoretical approaches that mostly derive from post-colonial and cultural studies. One of these concepts is cultural hybridity.

5.2 Cultural Hybridity – A Useful Concept for Archaeology?

As is well known, the essentialist notion of neatly separable cultures, societies and even "races" living in accordance with themselves and nature, is rooted in ideals of European romanticism of the nineteenth century that held "purity" in high esteem and equated "hybridity" with degeneration and decay. In the last two decades, the aforementioned re-assessment of intercultural contacts within cultural and post-colonial studies has led to a total reversal of this situation, in which now cultural hybridity is regarded as the rule and "purity" as a dangerous illusion (Ha 2005, 11–54). The question I would like to discuss is whether the concept of cultural hybridity really can help give a fresh approach to the sources of the field of prehistory and early history. Among the positive aspects of the application of the concept I would mention the emphasis on the elusiveness of alleged cultural borders, on the fluidity of the meaning of cultural forms, and on the dynamics of change provoked by flows of goods and ideas. All this can serve as an important antidote to assumptions of cultural purity, and this alone could indeed open-up new avenues for re-assessing the meaning of the units which are called archaeological cultures. Still, I see the need to address several points of criticism that have been in my opinion rightly raised against the concept of cultural hybridity.

First, it has been criticized that the use of the concept puts too much emphasis on geographic origins by assuming that they are the defining characteristic of culture, while it is the practice of integration that should be regarded as the decisive element of culture (Friedman 1997, 81; Hahn 2008b, 194–199). In light of this criticism,

I would stress the need to focus, as Hans-Peter Hahn (2004, 213–225; 2005, 99–107; 2008b, 195–200) and Gerd Spittler (2002) have pointed out, not on origins, but on the forms of appropriation of foreign ideas and objects. Only in this way one can avoid the diffusionist pitfalls of culture history and concentrate on the issue of clarifying what new forms are being created.

Second, on epistemological grounds the question arises of whether the dialectics of applying a concept like cultural hybridity do not necessarily require the existence of exactly that which one wishes to overcome, namely an opposite state characterized by a higher degree of purity (Kalra et al. 2005, 70–86). Accordingly, if the concept of cultural hybridity is assumed to apply only to specific cases, then there should be other cases that can be categorized at least as more unmixed and pure. If, however, the concept is deemed valid always and everywhere - which seems to be the position of most of its proponents - then doubts arise about the explanatory value of such a concept.

This line of thought leads us to ask whether it is possible to differentiate different forms and degrees of hybridity. In drawing on ideas of Mikhail Bakhtin (1981, 355–368), Pnina Werbner (1997) has proposed to make a distinction between what she calls "organic hybridity" and "intentional hybridity". With "organic hybridity" she refers to routine processes, in which ideas, words and objects are constantly borrowed and adopted from other groups of people in a relatively unreflected way, so that the sense of order and continuity within society is not disrupted. Compared to this, "intentional hybridity" refers to situations in which cultural forms coming from the outside are employed by social actors to distance themselves from other groups within a given society. Since this form of hybridity is deliberately chosen in opposition to an existing state of affairs, it represents a challenge to social order and identities (Werbner 1997, 5).

5.3 Imagined Worlds

The analysis of prehistoric and early historic sources has an extraordinary potential for widening the scope of our understanding of the effects of interculturality, because it confronts us with the material remains of societies that had been characterized by a true universe of differing systems of value and forms of social space. In order to fathom the transformative repercussions of such relations, it is necessary to change the approach towards items coming from the outside. Using them mostly for reconstructing past systems of exchange or for chronology archaeology has restricted them to their properties of being objects and of being foreign. Instead, as Hans-Peter Hahn has pointed out, what needs to be studied are the differing ways foreign cultural forms are integrated into a new context, in order to clarify whether their use followed patterns of practice comparable to or different from those in their region of origin. To accomplish this, it is necessary to focus on micro-contexts on the local level (Hahn 2008b, 199), irrespective of whether we are dealing with ethnographic or archaeological sources.

The main reason for the transformative potential of such acts of appropriation already in pre-modern contexts lies in the agency of social actors exercised through the prevalent forms of discourses and social practices. In combination with the particular structure of a society, this agency must have at all times ensured that impulses arriving from the outside were transformed by merging them with existing values and world views.

There are two closely intertwined aspects of how agency operates in this context. The first aspect is the one of *translation*, that is the discourses and practices through which the meaning of new foreign traits are made accessible in the course of the transfer from one society to another.

The second aspect derives from the *social imaginary*, that is the set of ideas which groups have about themselves and others as well as about the world they live in and the significance of material and immaterial traits received from the outside (Anderson 1983; Taylor 2004, 23–30). The negotiation of the meaning and value of foreign features is directly linked to how the surrounding world is conceived. Roland Robertson (1992, 54–75) has criticized World-Systems Theory for belittling the significance of cultural factors as ephemeral compared with those of economy. By taking the modern vision of geography and space for granted, World Systems Theory insinuates a universally applicable significance for economy, space and distance. The generally accepted view of the world as a coherent entity with continents, seas and other geographical features is, however, a relatively recent phenomenon. Before, based on differing social imaginaries, societies have conceived the shape and the meaning of the surrounding world in very different ways. Such views of the world were always at the same time world views (Robertson 1992, 69–77), inasmuch as they were linked with the values and convictions of a group, and the question of its position with regard to the wider cosmos and the natural and super-natural forces inhabiting it. But it would be overly simplistic to assume that this linkage between ideological concepts and views of the world is an aspect restricted to the past or to non-modern societies. As Robertson (1992, 66) emphasizes, ideas of how the world should be conceived and interpreted in modern globalization are likewise crucial for determining the directions in which economic interests will be pursued.

Ideologically charged cognitive concepts of the world are highly dynamic, inasmuch as the underlying presuppositions guide and give meaning to exchanges made with the outside and, at the same time, are subject to change due to the increase of knowledge gained in the course of such exchanges (Maran 2007, 4–5). For this reason I find it justified to use the term "global" when speaking about exchange in pre-modern times, because what was perceived as the "world" was culturally constituted and differed from group to group, something which is lost by retroactively imposing a contemporary view of the world as the only correct one.

Without textual sources to inform us about such issues, archaeology is not in a position to grasp ancient discourses about the structure and the meaning of the world and specific foreign features. But it is important to keep in mind that such inner-societal processes for the creation of meaning must have had an immediate bearing on the changing attitudes towards goods and ideas coming from the outside, since they were associated with the power of the forces of certain corners of the world (Helms 1988, 3–65; 1993, 46–51). What in principle is accessible to archaeology is the level of social practices - insofar as they left traces in material remains. By carefully studying find associations in closed micro-contexts, as well by observing indications for the manipulation of objects to fit new purposes, it is in some cases possible to clarify how foreign traits may have been integrated into such practices. Moreover, in rare cases of a sudden cultural re-orientation towards distant areas one can even specify which areas of the "world" were charged with a special meaning and through this get glimpses of how the surrounding world was conceived (Maran 2011).

In summary, the biggest problem I see in concepts like cultural hybridity and creolization is that in spite of their promise to overcome outdated obsessions with purity and origins, there is the danger of these very aspects sneaking in, so to say, through the back door. Moreover, if such concepts are thought to be generally applicable, they are too unspecific to be of any explanatory value. Although I would thus doubt the usefulness of the concept of cultural hybridity for interpreting prehistoric and early historic finds, the issues raised by the concept are undoubtedly of particular relevance for antiquity since they draw attention to the potential for transformation inherent in interculturality. In dealing with the appearance of foreign traits, the focus of attention must be placed on clarifying the ways of appropriation on a local level and on how, in the course of their integration into existing practices, new cultural forms were created. It seems to me that those cases designated as "intentional hybridity" by Werbner are of particular relevance to archaeology. Not only are they based on the conscious selection and employment of a whole array of specific foreign traits, but they also have a high transformative potential deriving from the agency of social groups which aim to change an existing order and to construct new social identities. I have stressed the need to take the social imaginary of a given group in consideration when discussing the question of how foreign cultural traits were assessed. For far too long intercultural contacts in antiquity as well as in modern times were viewed solely through the prisms of economy and politics. In doing this it came to be overlooked that a generally accepted view of the world must be taken as the absolute exception, rather than the rule. In a long historical perspective diverging concepts of the world must have played a crucial role in giving meaning to such contacts and to the foreign traits received through them.

References

Anderson, Benedict. 1983. *Imagined Communities*. London: Verso.
Bakhtin, Michail M. 1981. *The Dialogic Imagination*. Austin: University of Texas Press.
Bernbeck, Reinhard. 1997. *Theorien in der Archäologie*. Tübingen: Francke.
Childe, V. Gordon. 1929. *The Danube in Prehistory*. Oxford: Clarendon Press.
Friedman, Jonathan. 1997. "Global Crises, the Struggle for Cultural Identity and Intellectual Porkbarelling: Cosmopolitans versus Locals, Ethnics and Nationals in an Era of

De-hegemonisation." In *Debating Cultural Hybridity: Multi-Cultural Identities and the Politics of Anti-Racism*, edited by Pnina Werbner and Tariq Modood, 70–89. London and New Jersey: Zed Books.

Graebner, Fritz 1967. "Kulturkreise und Kulturschichten." In *Historische Völkerkunde*, edited by Carl August Schmitz 1967a, 28–54, Frankfurt a. Main: Akademische Verlagsgesellschaft.

Ha, Kien Nghi. 2005. *Hype um Hybridität. Kultureller Differenzkonsum und postmoderne Verwertungstechniken im Spätkapitalismus*. Bielefeld: Transcript Verlag.

Hahn, Hans Peter 2004. "Global Goods and the Process of Appropriation." In *Between Resistance and Expansion. Explorations of Local Vitality in Africa*. Beiträge zur Afrikaforschung 18, edited by Peter Probst and Gerd Spittler, 211–229. Münster: LIT Verlag.

Hahn, Hans Peter. 2005. *Materielle Kultur. Eine Einführung*. Berlin: Reimer.

Hahn, Hans Peter 2008a. "Lokale Kulturen und globale Verflechtungen. Handwerker, Traditionen und transkontinentale Bezüge." In *Same Same, but Different. Der Dokra-Weg der Ringe*, edited by Johanna Dahm, 86–95. Zürich: Niggli.

Hahn, Hans Peter 2008a. "Lokale Kulturen und globale Verflechtungen. Handwerker, Traditionen und transkontinentale Bezüge." In *Same Same, but Different. Der Dokra-Weg der Ringe*, edited by Johanna Dahm, 86–95. Zürich: Niggli.

Harris, Marvin. 1968. *The Rise of Anthropological Theory*. New York: Crowell.

Helms, Mary W. 1988. *Ulysses' Sail. An Ethnographic Odyssey of Power, Knowledge, and Geographical Distance*. Princeton: Princeton University Press.

Helms, Mary W. 1993. *Craft and the Kingly Ideal: Art, Trade, and Power*. Austin: University of Texas Press.

Kalra, Virinder S., Raminder Kaur, and John Hutnyk. 2005. *Diaspora and Hybridity*. London: Sage.

Maran, Joseph. 2007. "Seaborne Contacts between the Aegean, the Balkans and the Central Mediterranean in the 3rd Millennium BC: The Unfolding of the Mediterranean World." In *Between the Aegean and Baltic Seas. Prehistory across Borders, Proceedings of the International Conference Bronze and Early Iron Age Interconnections and Contemporary Developments between the Aegean and the Regions of the Balkan Peninsula, Central and Northern Europe, University of Zagreb, 11–14 April 2005. Aegaeum 27*, edited by Ioanna Galanaki, Helena Tomas, Yannis Galanakis, and Robert Laffineur, 3–24. Liège and Austin: Université de Liège and University of Texas.

Maran, Joseph. 2011. "Lost in Translation – The Emergence of Mycenaean Culture as a Phenomenon of Glocalisation." In *Interweaving Worlds: Systemic Interactions in Eurasia, 7th to 1st millennia BC. Proceedings of the Conference Ancient World Systems, Sheffield, 1st–4th April 2008 in Memory of Andrew Sherratt*, edited by. Tony Wilkinson, Susan Sherratt, and John Bennet, 282–294. Oxford: Oxbow.

Ratzel, Friedrich. 1967. "Über den anthropogeographischen Wert ethnographischer Merkmale." In *Historische Völkerkunde*, edited by Carl August Schmitz 1967a, 9–27. Frankfurt a. Main: Akademische Verlagsgesellschaft.

Robertson, Roland. 1992. *Globalization: Social Theory and Global Culture*. London: Sage.

Rössler, Martin. 2007. *Die deutschsprachige Ethnologie bis ca. 1960: Ein historischer Abriss*, Kölner Arbeitspapiere zur Ethnologie 1. Köln: Institut für Völkerkunde, Universität Köln.

Schmitz, Carl August. 1967a. *Historische Völkerkunde*. Frankfurt a. Main: Akademische Verlagsgesellschaft.

Schmitz, Carl August. 1967b. Vorwort. In *Historische Völkerkunde*, edited by Carl August Schmitz, 1–8. Frankfurt a. Main: Akademische Verlagsgesellschaft.

Spittler, Gerd. 2002. "Globale Waren – Lokale Aneignungen." In *Ethnologie der Globalisierung. Perspektiven kultureller Verflechtungen*, edited by Brigitta Hauser-Schäublin and Ulrich Braukämper, 15–30. Berlin: Reimer.

Streck, Bernhard. 2000. "Diffusion und Rekontextualisierung – Einführung." In *Afrika 2000. 17. Tagung der Vereinigung von Afrikanisten (VAD) in Deutschland, Leipzig, 30. März bis 1. April*

2000, edited by Ulf Engel, Adam Jones, and Robert Kappel. Leipzig: Institut für Afrikanistik der Universität Leipzig (CD).

Taylor, Charles. 2004. *Modern Social Imaginaries*. Durham: Duke University Press.

Veit, Ulrich. 1989. "Ethnic Concepts in German Prehistory: a Case Study on the Relationship between Cultural Identity and Archaeological Objectivity." In *Archaeological Approaches to Cultural Identity. One World Archaeology 10*, edited by Stephen J. Shennan. London: Routledge.

Werbner, Pnina. 1997. "Introduction: The Dialectics of Cultural Hybridity." In *Debating Cultural Hybridity: Multi-Cultural Identities and the Politics of Anti-Racism*, edited by Pnina Werbner and Tariq Modood, 1–26. London: Zed Books.

Werbner Pnina and Tariq Modood. 1997. *Debating Cultural Hybridity: Multi-Cultural Identities and the Politics of Anti-Racism*. London: Zed Books.

Chapter 6
Adjusting the Image – Processes of Hybridization in Visual Culture: A Perspective from Early Christian and Byzantine Archaeology

Ute Verstegen

Abstract Since Christian visual culture emerged from the substratum of antique pagan imagery in the late second – third century AD, the relationship between iconoclastic and iconophile views has oscillated in Christianity. The basis of the criticism against imagery was the ban imposed in the Old Testament, which was interpreted, depending on exegetical stringency, as a strict ban on either the production of images of God or of any representation of animated creatures. In the eighth century, the confrontation between the opposing inner-Christian positions culminated in the Byzantine Iconoclastic Controversy. With reference to the actual discourse of hybridity in cultural theory, this paper provides a case study of processes in the eighth century which took place in the Syro-Palestinian region during the clash of Christian and Muslim Arab religious ideas and visual cultures. Archaeological investigations of church interiors in this area have documented a trend towards geometrical motifs on the one hand, and deliberate destruction of older figural representations on the other: mosaic tesserae were removed from relevant places in floor mosaics and rearranged on the same spot into abstract or floral motifs. These discoveries raise the questions of the agents' identity and the backgrounds to these iconophobic acts.

Since Christian visual culture emerged from the substratum of antique pagan imagery in the late second and third century AD, the relationship between iconoclastic and iconophile views, between opponents and supporters of images in church buildings, has oscillated in Christianity. The basis of the criticism against imagery was the ban imposed on images in the Ten Commandments of the Old Testament. In Exodus 20:4–5 we read: "You shall not make for yourself an idol in the form of anything in heaven above or on the earth beneath or in the waters below. You shall not bow down to them or worship them." And in Deuteronomy 4:15–18: "Therefore watch yourselves very carefully, so that you do not become corrupt and make for yourselves an idol, an image of any shape, whether formed like a man or a woman, or like any animal on earth or any bird that flies in the air, or like any creature that moves along the ground or any fish in the waters below."

In Early Christianity these verses were interpreted, depending on exegetical stringency, either as a strict ban on the production of images of God or as one on any representation of animated creatures.[1] Concerning the manufacturing techniques of images, the ban was usually understood as an interdiction of three-dimensional cult statues, but sometimes even of two-dimensional representations. In the eighth century, the confrontation between the opposing inner-Christian positions culminated in the so-called Byzantine Iconoclastic Controversy.[2]

This paper provides a case study of processes in the eighth century which took place in the Syro-Palestinian region during the clash of Christian and Muslim Arab religious ideas and visual cultures. As a part of the Eastern Roman (or Byzantine) Empire, the region had experienced a period of economic prosperity in the sixth century; during the first half of the seventh century it had suffered two invasions: in 614, a raid by Sasanian troops from Persia, and, after a short period of Byzantine re-governance, the Islamic invasion of the 630s,[3] which ushered in permanent Islamic rule. The new rulers seem to have stayed tolerant towards the population, the overwhelming majority of which remained Christian throughout the Early Islamic period, especially during the Umayyad caliphate from 661 to 750 (Shboul and Walmsley 1998). Numerous examples of churches discovered in excavations prove that during this age, Christians continued to build, repair and refurnish churches (Schick 1995; Piccirillo 2002; Shiyyab 2006). The available historical and archaeological evidence for Christian communities in the Palestinian region diminishes at the beginning of the ninth century (Schick 1995, 2; Griffith 1997, 1998; Ribak 2007, 73). The same situation apparently occurred in the greater region of Syria (Shiyyab 2006, 214).

Archaeological investigations of church interiors in this area have documented an interesting break in the visual culture of the eighth century, which – as far as we can judge by the archaeological remains – primarily affected the mosaic pavements that were a standard feature in most late antique or Byzantine churches there (Avi-Yonah 1932, 1933; Ovadiah and Ovadiah 1987; Piccirillo 1993).[4]

---

[1] The literature on this topic is immense. For a current overview see Jäggi 2009, for a short summary see Helas 2003. Broad insights are given by Elliger 1930, Bredekamp 1975, Bryer and Herrin 1977, Dohmen and Sternberg 1987, Feld 1990, Möseneder 1997, Besançon 2001, and McClanan and Johnson 2005. Especially helpful are Baynes 1951, Stock 2007, and – on Western iconoclasm – Angenendt 2001, and Noble 2009.

[2] From the wide research available on this subject only some references shall be cited: Martin 1930 and Irmscher 1980 offer clear and still current summaries of the Byzantine Iconolastic Controversy; a short overview can be found in Lange 2007. The iconoclasm under Leo III has been analysed by Gero 1973. Grabar 1957 provides a collection of archaeological sources, which is expanded by Brubaker and Haldon 2001. The cultural roots of the Byzantine phenomenon are discussed by Barnard 1974.

[3] The 634 invasion of Syria (fall of Gaza, Bethlehem), followed by the final, August 636 battle at the river Yarmuk, and the falls of Jerusalem between 635 and 638, and Caesarea in 640.

[4] As Piccirillo 1998, 263 points out, in this region the habit of laying out mosaic pavements and wall mosaics persisted at least until the second half of the eighth century.

These pavements consisted of small mosaic cubes laid out in ornamental patterns, often featuring design elements such as depictions of people, animals, vegetation and architecture. Many of these mosaic floors additionally showed dedicational inscriptions which mention the date of dedication or completion of the church – giving archaeologists important information about the precise age of the building.

In these mosaic floors the change in the visual culture occurred in two ways: on the one hand, there was a trend towards newly laid pavements showing solely geometrical motifs (Schick 1995, 181–183; Piccirillo 1998, 269; Brubaker and Haldon 2001, 35; Piccirillo 2002, 243); in most cases, however, parts of older pavements which had depicted living things were deliberately destroyed and immediately repaired without recreating any figural representations. In his 1995 book on the Christian communities of Palestine from Byzantine to Islamic rule, Robert Schick documents more than fifty church mosaics with iconoclastic damage and more than seventy that remained undamaged.[5] Schick suggests that those mosaics with depictions of living things that survived might have been covered before the time the others were damaged (Schick 1995, 188f.). By the eighth century, as Schick argues, these churches may already have been abandoned or used for other purposes. Another explanation would be that the iconophobic actions resulted from selective decisions taken by local actors only, and were based on ideas that were not shared by all members of society.[6] To answer these questions, a closer look at different forms of image destructions is helpful.

6.1 An Example of Iconophobic Activity Without Repair: The Church at Kursi (Palaestina Secunda, Today Israel)

Only very few mosaics show clear signs of damage without subsequent repairs. One of them is the mosaic pavement of the church at Kursi on the east bank of Lake Tiberias (Fig. 6.1), which in late antiquity was part of the province of Palaestina Secunda, and in early Muslim times was under the custody of the jund al-Urdunn. Today the site belongs to Israel.

Ancient pilgrims commemorated the place as the spot where – according to Matthew 8:28–34, Mark 5:1–13 and Luke 8:32–37 – Jesus drove the demons out of a possessed man (or two) and transferred them to a herd of swine. The church and its related monastery were probably built in the fifth or at the beginning of the sixth century and partly destroyed and rebuilt in the seventh century (Ovadiah and Gomez de Silva 1981, 238–240 no. 233; Tzaferis 1984; Ovadiah and Ovadiah

---

[5] Adnan Shiyyab has assembled more than 60 churches in Palestine and Jordan showing clear signs of iconoclastic activities (Shiyyab 2006).

[6] Eliya Ribak concludes that in the provinces of Palestine, "iconoclasm appears in 21% of synagogues where human figures have been recognised and in 25% of churches with human figures" (Ribak 2007, 33).

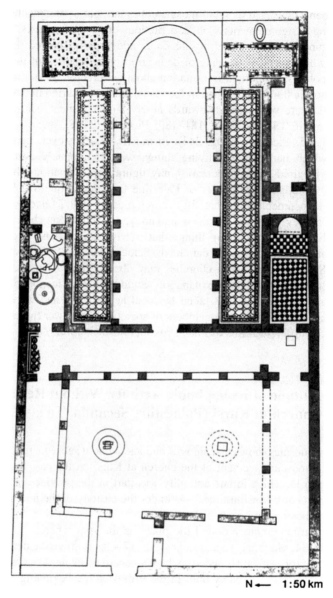

Fig. 6.1 Kursi (Israel), church, ground plan showing traces of mosaic pavements (Tzaferis 1993, 77)

1987, 103f.; Schick 1995, 195f. 377f. 387f.; Tzaferis 1993; Shiyyab 2006, 88–90; Ribak 2007, 182f.).

Set within the mosaics' ornamental framework (Figs. 6.2 and 6.3) are fields with depictions of plants, vegetables and fruit forming a repeating motif in a row (e.g. grapes, melons, pomegranates). Other rows have lost their pictures, because

Fig. 6.2 Kursi (Israel), church, mosaic in northern aisle, detailed view (Sebastian Watta, Nuremberg, 2009)

Fig. 6.3 Kursi (Israel), church, mosaic in northern aisle, detailed view (Sebastian Watta, Nuremberg, 2009)

they were destroyed and not subsequently repaired, leaving holes in the pavement. The current mortar fillings in the places of damage resulted from restoration work done after the excavation of the site in the 1970s.[7]

---

[7] For the original conditions see Ovadiah and Ovadiah 1987, pl. CIX.

In some fields slight traces of the motifs survived the ancient damage and show that they originally contained depictions, especially of birds. Only very few images of animals were left intact: two birds for example escaped damage because a fallen column covered them during the time of iconoclasm. The fallen column suggests in turn that the building was no longer used as a church and already at least partially destroyed, if not completely ruined. Pottery and coins from the Umayyad period indicate a later occupation and use of the ruined building as a stable. This later reoccupation lasted until the middle of the eighth century, so that the partial collapse must have occurred before then, supposedly at the beginning of the eighth century (Schick 1995, 195). As perpetrators of the damage Robert Schick thus suspects the later occupants of the site and identifies the deliberate damage as later vandalism (Schick 1995, 196). It is unknown whether these people were Christians or Muslims.[8]

6.2 An Example of Iconophobic Activity of Damage and Repair: The Church of Saint Stephen at Umm er-Rasas (Arabia, Today Jordan)

Contrary to what the example of Kursi suggests, mosaic images were usually damaged with care. This seeming paradox will be clarified in the following. In most cases considerable time and effort was spent to remove the mosaic tesserae from relevant places in the floor mosaics by plucking out the cubes individually or in small groups from the images. The surrounding areas, however, remained unscathed. Often the material was removed so precisely that the outlines of the image forms are still visible (Schick 1995, 194). Usually the created holes were refilled with mosaic tesserae, either by forming abstract patterns or by inserting geometrical or vegetative designs. In some cases it seems certain that the same mosaic cubes ripped out before were then mixed up and used to patch the gaps (Schick 1995, 195; Piccirillo 1998, 269; 2002, 243).[9] In these cases damage and repair took place more or less at the same time.

The site of Umm er-Rasas (ancient Kastron Mefa'a in the province of Arabia, in early Muslim time part of the jund Dimashq) in present Jordan, 70 km south of Amman, features the churches with the most significantly damaged and repaired mosaics. One of them is the Church of Saint Stephen (Figs. 6.4 and 6.5), which was built in the sixth or seventh century outside the city walls, redecorated in the eighth century, excavated in 1986 and analysed in terms of iconoclastic damage by Susanna Ognibene in her publication of 2002 (Ognibene 2002).

---

[8] Damage of that kind has also been found in the Palestinian Jewish synagogues of Na'aran and Meroth (Ribak 2007, 33). In Meroth the evidence suggests that only the eyes of the figures were destroyed. This alteration, combined with covering the mosaic with a flagstone floor, already took place before the Muslim reign, possibly at the end of the fifth or the beginning of the sixth century (Ribak 2007, 34).

[9] E.g. at Madaba (map church and cathedral), Nitl, Rihab, Umm er-Rasas, Zei.

6 Adjusting the Image – Processes of Hybridization in Visual Culture

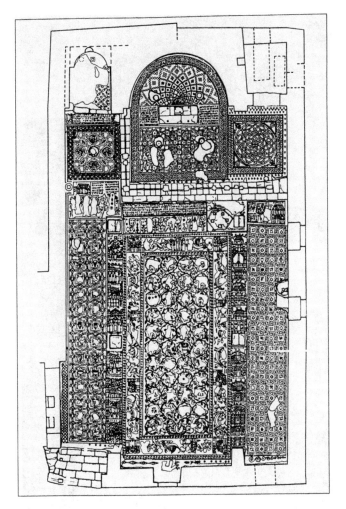

Fig. 6.4 Umm er-Rasas (Jordan), Church of St Stephen, ground plan, also showing mosaic pavements (Ognibene 2002, 52 fig. 4)

The church of Saint Stephen contains two dated mosaic floors (Piccirillo 1993, 36f. 233. 238f.; Piccirillo and Alliata 1994, 242–246; Schick 1995, 472–474; Blázquez 1996, 138; Ognibene 2002, 144). In the apse is a purely geometric mosaic dated by inscription to March 756, in the time of Bishop Job. There is a second inscription in the nave which appears to date to 785, but by analysing the repairs in this section meticulously, Robert Schick has argued convincingly that this date "appears to be incorrect and should be changed to 718" (Schick 1995, 472).[10]

---

[10] See also the drawing in Schick 1995, plate X. The present inscription has to be read as 785, in the time of Bishop Sergius, given as year 680 according to the era of the province of Arabia.

Fig. 6.5 Umm er-Rasas (Jordan), Church of St Stephen, aerial view (Piccirillo and Alliata 1994, 135 fig. 23)

The explanation given for the different original date is that the inscription was damaged around that date. The person who repaired the damage didn't know Greek as can be recognised by the incorrect use of individual letters. A few coloured mosaic cubes in the otherwise pure white background give a hint of which part was damaged and then restored by the worker. The first letter of the date seems to be original. It is a Greek X, symbolising 600 in the system of the milesian numerals. The following Greek letter Π symbolising 80 is a restoration. Instead of it, Schick argues, originally there were the letters IΓ symbolising 13 (I = 10, Γ = 3). Piccirillo and Alliata 1994, 244–246 and Ognibene 2002, 79 follow Schick in this argumentation. The restoration of the date was completed before the church was abandoned.

Fig. 6.6 Umm er-Rasas (Jordan), Church of St Stephen, mosaic floor in the nave, view to the east (Ute Verstegen, Nuremberg, 2001)

Pottery sherds and coins that were found during the excavation indicate that the building complex existed until the ninth or tenth century, when it was abandoned and finally collapsed (Schick 1995, 474; Ognibene 2002, 145).[11]

The eighth century church's nave mosaic is one of the largest and exemplifies the highest quality to be found in the region (Figs. 6.6 and 6.7). Its rectangular middle panel shows a continuous vine scroll forming medallions once filled with single images of people and animals, as well as a central basket which still remains. The rectangle is framed by a zone with black background presenting fishing scenes – a so-called Nilotic scene – while in the second outer frame the most important cities of the region (including e.g. Kastron Mefa'a, Jerusalem and Gaza) are depicted as vignettes, a typical late antique manner of architectural representation. The side aisles were paved with mosaics showing round and square fields with depictions of small animals, especially birds. In front of the altar zone, at the eastern end of the nave, is a panel (Fig. 6.8) that contains a long dedicatory inscription mentioning the officiating bishop Sergius, the patron saint Stephanos, the name of the city and the date of the mosaic's completion. Originally, seven benefactors separated by fructified trees were represented underneath these lines.

---

[11] The mosaics of the two churches at Umm er-Rasas were covered with a layer of silt and ash. This indicates that the buildings were abandoned for some time before their collapse. Obviously the buildings were not extensively robbed before they collapsed because many fragments of the interior furnishings - such as columns, chancel screens, and reliquaries - were found inside. The latest pottery sherds found in the area of the two churches of Bishop Sergius and Saint Stephen have been Early Islamic, perhaps datable to the ninth century.

Fig. 6.7 Umm er-Rasas (Jordan), Church of St Stephen, mosaic floor in the nave, view to the west (Ute Verstegen, Nuremberg, 2001)

Fig. 6.8 Umm er-Rasas (Jordan), Church of St Stephen, mosaic pavement at the east end of the nave with an inscription formerly dating to 718 (changed to 785) (Piccirillo and Alliata 1994, 140 fig. 30)

While the architectural and vegetative motifs of all these mosaics remained intact, all depictions of people and animals were thoroughly damaged, either in part or in total. A detailed view (Fig. 6.9a, b) suggests a slight tendency to confine the damage to the heads of people and animals, sometimes also to the limbs, whereas the torsos were left unscathed.[12] By destroying the parts of the body that enable options for activity – hands, feet, mouth and eyes – it seems that the figures should be rendered innocuous.

---

[12] Another example for this *modus operandi* can be found in the lower church at el-Quweisma. For various examples see Schick 1995, 200.

6 Adjusting the Image – Processes of Hybridization in Visual Culture

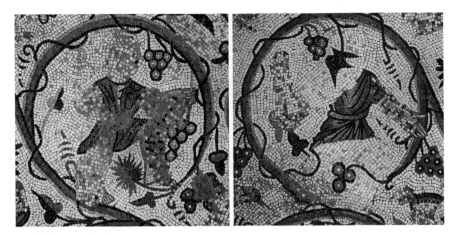

Fig. 6.9 Umm er-Rasas (Jordan), Church of St Stephen, central mosaic panel. Figural representations of standing people with damaged faces and extremities (Ognibene 2002, 205 photo 33 (a), 217 photo 38 (b))

Fig. 6.10 Umm er-Rasas (Jordan), Church of St Stephen, northern aisle. Undamaged section of mosaic with depiction of a fish on a plate (Ognibene 2002, 353 photo 106)

In some cases the original images were replaced by decorative motifs of geometrical or floral type. This can be studied best in the panel with the seven benefactors (Fig. 6.8), which shows that only the figures were obliterated, while the inscriptions with the names of the benefactors were kept unchanged. Clearly, there was no intention of erasing the memory of the donators.

Only two birds in the southern aisle, some little fish and squid in the Nilotic scene and one of two fish on a plate (Fig. 6.10) were left intact. Maybe the birds

Fig. 6.11 Umm er-Rasas (Jordan), Church of St Stephen, frieze with Nilotic scene surrounding the central mosaic panel. Damaged mosaic formerly showing animals and fishing *amorini*, at the left a patch of the iconophobic phase depicting a fish (Bowersock 2006, 79 fig. 3.9)

were overlooked, or some furnishing stood on top of them at the time of the iconoclastic activity. Schick suggests that the fish on the plate was considered dead – which means it was not considered to be a living creature according to the instructions of the Ten Commandments or to Muslim conceptions – and therefore was omitted (Schick 1995, 473). Strangely enough, in the Nilotic scene the workers who repaired the damage placed a fish in the patch (Fig. 6.11).

Discoveries like these in Umm er-Rasas raise the question of who were the agents and what were the backgrounds to these iconophobic acts. An important question is, for example, whether the destructors and repairers of the mosaics were the same people. Cases which show that the same tesserae were removed, mixed up, and then reinserted, indicate that damage and repair occurred at the same time.

One would largely assume that the new Muslim population was responsible for these acts of destruction. However, the replacement of a damaged section with a cross (Fig. 6.12) in the mosaic pavement of Saint Stephen in Umm er-Rasas suggests that the repairers were themselves Christians and had an interest in repairing the damaged mosaics, because the churches were still used by Christian congregations. This evidence finds a parallel in another damaged and repaired mosaic in the church at Masuh (Fig. 6.13), located between Umm er-Rasas and Amman (Piccirillo 1993, 252; Schick 1995, 404f.; Shiyyab 2006, 109). There the damaged sections were carefully repaired using larger mosaic cubes than those used in the original mosaic. In another case at Masuh the patch included the representation of a church building, which also hints at the Christian origin of the repairs. The carefulness of the eradication and the repair also indicates that the actors were themselves Christians. But what was their motivation behind these actions?

6 Adjusting the Image – Processes of Hybridization in Visual Culture

Fig. 6.12 Umm er-Rasas (Jordan), Church of St Stephen. Detail of the first register of the central mosaic panel showing a cross in the filling used to repair iconophobic damage (Ognibene 2002, 163 photo 11 and tavola 3)

Fig. 6.13 Masuh (Jordan), church. Detail of the mosaic pavement showing a cross in the filling used to repair iconophobic damage (Schick 1995, plate 21)

6.3 Early Christian Critique of Images

In the Byzantine Empire and the Muslim regions the dispute over images peaked in the eighth and ninth centuries. Within a few years in the same decade of the eighth century there seem to have been two distinct and universal prohibitions of images, one by the Muslim caliph and one by the Byzantine emperor.

An early sign of the upcoming iconoclastic movement in Byzantium came when in 730 the Byzantine emperor Leo III (r. 717–741) forbade the veneration of religious images (Hausammann 2004, 257–259).[13] He banned all representations of revered persons on icons, referring to Christ, the Virgin Mary, martyrs and saints. And indeed, between 730 and 787 (and again from 815 to 843) the production of icons that included images of Christ, the Virgin, and the saints was stopped. At the same time, in some places, especially in Constantinople, icons of that type were eliminated. There is, for example, clear evidence of an iconoclastic removal of mosaic depictions in Constantinople's Hagia Sophia and in the church of the Koimesis at Nicaea (today's İznik in Turkey, not far from Constantinople) some time during the 760s (Brubaker and Haldon 2001, 20–22).

The prohibition only referred to religious imagery. There is no evidence, however, that the Byzantine iconoclasts rejected *any* type of image depicting people and animals. In the life of St Stephen the Younger, who died in 767, there is a passage giving us an impression of the iconoclastic actions under Leo III's son Constantine V[14]:

"And wherever there were venerable images of Christ or the Mother of God or the saints, these were consigned to the flames or were gouged out or smeared over. If, on the other hand, there were pictures of trees or birds or senseless beasts, and, in particular, satanic horse-races, hunts, theatrical and hippodrome scenes, these were preserved with honour and given greater lustre."[15]

The tone of the passage shows clearly that the author dissents from the iconoclastic actions. He also did not approve of imagery depicting typical 'leisure activities' of Byzantine society, which had always been a matter of critique in religious circles. Iconoclasm in the Byzantine Empire thus differed fundamentally from the archaeologically observed actions of damage to church mosaic floors in the former provinces of Palestine and Arabia. This allows us to presume that the

---

[13] The exact beginning of Leo III's iconoclasm is not handed down in the written sources. Probably one of his first actions was the destruction of the icon of Christ at the Chalke portal leading to the imperial palace in Constantinople in 726.

[14] Although the text was written by Stephen the deacon (of the Great Church in Constantinople) at the beginning of the ninth century according to his own statement, the iconophile passages may have been added as late as the end of the iconoclastic controversy in the middle of the ninth century. See Auzépy 1997.

[15] Vita Stephani iunioris (Patrologia Graeca 100, col. 1113), translation by Mango 1993, 152.

damage was not inspired by Byzantine practices.[16] This is the reason why the most prominent researcher of mosaics in the Middle East, the Italian Michele Piccirillo, refused to describe the damage as "iconoclastic", and instead called it "iconophobic" (Piccirillo 1996).

Leo III was not the first Christian ruler to criticize the veneration of icons. Already from the fifth to the seventh centuries, Christianity had struggled with the internal dogmatic dispute about the human and divine natures of Christ. As a result of and in opposition to the council of Chalcedon held in 451, where the double nature of Christ (perfect in divinity and perfect in humanity) was declared to be orthodox belief, the so-called Monophysite churches sprung up and spread over Syria, the Levant, Egypt and parts of Asia Minor (today's Turkey) (Hausammann 2004, 1–145). Monophysites argued that Christ has only one nature, his humanity being absorbed by his deity. While the 'Chalcedonian' orthodoxy – also enforced by the Byzantine Emperors – came to take hold in the central regions of Syria and Palestine from the later fifth century onward (Griffith 2008, 6), in the hinterland and in the monastic milieu Monophysitism was widely accepted, so that in some regions both persuasions co-existed (Mundell 1977, 64; Griffith 2008, 5–8). There are some indications in the archaeological records that in churches used by Monophysite congregations there was a tendency to avoid representational, figurative art by favouring symbolical representations like the cross, sometimes adding trees, vines and, on occasion, architectural scenes or Eucharistic vessels (Mundell 1977, 64–70; King 1985, 272–276). Hence, already before Islam there was a tendency among certain Christian groups in the Near East to adopt non-figurative motifs in their churches.

Additionally, even before Leo III's actions, there was a debate over icons in Asia Minor (Gero 1973, 85–93; Hausammann 2004, 252–257). Literary evidence shows that Jews and Arabs criticized Christians and urged them to act against images (Hausamann 2004, 256f.). In 724, the patriarch of Constantinople, Germanos, who later refused to sign Leo III's iconoclastic edict, wrote to Thomas of Claudiopolis concerning a policy of iconoclasm that Thomas had locally enforced (Mansi 1960, XIII 107–128A). The correspondence has been preserved in the proceedings of the Second Council of Nicaea in 787, which had assembled to condemn iconoclasm. The acts also refer to a number of Jewish destructions of images[17] (Mansi 1960,

---

[16] In addition, Byzantine iconoclasm was turned down by the Christian church hierarchy in the east. It was condemned by local synods and patriarchs in 760, 764 and 767 (Brubaker and Haldon 2001, 35).

[17] In the sixth century, Jewish communities also showed a revulsion for figural representations which previously had been accepted in synagogues (King 1985, 26; Fine 2000). Eliya Ribak has observed that "iconoclasm also affected both churches and Jewish synagogues in the same way and in the same locations, suggesting a shared theology of images" (Ribak 2007, 78). Interestingly, Samaritan synagogues in Palestine that were likewise decorated with mosaic floors were not affected by iconoclasm. The reason for this was that originally they did not depict living creatures on their mosaic pavements or any other religious object (Ribak 2007, 33, 78).

XIII 24E–32A), but it is unclear if this does not reflect the typical hostility towards Jews in iconophile literature.

In the 720s, the atmosphere of criticism against images in the Near East intensified, as internal and local Christian controversies raged on and Jewish and Muslim attitudes hardened against images.

6.4 Muslim Attitudes Towards Images

The emergence of Muslim opposition to images has been an intense field of study.[18] While the Qur'ān does not contain a prohibition against images per se – except if used as idols – Muslim attitudes towards images are documented in the *ḥadīṯ*, the oral heritage relating to the statements and actions of the prophet Muhammad written down in the late eighth and ninth centuries. They show an opposition to depictions of any living being that possesses *rūḥ*, the "breath of life", because these depictions were seen as a blasphemous imitation of God's power of creation (Shiyyab 2006, 2–18). As plants and trees were not considered to contain the breath of life, their depiction was not forbidden (Shiyyab 2006, 15–17, Belting 2008, 75). According to the *ḥadīṯ*, another possibility of keeping an existing figural representation was to cut off the head of the figure or remove other basic parts of the body to eliminate the viability of the depicted creature (Shiyyab 2006, 14f.). This Muslim attitude corresponds much better than Byzantine iconoclasm with the archaeological evidence in the mosaics. On the other hand, there are references in the *ḥadīṯ* suggesting that images shown on carpets or pillows or on other objects used to sit or step on are not regarded as condemnable (Shiyyab 2006, 17f.). But since these cases only refer to textile decorations, mosaic floors may still have posed a problem because they were immovable and made of another, durable material.

Some years before Leo III's edict, the Umayyad caliph Yazīd II (r. 720–724) had issued a ban on images of all living things (Vasiliev 1955–56). The specific date of this edict is unknown because of differing documentations in the literary traditions: it was issued either in the year 721 or in the year 723 (Shiyyab 2006, 22–37). Curiously enough, Yazīd's ban was acknowledged early in Byzantine sources, but is absent from early Muslim sources until the tenth century, when parts of the story appear but the destruction of images in churches still goes unmentioned (Shiyyab 2006, 31–34). The earliest account of Yazīd's edict is given in 787. A presbyter of Jerusalem named John delivered it to the iconophile Second Council of Nicaea (Mansi 1960, XIII 195E–200C). He reports that a Jewish sorcerer in Tiberias promised Yazīd that he would rule for 30 years if he would enforce the order throughout the caliphate:

---

[18] There is also an extensive bibliography on the Muslim attitudes towards images. See for instance the overview chapters in Barnard 1974, 10–33, Besançon 2000, 77–81, and Belting 2008, 67–80 with further references, and the publications of Paret 1960, Paret 1976–77, Grabar 1977, King 1985, Shiyyab 2006, and Naef 2007.

"that every kind of pictorial representation, on boards or in wall-mosaic or on holy vessels or altar-cloths, or anything else of the sort that is found in all Christian churches, should be obliterated and entirely destroyed; not only these, but also all the effigies that are set up as decoration in the marketplaces of cities" (translation in Schick 1995, 21).

John continues that the Christians preferred to flee and not to destroy holy icons with their own hands, so that the Emirs who had been charged with this task had to impose it on Jews and Arabs.

But, as we have seen, this literary tradition does not accord with the archaeological evidence which points to the Christians themselves carefully disfiguring and repairing the mosaics. The aim of the actors was *not* to remove all traces of the images. Often the outlines of the depictions remained visible, or traces of them were left intact. The images were, in a way, 'camouflaged'. Keeping in mind the Muslim attitude towards images as documented in the *ḥadīt*, Robert Schick argues that the Christians who carried out the damage and repairs acted under duress (Schick 1995, 218f.). Muslim government officials may have ordered the destruction of images in the churches, and the Christians "may then have done the damage themselves to forestall others from doing it" (Schick 1995, 219). As in some churches undamaged and damaged and repaired images coexist within the same pavement, Glen Bowersock assumed recently "that the unexpected order to destroy images was in force for a very short time" (Bowersock 2006, 103). Perhaps Yazīd, who died in 724, formulated his ban only a few months before his death, which could explain the archaeological evidence.

Besides Yazīd's edict there are no references, neither by Christian nor by Muslim authors, to image-breaking under other Umayyad caliphs. G.B.R. King therefore concludes that Yazīd's action was "a rarity worthy of comment" (King 1985, 267) and that under normal circumstances the Muslim rulers would have allowed the use of icons and figural representations inside Christian churches.

There is no certainty, however, as to whether the workers who carried out the damage on the mosaics really acted under pressure. In his analysis of the Muslim contribution to the iconophobic activities in Jordan and Palestine, Adnan Shiyyab concludes that the Christians acted voluntarily, because at the same time and in the same region churches existed or were newly built that contained pictorial representations which remained unharmed (Shiyyab 2006, 3). Peter Baumann supposes that those Christians who destroyed images in their churches did so in order to prove their loyalty to their new Muslim rulers (Baumann 1999, 48).

Recent studies have called attention to another possible explanation for the observed phenomenon: the early Muslim use of existing Christian churches for prayer. As Suliman Bashear has shown, Muslim prayer in churches was common practice during the seventh and eighth centuries (Bashear 1991). The fact that in some churches the images in the eastern zone remained intact may be explained by the prohibition that stopped Muslims from entering the cleric's zones in churches (Piccirillo 1998, 278). Bowersock uses these observations to explain the background of Yazīd's actions: he supposes that the Muslim utilization of Christian churches for prayer was the reason why the caliph intended to apply the strict specifications for mosques, among which was the renunciation of figural representations, to churches, too (Bowersock 2006, 109f.).

6.5 The Emergence of a Hybrid Visual Culture

At the end of the seventh and the beginning of the eighth century, the new Muslim rulers forced a campaign of publicly and symbolically claiming the occupied territories for Islam and setting up a new religious hegemony.[19] Concurrently, they developed their own architectural and visual culture which to this day is well known. Major examples are the famous Dome of the Rock in Jerusalem and the Umayyad Great Mosque in Damascus, which had been the caliphal capital and thus the Muslim political power base since the reign of caliph Mu:āwiya (r. 41–60/ 661–680). Founded by the Umayyad caliph al-Walīd b. 'Abd al-Malik (r. 86–96/ 705–715), the Umayyad mosque was built during his reign from 705 to 715, which corresponds more or less with the time when the mosaic floor was laid in the nave of Saint Stephen's church at Umm er-Rasas.

In spite of several fires that destroyed important parts of the mosque's interior, the building still shows traces of lavish decoration with marble revetments and mosaics. The walls in the western colonnaded portico – in Arabic called riwāq – of the court of the Damascus Mosque are covered with sophisticated, polychrome glass mosaics depicting motifs that can be compared to those in the visually 'cleaned' Christian mosaics (Figs. 6.14 and 6.15). Framed with ornaments, the Damascene mosaics show architectural representations in a landscape with fruit trees and a river, which alludes to paradise. There is not a single image of a person or an animal. The motif of the vine scrolls that features on the central panel in Umm er-Rasas is present here, too: firstly, there are depictions of vine branches set with gold glass mosaic tesserae in some of the architectural representations of the riwāq mosaics. Secondly, a gilded marble vine frieze (Fig. 6.15) with clusters of grapes and pomegranates – both a Muslim symbol for paradise and for cosmic monarchy – once encircled the interior of the prayer hall (Flood 2001, 238, figs. 28, 32, 33).

It is often emphasized that the Umayyad Muslim architectural and visual culture derived from artistic traditions of pre-Islamic Syria and Byzantium, which were restructured and reshaped for the specific requirements of Muslim society. In his book about the Great Mosque of Damascus, published in 2001, Finbarr Flood describes this process as "a type of inter-cultural translation" determined by various factors such as the specific religious needs of the Muslim community and the necessity to communicate with a wider, non-Muslim audience (Flood 2001, 237). The attempt to develop a new visual culture shows the necessity of defining oneself

---

[19] For an overview of the diverse activities associated with this campaign see for example Griffith 2008.

Fig. 6.14 Damascus (Syria), Great Umayyad mosque, western *riwāq*, wall mosaic (Carola Jäggi, Nuremberg, 2005)

Fig. 6.15 Damascus (Syria), Great Umayyad mosque, western *riwāq*, wall mosaic (Carola Jäggi, Nuremberg, 2005)

as different in relation to pre-existing cultural groups like Jews and especially Christians. At the same time, the new imagery should also be 'legible' to a certain degree to these previous groups. In his 1988 study of the Damascus mosaics,

Klaus Brisch argues that the depictions in the riwāq are paradisiacal in theme, and notes that the images were also "a missionary act of *propaganda fidei*, an invitation to the Jewish and Christian subjects of the Islamic ruler to convert. Just as the inscriptions inside the Dome of the Rock at Jerusalem appeal in particular ... to the Christians under Islam, defining clearly what they may retain of their former religion and what they must abandon, so the mosaics at Damascus could have provided them with a vision of Paradise similar to the one with which they were familiar, yet which had the appeal of its glorious artistic language." (Brisch 1988, 18)

It is interesting that even during his lifetime, al-Walīd was accused by Muslim fellows of building mosques in the style of churches.[20] This response does not astonish modern scholars, because of the many references in Muslim sources attesting the Umayyad builders' high esteem for Byzantine craftsmanship, which manifested itself in the immediate employment of Byzantine workmen and artists in the construction and decoration of new Muslim religious buildings (Gibb 1958, 225–229; El Cheikh 2004, 55–60). In the tenth century, the Arab geographer al-Muqaddasī wrote that for the construction of the mosque in Damascus, Caliph al-Walīd gathered artisans from Persia, India, the Maghrib, and also Byzantium; furthermore, the Byzantine Emperor himself sent implements and mosaics as gifts for the building. This Byzantine commitment may not have been voluntary since al-Muqaddasī also mentioned that al-Walīd threatened the emperor with the destruction of churches in the Muslim regions if his requirements were not fulfilled (El Cheikh 2004, 57). According to a tradition related in the annals of the Persian historian at-Tabarī (838/9–923), a similar transaction occurred when al-Walīd began building the mosque of the Prophet in Medina in 707. The Byzantine emperor not only sent 100,000 mithqāl (which corresponds to 425 kg) of gold, but also 100 workmen and 40 loads of mosaic cubes. The emperor also allegedly ordered a search for mosaic cubes in destroyed cities, and had them sent to al-Walīd (Gibb 1958, 225; El Cheikh 2004, 57; another tradition after al-Samhūdī is given in Wüstenfeld 1860, 73; Gibb 1958, 229).

Comparing the elements of the iconographical repertoire of the original church mosaic with the decoration of the mosque yields strong analogies (Fig. 6.16). There are rows of fructified trees on the banks of streams (the ornamental frieze pattern of the spiral meander wave at the bottom of the benefactors' panel can also be interpreted as a symbol for water), rows of architectural vignettes, and vine scrolls. In the mosque, of course, symbols of the cross are absent. Moreover, the mosque's wall mosaics differ from the church pavement in that they use more lavish materials, e.g. mother-of-pearl, or gold glass mosaic tesserae for the background. This practice was common albeit characteristic only of ambitiously decorated Byzantine churches, and not employed for mosaic floors because the material was too easily destroyed by people walking on it. Another difference is the high artistic quality of the mosque's mosaics, which match the highly ambitious architectural

---

[20] At least later Medieval sources hand down this tradition, e.g. al-Samhudi in his chronicle of Medina, in most parts finished in 886/1481, cf. Wüstenfeld 1860, 74. See the whole passage concerning "Architecture and its audiences" in Flood 2001, 213–236.

6 Adjusting the Image – Processes of Hybridization in Visual Culture

Fig. 6.16 Damascus (Syria), Great Umayyad mosque, photo of the *qibla* wall before the fire of 1893 (Flood 2001, fig. 28)

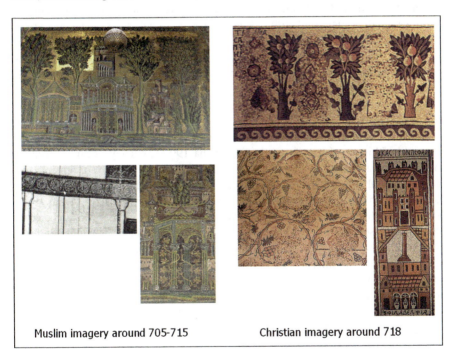

Fig. 6.17 Umm er-Rasas (Jordan), Church of St Stephen, and Damascus (Syria), Great Umayyad mosque. Comparative set of elements of the imagery (Ute Verstegen, 2011)

decoration in one of the capital's prestigious buildings. Of course, such an artistic level cannot be expected in a monument built by the local population in a peripheral area. Nevertheless, the mosaic pavements of Saint Stephen at Umm er-Rasas are among the best of the time and region (Fig. 6.17). After the iconophobic destruction that eliminated the images of all living beings, the church mosaic approximated Muslim imagery even more. Muslims visiting the site may have felt familiar with the imagery, but a Christian visitor may well have noticed the 'camouflage' and superficial adoption of the new requirements. The imagery 'created' by damage and repair may therefore be called 'hybrid'.

6.6 Discussing Historical Visual Cultures in the Context of the Actual Discourse of Hybridity

Over the last decades, the terms 'hybridity' and 'hybridization' acquired a new semantic dimension in the context of post-colonial studies. Originally associated with biological mixtures, in social and cultural theory the term 'hybridization' is now used in the notion of the intermixing and amalgamation of formerly separated social and cultural phenomena, especially of ethnic and national identities (Hall 1994; Said 1994; Bhabha 1994; Seibel 2008). The analytical concept of hybridization clearly refuses a strictly dualistic model and instead hinges on an "either-and-or" approach ("Entweder-und-oder-Modell"), as Elka Tschernokoshewa calls it (Tchernokoshewa and Juri-Pahor 2005, 23f.), where differences are not negated, and thus permits to describe complex and interwoven, sometimes even contradictory social and cultural processes. Products that emerge from such processes are called 'hybrids'.

Homi K. Bhabha shows that processes of hybridization tend to "emerge in moments of historical transformation" (Bhabha 1994, 2). They occur in instable societies, characterized by unequal power relations, an atmosphere of tension and violence, and the disruption of cultural traditions. In a wider perspective "hybridity has existed wherever civilizations conflict, combine, and synthesize" (Stam 1999, 60). Bhabha observes that in colonial situations the clashing cultures do not coexist, but find themselves in a "Culture's In-Between" that includes unequal "cultural times" (Bhabha 1998, 56) caused by differing pasts which implicate differing foresights.[21] For the analyses of historical cultural objects and phenomena these observations turn the focus onto the issue of how 'foreign' elements were appropriated and incorporated into a particular cultural setting. Therefore it is necessary to distinguish precisely between the diverse parts of entangled 'familiar' and 'foreign' components of these objects and phenomena.[22]

---

[21] Bonz and Struve 2006, 143 describe this phenomenon as the "Gleichzeitigkeit von Ungleichzeitigkeiten verschiedener Kulturen".

[22] For the nascent discourse on this topic in the fields of art history and archaeology see Borgolte and Schneidmüller 2009, and the contributions of Philipp Stockhammer and Joseph Maran in the present volume. Dealing with the artistic changes of the 1990s, which were caused by the influences of the so-called new media, Christian W. Thomsen may be considered as a precursor of the debate (Thomsen 1994).

The example shown in this paper offers rare evidence for such cultural processes in the early history of Christianity. Unfortunately, besides the archaeological evidence there are no historical written sources which shed light on the motifs and self-conceptions of those that inflicted the iconophobic damage on the church mosaics. In their manner of destroying figural representations they followed principles towards imagery which the new Muslim rulers of the region may have introduced to them. At any rate, their actions resulted in the creation of hybrids, which include traditional Christian imagery reduced to those elements which were also acceptable to Muslim religious convictions. This process of hybridization was simultaneously a mode of appropriation and one of resistance, because parts or at least outlines of the destroyed mosaic sections remained visible and recognizable to someone familiar with the traditional iconography and the modes of representation. In 1933, Michael Avi-Yonah used the term "palimpsest mosaic" (Avi-Yonah 1933, 73) to describe those mosaics with 'camouflaged', but in their outlines still visible figures.[23] In the hybridity discourse, Robert Stam has again drawn attention to the frequently observed "palimpsestic aesthetics" of cultural objects that are created in processes of cultural hybridization (Stam 1999),[24] so that the palimpsest phenomenon might be one of the core indications for objects of that kind.

If we assume that the iconophobic actions were caused by Muslim intervention, further evidence for an almost hidden aspect of resistance to it can be observed in the symbols of the cross found in the fillings of the damaged mosaic sections. While it has always been the most important symbol in Christianity, the cross also became the principal sign of the Byzantine Empire in the course of the seventh century. Its prominence and ubiquity, e.g. on Byzantine coinage, often caused Muslim rulers to eradicate the sign from any Muslim context, to forbid its display in public, and sometimes even physically to attack and destroy crosses (King 1985).

Against this, once Muslim governors started to develop a new visual culture for their religious building programme, their imagery relied greatly on elements of the traditional Christian iconographical repertoire.[25] Thus, for a short time in the eighth century, Christians and Muslims in the Syro-Palestinian region shared a visual culture which had developed by processes of hybridization and was branded by the mark of hybridity.

---

[23] He talked of the mosaic floor at Khirbet 'Asida as "a curious case of a 'palimpsest' mosaic, with the animals' forms recognizable among the later flowers".

[24] I owe this reference to Hans Peter Hahn.

[25] Flood 2001, 224 n. 171 underlines that the imagery of the Umayyad mosaics is very similar to the iconoclastic decoration of Monophysite churches; see the discussion above.

References

Angenendt, Arnold. 2001. "Der römische und gallisch-fränkische Anti-Ikonoklasmus." *Frühmittel-alterliche Studien* 35: 201–225.

Auzépy, Marie-France. 1997. *La vie d'Étienne le Jeune par Étienne le Diacre: Introduction, édition et traduction*. Aldershot: Variorum.

Avi-Yonah, Michael. 1932. "Mosaic Pavements in Palestine." *Quarterly of the Department of Antiquities in Palestine* 2: 136–181.

Avi-Yonah, Michael. 1933. "Mosaic Pavements in Palestine." *Quarterly of the Department of Antiquities in Palestine* 3: 26–47, 49–73.

Barnard, Leslie W. 1974. *The Graeco-Roman and Oriental Background of the Iconoclastic Controversy*. Byzantina Neerlandica 5. Leiden: Brill.

Bashear, Suliman. 1991. "Qibla Musharriqa and Early Muslim Prayer in Churches." *The Muslim World* 81: 267–282, accessed February 11, 2011, doi: 10.1111/j.1478-1913.1991.tb03531.x.

Baumann, Peter. 1999. *Spätantike Stifter im Heiligen Land: Darstellungen und Inschriften auf Bodenmosaiken in Kirchen, Synagogen und Privathäusern*. Spätantike - frühes Christentum - Byzanz, Reihe B: Studien und Perspektiven 5. Wiesbaden: Reichert.

Baynes, Norman H. 1951. "Idolatry and the Early Church." *The Harvard Theological Review* 44: 39–106.

Belting, Hans. 2004. *Bild und Kult: Eine Geschichte des Bildes vor dem Zeitalter der Kunst*. 6th ed. Munich: Beck.

Belting, Hans. 2008. *Florenz und Bagdad: Eine westöstliche Geschichte des Blicks*. Munich: Beck.

Besançon, Alain. 2000. *The Forbidden Image: An Intellectual History of Iconoclasm*. Chicago: University of Chicago Press.

Bhabha, Homi K. 1994. *The Location of Culture*. London: Routledge.

Bhabha, Homi K. 1998. "Culture's In-Between." In *Questions of Cultural Identity*, edited by Stuart Hall and Paul du Gay, 53–60. London: SAGE Publications.

Blázquez Martínez, José M. 1996. "Arte bizantino antiguo de tradición clasica enl desierto jordano: Los mosaicos de Um er-Rasas." *Goya* 1996, H. 255: 130–143.

Bonz, Jochen, and Karin Struve. 2006. "Homi K. Bhabha: Auf der Innenseite kultureller Differenz: 'in the middle of differences'." In *Kultur: Theorien der Gegenwart*, edited by Stephan Moebius and Dirk Quadflieg, 140–153. Wiesbaden: Verlag für Sozialwissenschaften.

Borgolte, Michael, and Bernd Schneidmüller, eds. 2009. *Hybride Kulturen im mittelalterlichen Europa: Vorträge und Workshops einer internationalen Frühlingsschule*. Europa im Mittelalter 16. Berlin: Akademie-Verlag.

Bowersock, Glen W. 2006. *Mosaics as History: The Near East from Late Antiquity to Islam*. Cambridge, Mass.: Belknap Press of Harvard University Press.

Bredekamp, Horst. 1975. *Kunst als Medium sozialer Konflikte: Bilderkämpfe von der Spätantike bis zur Hussitenrevolution*. Edition Suhrkamp 763. Frankfurt am Main: Suhrkamp.

Brisch, Klaus 1988. "Observations on the Iconography of the Mosaics in the Great Mosque at Damascus." In *Content and Context of Visual Arts in the Islamic World: Papers from a Colloquium in Memory of Richard Ettinghausen, Institute of Fine Arts, New York University, 2 – 4 April 1980*, Monographs on the Fine Arts 44, edited by Priscilla Soucek, 13–20. University Park: The Pennsylvania State University Press.

Brubaker, Leslie, and John Haldon. 2001. *Byzantium in the Iconoclast Era (ca 680 – 850): The Sources: An Annotated Survey*. Birmingham Byzantine and Ottoman Monographs 7. Aldershot: Ashgate.

Bryer, Anthony, and Judith Herrin, eds. 1977. *Iconoclasm: Papers given at the ninth Spring Symposium of Byzantine Studies, University of Birmingham, March 1975*. Birmingham: Centre for Byzantine Studies University of Birmingham.

Derfler, Steven L. 2003. "The Byzantine Church at Tel Kerioth and Religious Iconoclasm in the 8th Century: The 1991–1994 Seasons of Excavation." *ARAM* 15: 39–47, accessed February 11, 2011, doi: 10.2143/ARAM.15.0.504524.

Dohmen, Christoph, and Thomas Sternberg, eds. 1987. *... kein Bildnis machen: Kunst und Theologie im Gespräch*. Würzburg: Echter.
El Cheikh, Nadia Maria. 2004. *Byzantium Viewed by the Arabs*. Harvard Middle Eastern Monographs, 36. Cambridge, Mass.: Harvard University Press.
Elliger, Walter. 1930. *Die Stellung der alten Christen zu den Bildern in den ersten vier Jahrhunderten: Nach den Angaben der zeitgenössischen kirchlichen Schriftsteller*. Leipzig: Dieterich.
Feld, Helmut. 1990. *Der Ikonoklasmus des Westens*. Studies in the history of Christian thought 41. Leiden: Brill.
Fine, Steven. 2000. "Iconoclasm and the art of late-antique Palestinian synagogues." In *From Dura to Sepphoris: Studies in Jewish art and society in late antiquity*. Journal of Roman archaeology, Supplementary series 40, edited by Lee I. Levine and Zeev Weiss, 183–194. Portsmouth, RI: Journal of Roman Archaeology.
Flood, Finbarr Barry. 2001. *The Great Mosque of Damascus: Studies on the Makings of an Umayyad Visual Culture*. Islamic history and civilization 33. Leiden: Brill.
Gero, Stephen. 1973. *Byzantine Iconoclasm during the Reign of Leo III: With Particular Attention to the Oriental Sources*. Corpus Scriptorum Christianorum Orientalium 346, Subsidia 41. Louvain: Corpus Scriptorum Christianorum Orientalium.
Giakalis, Ambrosios. 2005. *Images of the Divine: The Theology of Icons at the Seventh Ecumenical Council*. Studies in the history of Christian thought 122. Rev. ed. Leiden: Brill.
Gibb, Hamilton A. R. 1958. "Arab-Byzantine Relations under the Umayyad Caliphate." *Dumbarton Oaks Papers* 12: 219–233.
Grabar, André. 1957. *L' iconoclasme byzantin: Dossier archéologique*. Paris: Collège de France.
Grabar, Oleg. 1977. "Islam and Iconoclasm." In *Iconoclasm: Papers given at the ninth Spring Symposium of Byzantine Studies, University of Birmingham, March 1975*, edited by Anthony Bryer and Judith Herrin, 45–52. Birmingham: Centre for Byzantine Studies University of Birmingham.
Griffith, Sidney H. 1997. "Byzantium and the Christians in the World of Islam: Constantinople and the Church in the Holy Land in the Ninth Century." *Medieval Encounters* 3: 231–265.
Griffith, Sidney H. 1998. "What has Constantinople to do with Jerusalem? Palestine in the Ninth Century: Byzantine Orthodoxy in the World of Islam." In *Byzantium in the Ninth Century: Dead or Alive?*. Society for the Promotion of Byzantine Studies Publications 5, edited by Leslie Brubaker, 181–194. Aldershot: Ashgate/Variorum.
Griffith, Sidney H. 2008. "John of Damascus and the Church in Syria in the Umayyad Era: The Intellectual and Cultural Milieu of Orthodox Christians in the World of Islam." *Hugoye. Journal of Syriac Studies* 11, no. 2. Accessed February 28, 2010. http://syrcom.cua.edu/Hugoye/Vol11No2/HV11N2Griffith.html.
Hall, Stuart. 1994. *Rassismus und kulturelle Identität*. Das Argument 226. Hamburg: Argument-Verlag.
Hausammann, Susanne. 2004. *Alte Kirche, vol. IV: Das Christusbekenntnis in Ost und West*. Neukirchen-Vluyn: Neukirchener Verlag.
Helas, Philine. 2003. "Ikonoklasmus." In *Metzler-Lexikon Kunstwissenschaft: Ideen, Methoden, Begriffe*, edited by Ulrich Pfisterer, 155–158. Stuttgart: Metzler.
Irmscher, Johannes. 1980. *Der byzantinische Bilderstreit: Sozialökonomische Voraussetzungen - ideologische Grundlagen - geschichtliche Wirkungen*. Leipzig: Koehler & Amelang.
Jäggi, Carola. 2009. "Das kontrollierte Bild: Auseinandersetzungen um Bedeutung und Gebrauch von Bildern in der christlichen Frühzeit und im Mittelalter." In *Medien unter Kontrolle*, edited by Sven Grampp, Daniel Meier, and Sandra Rühr, 18–31. Erlangen: Buchwissenschaft / Universität Erlangen-Nürnberg. Accessed February 28, 2010. http://www.buchwiss.uni-erlangen.de/forschung/publikationen/Medien-unter-Kontrolle.pdf.
King, G. R. D. 1985. "Islam, Iconoclasm, and the Declaration of Doctrine." *Bulletin of the School of Oriental and African Studies, University of London* 48: 267–277.

Lange, Günter. 2007. "Der byzantinische Bilderstreit und das Bilderkonzil von Nikaia (787)." In *Handbuch der Bildtheologie, vol. I: Bild-Konflikte*, edited by Reinhard Hoeps, 171–190. Paderborn: Schöningh.
Mango, Cyril. (1972)1993. *The Art of the Byzantine Empire 312 – 1453: Sources and Documents*. Medieval Academy Reprints for Teaching 16. Reprint,Toronto: University of Toronto Press.
Mansi, Giovanni Domenico. 1960. *Sacrorum conciliorum nova et amplissima collectio*. Unveränd. Nachdr. d. Ausg. Paris 1901–1927. Graz: Akademische Druck- u. Verlagsanstalt.
Martin, Edward J. (1930)1978. *A History of the Iconoclastic Controversy*. Church Historical Society's publications 2. Reprint,London: Society for Promoting Christian Knowledge.
McClanan, Anne L. and Jeff Johnson, eds. 2005. *Negating the Image: Case Studies in Iconoclasm*. Aldershot: Ashgate.
Möseneder, Karl, ed. 1997. *Streit um Bilder: Von Byzanz bis Duchamp*. Berlin: Reimer.
Mundell, Marlia. 1977. "Monophysite Church Decoration." In *Iconoclasm: Papers given at the ninth Spring Symposium of Byzantine Studies, University of Birmingham, March 1975*, edited by Anthony Bryer, and Judith Herrin, 59–74. Birmingham: Centre for Byzantine Studies University of Birmingham.
Naef, Silvia. 2007. *Bilder und Bilderverbot im Islam: Vom Koran bis zum Karikaturenstreit*. Munich: Beck.
Noble, Thomas F. X. 2009. *Images, Iconoclasm, and the Carolingians*. Philadelphia, Oxford: University of Pennsylvania Press, Oxford Creative Marketing.
Ognibene, Susanna. 2002. *Umm al-Rasas: La chiesa di Santo Stefano ed il "Problema iconofobico"*. Rome: L'Erma di Bretschneider.
Ovadiah, Asher, and Carla Gomez de Silva. 1981. "Supplementum to the Corpus of the Byzantine Churches in the Holy Land, Part I: Newly Discovered Churches." *Levant* 13: 200–261.
Ovadiah, Asher, and Ruth Ovadiah. 1987. *Hellenistic, Roman and Early Byzantine Mosaic Pavements in Israel*. Bibliotheca Archaeologica 6. Rome: L'Erma di Bretschneider.
Paret, Rudi 1960. "Textbelege zum islamischen Bilderverbot." In *Das Werk des Künstlers: Studien zur Ikonographie und Formgeschichte: Hubert Schrade zum 60. Geburtstag dargebracht von Kollegen und Schülern*, edited by Hans Fegers, 36–48. Stuttgart: Kohlhammer.
Paret, Rudi. 1976–77. "Die Entstehungszeit des islamischen Bilderverbots." *Kunst des Orients* 11: 158–181.
Piccirillo, Michele. 1993. *The Mosaics of Jordan*. Amman: American Center of Oriental Research.
Piccirillo, Michele. 1996. "Iconofobia o iconoclastia nelle chiese di Giordania?" In *Bisanzio e l'Occidente. Arte, archeologia, storia. Studi in onore di Fernanda de' Maffei*, edited by Claudia Barsanti and Alessandra Acconci, 173–191. Rome: Viella.
Piccirillo, Michele. 1998. "Les mosaïques d'époque omeyyade des églises de la Jordanie." *Syria* 75: 263–278.
Piccirillo, Michele. 2002. *L' Arabia cristiana: Dalla provincia imperiale al primo periodo Islamico*. Milan: Jaca Book.
Piccirillo, Michele, and Eugenio Alliata. 1994. *Umm al-Rasas Mayfa'ah, vol. I: Gli scavi del complesso di Santo Stefano*. Jerusalem: Studium Biblicum Franciscanum.
Ribak, Eliya. 2007. *Religious Communities in Byzantine Palestine: The Relationship between Judaism, Christianity and Islam, AD 400–700*. BAR International series 1646. Oxford: Archaeopress.
Said, Edward W. 1994. Culture and Imperialism. New York: Vintage.
Schick, Robert. 1995. *The Christian Communities of Palestine from Byzantine to Islamic Rule: A Historical and Archaeolgical Study*. Studies in Late Antiquity and Early Islam 2. Princeton, NJ: Darwin Press.
Seibel, Klaudia. 2008. "Hybridisierung." In *Metzler Lexikon Literatur- und Kulturtheorie. Ansätze - Personen – Grundbegriffe*, 4th ed., edited by Ansgar Nünning, 297. Stuttgart: Metzler.
Shboul, Ahmad, and Alan Walmsley. 1998. "Identity and Self-Image in Syria-Palestine in the Transition from Byzantine to Early Islamic Rule: Arab Christians and Muslims." *Mediterranean Archaeology* 11: 255–287.

Shiyyab, Adnan. 2006. *Der Islam und der Bilderstreit in Jordanien und Palästina: Archäologische und kunstgeschichtliche Untersuchungen unter Berücksichtigung der "Kirche von Ya'mun"*. Kunstwissenschaften 14. Munich: Utz.

Speck, Paul. 1990. *Ich bin's nicht, Kaiser Konstantin ist es gewesen: Die Legenden vom Einfluß des Teufels, des Juden und des Moslem auf den Ikonoklasmus*. Poikila Byzantina 10. Bonn: Habelt.

Stam, Robert. 1999. "Palimpsestic Aesthetics: A Meditation on Hybridity and Garbage." In *Performing Hybridity*, edited by Joseph May and Jennifer Natalya Fink, 59–78. Minneapolis: University of Minnesota Press.

Stock, Alex. 2007. "Frühchristliche Bildpolemik. Das Neue Testament und die Polemik des 2. Jahrhunderts." In *Handbuch der Bildtheologie, vol. I: Bild-Konflikte*, edited by Reinhard Hoeps, 120–138. Paderborn: Schöningh.

Thomsen, Christian W, ed. 1994. *Hybridkultur: Bildschirmmedien und Evolutionsformen der Künste: Annäherungen an ein interdisziplinäres Problem*. Arbeitshefte Bildschirmmedien 46. Siegen: DFG Sonderforschungsbereich 240.

Tschernokoshewa, Elka, and Marija Juri-Pahor. 2005. *Auf der Suche nach hybriden Lebensgeschichten: Theorie - Feldforschung - Praxis*. Hybride Welten 3. Münster: Waxmann.

Tzaferis, Vassilios. 1984. "The Early Christian Basilica of Kursi." In *Actes du Xe Congrès International d'Archéologie Chrétienne, Thessalonique 28 septembre – 4 octobre 1980*. Πρακτικά του 10ου Διεθνούς Συνεδρίου Χριστιανικής Αρχαιολογίας, Θεσσαλονίκη 28 Σεπτεμβρίου – 4 Οκτοβρίου 1980, vol. II: Communications, B': Ανακοινώσεις, 605–611. Studi di antichità cristiana 27. Città del Vaticano, Thessaloniki.

Tzaferis, Vassilios. 1993. "The Early Christian Monastery at Kursi." In *Ancient Churches Revealed*, edited by Yoram Tsafrir, 77–79. Jerusalem: Israel Exploration Society.

van Reenen, Dan. 1990. "The Bilderverbot: A New Survey." *Der Islam* 67: 27–77.

Vasiliev, Alexander Alexandrovich. 1955–56. "The Iconoclastic Edict of the Caliph Yazid II. A.D. 721." *Dumbarton Oaks Papers* 9–10: 23–47.

Wüstenfeld, Ferdinand. 1860. *Geschichte der Stadt Medina im Auszuge aus dem Arabischen des Samhûdi*. Abhandlungen der K. Ges. d. Wiss. zu Göttingen 9. Göttingen: Dieterich.

Chapter 7
Transfer of German Human Resource Management Practices: Replication, Localization, Hybridization

Torsten M. Kühlmann

Abstract This paper examines the transfer of human resource (HR) practices from German parent companies to their Chinese subsidiaries. Based upon a review of the literature we outline important determinants and outcomes of cross-border transfers in HR-practices. The review suggests that transferring the best practices is a "sticky" process often requiring local adaptation and hybridization. Following a section describing our research methods, the third section presents data on the transfer process from in-depth interviews with German expatriates in China. The interviews centred on the question: what practices are transferred by what processes and with what effects from German parent companies to their Chinese subsidiaries? The results of the analysis challenge the view that the cross-border transfer of organizational practices regularly involves adaptation to local institutions/national cultures in order to be effective in a new context. The discussion traces out the implications of the findings, in particular for cross-border transfer within multinational corporations.

The terms 'hybrid' and 'hybridization' are currently being used in different disciplines and contexts. Recently this term received the attention of a broader, non-academic public when the Japanese car manufacturer Toyota introduced its hybrid car 'Prius' worldwide in 2001. It is the first mass-produced hybrid vehicle combining a conventional combustion engine with an electric propulsion system. With reference to international management literature and practice, the term hybridization is deeply embedded in the ongoing debate about the desirability and the feasibility of replicating or localizing management principles and practices in multinational corporations (MNCs). A popular formulation of hybridization in the international management literature has been proposed by Tolliday et al. (1998). Based upon their research on production models in the automobile industry, they consider hybridization as the "insertion of a business system into a new society or context, and the processes of adaptation and learning involved" (Tolliday et al. 1998, 3f). Hybridization can be regarded as the pursuit of transferring the 'essence' of a business model or practice, but in a reinterpreted and reinvented form that better fits the different institutional and cultural context. For Boyer et al. (1998), hybridization is a third approach to the cross-border transfer of management principles and practices between the strict replication of the home-country way of doing business in the foreign context, and the radical adoption of the local practices of the host country in which the subsidiaries are operating.

This paper considers the transfer of human resource management (HRM) practices from German parent companies to their Chinese subsidiaries. First, three different approaches to managing the operations of a MNC in different national contexts are discussed. Following a section describing research methods, the third section presents data on the transfer process from a survey of German MNCs operating in China. The discussion traces out the implications of the findings, in particular for the cross-border transfer of HRM practices within MNCs.

7.1 Approaches to the Transfer of Management Practices to Foreign Subsidiaries

The objective of this paper is to explore the degree to which HRM practices of German MNCs operating in China imitate those of the German headquarters ('replication'), are adapted to local conditions ('localization'), or combine characteristic elements from both German and Chinese HRM ('hybridization'). Many scholars argue that the ability of a parent company to transfer HRM practices to overseas subsidiaries is a primary resource for its competitive advantage in the global market place (Nohria and Ghoshal 1997; Fenton-O'Creevy and Gooderham 2003). But we know relatively little about which HRM practices are due to be transferred, which adaptations have to be made, and how the employees affected by the transferred HRM practices react (Björkman and Lervik 2007; Flood et al. 2003; Gamble 2003). What we know from case studies and surveys is that the recruitment, development and retention of employees continues to pose a difficult problem for Western companies operating in China (Björkman and Lu 1999; Braun and Warner 2002).

7.2 Replication

Proponents of the replication approach to international management suggest that MNCs transfer their management practices from their headquarters and home country to operations in other countries ('country-of-origin effect'; Harzing and Sorge 2003; Lao and Ngo 2001; Mayrhofer and Brewster 1996; Pudelko and Harzing 2007). Some specific assumptions drive MNCs toward a replication approach (Chen and Wilson 2003):

1. Managers in the MNC may assume that their management practices constitute the sole best approach, and are superior in all contexts. Refusing to adopt them would be completely irrational.
2. They may believe that standardization in management practices is required to attain operational effectiveness and efficiency in international business activities.
3. The MNC may look back at a history of successful replications of management practices in different contexts. That heritage forms a basis for expecting positive outcomes for other replicational approaches as well as experience-based support to guide the implementation.

7.3 Localization

Alternatively, followers of the localization approach argue that MNCs will conform to the formal rules and unwritten norms and values of certain country-specific institutional and cultural contexts ('host-country effect'; Boyer and Hollingsworth 1997; Kostova and Roth 2002; Mueller 1994; Myloni et al. 2004; Sorge 2004). Variations in organizational practices are made to keep in line with different institutional settings and cultural traditions. Assumptions in the MNC operating in favour of localization are as follows:

1. Managers may believe that practices are born and reinforced in specific national contexts. What works in the domestic environment does not necessarily work in a foreign environment. Misfits between managerial practices, their underlying values and assumptions and given local culture and institutions would make the replication of home country practices either inappropriate or even illegal in the foreign environment.
2. In different national contexts there may be different practices that are functional equivalents to the practices in the home country of the MNC.
3. Not imposing home country practices, but adopting host country practices appears to be well-suited to convincing local employees that their routines and knowledge will be valued by the parent company, as well as to overcoming any potential resistance on their part.

7.4 Hybridization

Empirical research (Björkman and Lu 2001; Boyer et al. 1998; Brewster et al. 2008; Dörrenbächer 2002; Ferner et al. 2005) reveals that managing foreign operations in MNCs resides between these two polar approaches of replication and localization. A cross-border transfer of an invariant model of management constitutes an exception, as does a complete adoption of specific local practices. The approach of hybridization offers a third avenue to managing business in countries different from one's own home country. Whilst MNCs strive to transfer successful practices across national borders, constraints set by national-specific institutions and cultural conditions will hinder this intention. Thus, MNCs have to take account of local differences, and the practices established should blend both country-of-origin practices as well as practices similar to those in the countries in which the MNC operate. The logic underlining the approach of hybridization can be reconstructed as follows:

1. The managers of the parent company believe that they have developed a successful model for managing a MNC, but do not assume that their way transcends the contexts in which it operates. The recognition of the relativity of superiority opens the way to a plurality of models that can co-exist because they are better adapted to different contexts.
2. The institutional as well as the cultural constraints of the local society are permissive enough to enable the introduction and integration of country-of-origin elements in the local HRM system.
3. Blending management practices originating in the home country with those from the host country of the MNC may create a complementary or at least compatible set of practices that is capable of delivering greater success compared to the host country competition.

7.5 Transferring HRM Practices from German Headquarters to Chinese Subsidiaries

Up to now we have addressed issues of replication, localization and hybridization in the domain of general management practices. All of the arguments given above can also be found in the specific debate about the simultaneous pressures towards company-wide replication and localization of HRM practices. HRM includes management functions like recruitment, training and development, remuneration, job design and career planning. HRM is an area of management where the forces toward localization are relatively high, given that the addressees have to accept and feel committed to the measures taken by the HR managers (Brewster et al. 2008; Chen and Wilson 2003; Rosenzweig and Nohria 1994). HRM practices are directly related to divergent institutional environments as well as to cultural differences (Björkman and Lu 1999; Ferner et al. 2005; Braun and Warner 2002; Saka 2004; Tempel et al. 2006). Mainstream literature suggests that transferring HRM practices that are rated as successful in the parent company may provoke conflicts between the actors and resistance to change. Depending on the different institutional and cultural contexts in which MNC are operating, their foreign subsidiaries have multiple capacities to confront transfer or to modify transferred practices according to their own interests (Morgan and Kristensen 2006; Oliver 1991). Many examples can be found of practices, that had to be adapted to the local context so as not to be culturally offensive or institutionally illegitimate (Björkman and Lu 1999; Boyer et al. 1998). Thus, the aim here will be to explore replication, localization and hybridization using the area of HRM.

To study the transfer of HRM practices we chose China as our field of investigation. That choice was guided by three lines of reasoning:

1. China has become a major trade partner as well as a destination for foreign investment for many German companies from different industries. Most large German multinational companies have established manufacturing operations in China.
2. Doing business in China means acting within a rather different socio-cultural and institutional context to that in Germany. Chinese management of human resources differs in many aspects from that found in Germany. German companies view employees as a valuable asset. They attach value to systematic recruitment, selection, training, performance appraisal, career planning and incentive schemes. This diligence is rarely found in Chinese companies. It has also been argued that there are a number of Chinese national culture characteristics that make any transfer of Western or German HRM practices problematic. These include the importance of saving face and harmony in social relationships, respect for authority, an indirect verbal style; nepotism in staffing practices and "cash mentality" in compensation preferences (Björkman and Lu 1999; Björkman et al 2008). A summary of the diverse conceptions of HRM in Germany and China is given in Table 7.1.
3. The institutional forces to practice a HRM mode with Chinese characteristics have currently diminished, because the economic reforms have introduced elements of Western market economy such as labour markets, pay for performance or job contracts of limited duration (Ding et al. 2000). The central government's role in regulating industrial relations and human resource issues has declined. Which is to say, the parent companies' pressures to replicate their HRM practices are no longer counterbalanced by strong Chinese institutional forces to adopt characteristically Chinese approaches to HRM.

Table 7.1 National differences in the conception of HRM

Germany	China
High-quality vocational training system	Rudimentary vocational training system
High investment in staff development	Low investment in staff development
Performance-based selection criteria	Guanxi-based selection criteria
Long-term orientation in career pattern	Short-term orientation in career pattern
Co-determination giving workers substantial rights	Weak control over entrepreneurial arbitrariness
Democratic leader behaviour	Paternalistic leader behaviour
Two-way communication between management and employees	Top-down communication
Emphasis on just wages	Emphasis on high wages
Job enrichment	Division of labour

Within the Chinese context, individual performance appraisal is a practice that might illustrate different options for introducing HRM in a Chinese subsidiary. In German companies, performance appraisals are typically centred on the annual appraisal interview between the employee and his superior, confronting the employee with his superior's written evaluation of his past performance using a list of pre-set criteria or objectives. Conventional wisdom holds that Chinese superiors are unwilling to give their subordinate poor ratings because that would provoke a loss of face and impact negatively on interpersonal relationships.

Replication would imply a simple export of the original practice from the German company, without paying any attention to possible constraints and resistance arising from the values of face and harmony in Chinese life. Although risky, this approach is not unfeasible. For example, the Haier Corporation, one of the leading Chinese producers of household appliances, posts monthly appraisals of its managers in the company cafeteria (Pucik 1985).

Localization in the Chinese context would mean adopting the traditional Chinese means of performance evaluation: the employee himself authors a written self-assessment and hands it over to his superior.

According to the hybridization approach, one would set aside the formal rating system and the annual appraisal interview and instead include performance related remarks in the superior's daily routine of instructing and monitoring the employee. Thus, the hybrid practice combines German practice elements (i.e. the superior evaluates) and Chinese practice elements (i.e. the superior acts as a teacher, gives advice without threatening face and harmony).

7.6 Methods

7.6.1 Data Collection and Sample

Data were collected by means of a mail survey. Questionnaires were addressed to the heads of HRM departments at 100 German companies operating in China. A total of 74 companies participated in the survey. The sample covers a broad range of industries. About one third of the companies employed less than 100 people. Most of the subsidiaries were wholly foreign-owned enterprises. Detailed information on the industries, legal form and workforces are given in Table 7.2.

7.6.2 Measures

A questionnaire was developed after an extensive review of the literature on HRM practices in large and medium-sized German companies. To minimize the risk of creating misunderstandings, four HRM managers participated in a pre-test focusing

7 Transfer of German Human Resource Management Practices

Table 7.2 Sample characteristics (n = 74)

	Category	%
Industry	Electronics	31.0
	Automotive	13.5
	Machinery	21.6
	Chemicals	8.1
	Engineering	8.1
	Textiles	5.4
	Other	12.1
Legal form	Joint venture	16.2
	Wholly foreign-owned subsidiary	81.0
	Other	2.7
Number of employees	<100	29.7
	100–1,000	35.1
	>1,000	35.1

both on content and design of the questionnaire. The standardized questionnaire offers short descriptions of German HRM practices. For each practice the respondents were asked to indicate on Likert-type scales the level of its transfer to Chinese subsidiaries, the amount of adaptation to the Chinese context, and the degree of success in its application to the Chinese subsidiary.

7.7 Results

Most of our respondents maintain that they introduced German-style HRM practices in their Chinese operations on a large scale. However, many transferred practices have been adapted at least to some extent to local Chinese conditions (Table 7.3).

Table 7.3 reports the frequencies of localization, replication and hybridization of different HRM practices. Hybridization by combining both German and Chinese elements appears to be the most common approach to HRM in Chinese subsidiaries.

Localizing HRM practices clearly is the exception and not the rule. While hybridization appears to be the general case, the replication of practices originating in the German parent company is an alternative, but less frequently followed proceeding.

In order to get more insight into the success of the replication approach as opposed to the hybridization approach, we asked our respondents to assess the outcomes associated with both transfer approaches. Our data (see Table 7.4) indicates that both approaches seem to be successful in most companies and across most of the practices under study. For the majority of practices the success rate is slightly biased towards the pure replication approach.

Table. 7.3 Replication, localization, and hybridization of HR practices

Practice	Not transferred (%)	Replication (%)	Localization (%)	Hybridization (%)
Web recruiting	23	19	5	53
Employment ad in newspapers	54	14	5	27
Selection interview	19	27	3	51
Selection test	70	7	1	23
Assessment centre	51	22	3	23
Job enrichment	49	15	1	35
Self-regulating workgroup	60	15	1	24
Vocational training	19	31	1	50
Management development	28	38	0	34
Performance appraisal	35	28	4	32
Goal setting	41	18	7	34
Career planning	47	16	1	35
Pay for performance	33	36	3	29
Profit-sharing plan	38	26	4	32

Table 7.4 The success of replication versus hybridization

Practice	Replication successful (%)	Hybridization successful
Web recruiting	100	79
Employment ad in newspapers	80	74
Selection interview	100	71
Selection test	80	44
Assessment centre	75	65
Job enrichment	91	54
Self-regulating workgroup	64	41
Vocational training	87	86
Management development	54	60
Performance appraisal	67	79
Goal setting	62	64
Career planning	75	73
Pay for performance	44	95
Profit-sharing plan	47	65

7.8 Discussion

This study presents evidence of a strong disposition to introduce practices from the parent company to business operations in China. Our findings reflect the importance which practitioners assign to this area of management. It is argued that the management of human resources represents an increasingly critical factor for a company wishing to attain competitive advantages in the worldwide marketplace. Thus, practices which contribute to the company's success should be spread to all units. Our findings suggest that the transfer of many HRM practices results in hybrid practices that deviate both from the original approach and from the corresponding local way of dealing with HRM issues. The headquarters does not necessarily prescribe the standard, and the foreign subsidiary does not necessarily act as a passive recipient of pre-existing practices from the parent company. However, this does not mean that replication is always excluded. The significant amount of practices which have been replicated in China underlines the fact that transfer processes cannot be understood as a mechanical balance between the parent company's pressure to replicate and the subsidiary's wishes to localize, but the outcome of a selective transfer strategy.

The companies participating in our study were predominantly successful in transferring HRM practices with and without adaptations to the Chinese context. This finding confirms two different developments in Chinese business systems. First, in the wake of the extensive economic reforms China has launched in the last two decades, HR managers have been given more discretion in how to handle human resource issues. While progress in adopting market-oriented HR models has been low in Chinese state-owned companies, foreign-owned companies have heavily utilized that freedom now granted to them to transfer HRM practices from parent companies to their Chinese subsidiaries.

Second, our study reveals that cultural differences do not present an insurmountable barrier to the transfer of HRM practices. This evidence is in line with an increasing number of studies showing converging conceptions of Western and Asian managers of "good business" practices (Björkman et al. 2008; Gamble 2003; Pudelko and Harzing 2007; Ralston et al. 2006). Claims about the dysfunctional impact of cultural misfits in international HRM may be overemphasized and the adaptive capacity of people who hold distinct cultural orientations may be underestimated.

The findings must be viewed in the light of the study's limitations. The study explored HRM practices of German parent companies operating in China. Generalizations from these findings should thus be treated with caution and take into consideration the unique characteristics of the German HRM model, as well as the specific attributes of the cultural and institutional context of China.

The study analysed HRM practices and the results cannot be automatically generalised to other areas of organizational practices, such as marketing or research & development. Similar analyses of different management areas would help to clarify whether the relationship between localization, replication and hybridization holds for management practices in general or are specific to the HRM function.

Another limitation is the use of one respondent per company, making it impossible to control the data for response biases. Our measures are based on the perceptions and assessments of German HR managers. It could thus be argued that more objective measures (archival data) of the practices and the inclusion of Chinese respondents would offer a more valid description of actual HRM practices. HRM practices seen as replicated by the German respondents might have be seen subtly transformed into a hybrid from a Chinese perspective.

The study mainly deals with the content of replication, localization and hybridization and does not identify the specific determinants and mechanisms leading to different approaches for the implementation of HRM practices in China. In-depth interviews would help in improving our understanding of the reasons for transfer, the means through which practices are transferred (e.g. instructions expatriate assignments), and the factors that impede or facilitate success (e.g. dependency of subsidiary, and institutional and cultural distance between home and host country). That might be a major area for future research.

This study has some implications for the practice of international human resource management. Existing research on management practice transfer pays a lot of attention to cultural and institutional differences between the home country of the parent company and the subsidiary's host country (Gooderham et al. 2009; Kostova 1999; Liu 2004). But, there is no evidence from our research that German HRM practices have to be thoroughly adapted to the Chinese institutional and cultural context in order to make them a success. One can assume that a substantial overlap in the understanding of "good management" on the German and Chinese side often makes a hybridization or localization of HRM practices dispensable. On the contrary, MNCs should refrain from localizing practices that domestic Chinese companies themselves increasingly assess as outdated and not fitting for the changing Chinese business environment. Practices that were proved successful in the parent country can be replicated in Chinese operations. Adaptations may be made subsequently, if at all necessary. Societal values and institutional norms prevalent in China can be challenged and modified when Chinese employees encounter German style HRM in times of cultural change and ideological disorientation.

References

Björkman, Ingmar, and Yuan Lu. 1999. "The management of human resource in Chinese-Western joint ventures." *Journal of World Business* 34 (2): 1–19.
Björkman, Ingmar, and Yuan Lu. 2001. "Institutionalization and bargaining power explanations of HRM practices in international joint-ventures – the case of Chinese-Western joint ventures." *Organization Studies* 22 (3): 491–512.
Björkman, Ingmar, and Lervik, Jon E. 2007. Transferring HR practices within multinational companies. Human Resource Management Journal 17 (4): 320–335.
Björkman, Ingmar, Adam Smale, Jennie Sumelius, Vesa Suutari, and Yuan Lu. 2008. "Changes in institutional context and MNC operations in China: Subsidiary HRM practices in 1996 vs. 2006." *International Business Review* 17 (2): 146–158.
Boyer, Robert, and J. Rogers Hollingsworth. 1997. "From national embeddedness to spatial and institutional nestedness." In *Contemporary capitalism: The embeddedness of institutions*, edited by Robert Boyer and J. Rogers Hollingsworth, 433–484. Cambridge: Cambridge University Press.
Boyer, Robert, Elsie Charron, Ulrich Jürgens, and Steven Tolliday. 1998. *Between imitation and innovation - The transfer and hybridization of productive models in the international automobile industry*. Oxford: Oxford University Press.
Braun, Werner H., and Malcolm Warner. 2002. "Strategic human resource management in western multinationals in China." *Personnel Review* 31 (5): 553–579.

Brewster, Chris, Geoffrey Wood, and Michael Brookes. 2008. "Similarity, isomorphism or duality? Recent survey evidence on the human resource management policies of multinational corporations." *British Journal of Management* 19 (4): 343–364.

Chen, Shaohui, and Marie Wilson. 2003. "Standardization and localization of human resource management in Sino-foreign joint ventures." *Asia Pacific Journal of Management* 20 (3): 397–408.

Ding, Daniel Z., Keith Goodall, and Malcolm Warner. 2000. "The end of the "Iron Rice-Bowl": Whither Chinese human resource management?" *International Journal of Human Resource Management* 11 (2): 217–236.

Dörrenbächer, Christoph. 2002. *National business systems and the international transfer of industrial models in multinational corporations: Some remarks on heterogeneity*. WZB Discussion Paper FS I 02–102. Berlin: Social Science Research Center.

Fenton-O'Creevy, Mark, and Paul N. Gooderham. 2003. "International management of human resources." *Beta: Scandinavian Journal of Business Research* 17 (1): 2–5.

Ferner, Anthony, Phil Almond, and Trevor Colling. 2005. "Institutional theory and the cross-national transfer of employment policy: The case of 'workforce diversity' in US multinationals." *Journal of International Business Studies* 36 (3): 304–321.

Flood, Patrick C., Nagarajan, Ramamoorthy, and Wenchuan Liu. 2003. "Knowledge and innovation: Diffusion of HRM systems." *Beta: Scandinavian Journal of Business Research* 17 (1): 59–68.

Gamble, Jos. 2003. "Transferring human resource practices from the United Kingdom to China: The limits and potential for convergence." *International Journal of Human Resource Management* 14 (3): 369–387.

Gooderham, Paul, Odd Nordhaug, and Kristen Ringdal. 2009. "National embeddedness and calculative human resource management in US subsidiaries in Europe and Australia." *Human Relations* 59 (11): 1491–1513.

Harzing, Anne-Wil K., and Arndt M. Sorge. 2003. "The relative impact of country-of-origin and universal contingencies on internationalization strategies and corporate control in multinational enterprises: Worldwide and Europe perspectives." *Organization Studies* 24 (2): 187–214.

Kostova, Tatiana.1999. "Transnational transfer of strategic organisational practices: A contextual perspective." *Academy of Management Review* 24 (2): 308–324.

Kostova, Tatiana, and Kendall Roth. 2002. "Adoption of an organizational practice by subsidiaries of multinational cooperations." *Academy of Management Journal* 45 (1): 215–233.

Lao, Chung-Ming, and Hang-Yue Ngo. 2001. "Organizational development and firm performance: A comparison of multinational and local firms." *Journal of International Business Studies* 32 (1): 95–114.

Liu, Wenchuan. 2004. "The cross-national transfer of HRM practices in MNCs: An integrative research model." *International Journal of Manpower* 25 (6): 500–517.

Mayrhofer, Wolfgang and Chris Brewster. 1996. "In praise of ethnocentricity: Expatriate policies in European multinationals." *International Executive* 38 (6): 749–778.

Morgan, Glenn and Peer Hull Kristensen. 2006. "The contested space of multinationals: Varieties of institutionalism, varieties of capitalism." *Human Relations* 59 (11): 1467–1490.

Mueller, Frank. 1994. "Societal effect, organizational effect and globalization." *Organization Studies* 15 (3): 407–428.

Myloni, Barbara, Anne-Wil K. Harzing, and Hafiz Mirza. 2004. "Human resource management in Greece: Have the colors of culture faded away?" *International Journal of Cross Cultural Management* 4 (1): 59–76.

Nohria, Nitin, and Sumantra Ghoshal. 1997. "The differentiated network; organizing multinational corporations for value creation." San Francisco: Jossey-Bass.

Oliver, Christine. 1991. Strategic responses to institutional processes. *Academy of Management Review* 16 (1): 145–179.

Pucik, Vladimir. 1985. "Strategic human resource management in a multinational firm." In *Strategic management of multinational cooperations: The essentials*, edited by Heidi Vernon-Wortzel and Lawrence Wortzel, 424–435. New York: John Wiley.

Pudelko, Markus, and Anne-Wil Harzing. 2007. "Country-of-origin, localization, or dominance effect? An empirical investigation of HRM practices in foreign subsidiaries." *Human Resource Management* 46 (4): 535–559.

Ralston, David A., James Pounder, Carlos W. H. Lo, Yim-Yu Wong, Carolyn P. Egri, and Joseph Stauffer. 2006. "Stability and change in managerial work values: A longitudinal study of China, Hong Kong and the US." *Management and Organization Review* 2 (1): 67–94.

Rosenzweig, Philip M., and Nitin Nohria. 1994. "Influences on human resource development practices in multinational corporations." *Journal of International Business Studies* 25 (2): 229–251.

Saka, Ayse. 2004. "The cross-national diffusion of work systems: Translation of Japanese operations in the UK." *Organization Studies* 25 (2): 209–228.

Sorge, Arndt. 2004. "Cross-national differences in human resources and organization." In *International human resource management*, edited by Anne-Wil Harzing and Joris van Ruysseveldt, 117–139. London: Sage.

Tempel, Anne, Hartmut Wächter, and Peter Walgenbach. 2006. "The comparative institutional approach to HRM in MNCs – Contributions, limitations and future potential." In *Global, national and local practices in multinational companies*, edited by Mike Geppert and Michael Mayer, 17–37. New York: Palgrave.

Tolliday, Steven, Robert Boyer, Elsie Charron, and Ulrich Jürgens. 1998. Introduction. In *Between imitation and innovation – The transfer and hybridization of productive models in the international automobile industry*, edited by Robert Boyer, Elsie Charron, Ulrich Jürgens and Steven Tolliday, 1–19. Oxford: Oxford University Press.

Chapter 8
From Comparative Politics to Cultural Flow: The *Hybrid* State, and Resilience of the Political System in India

Subrata K. Mitra

Abstract The status of the state in India as a modern, electoral democracy is well established. But, while the country responds positively to most items on formal check lists of democracy and stateness, doubts persist because of its anomalous characteristics in areas crucial to modern democratic states. The emergency provisions built into India's constitution, the practice of relinquishing state power to the military under the Armed Forces Act in areas considered 'disturbed', hybrid civil institutions that undertake the role of the military, capitulation to social actors and ethnic groups in communal riots and, most importantly, glaring failures to protect secularism and individual rights – the ultimate symbols of high modernity – are seen as "functional" lapses of this hybrid state. I argue in this chapter that rather than being merely a diminished sub-type of liberal democracy and modernity, the state in India resembles a manifold – an embodiment of the "*avatars* [incarnations] of Vishnu" (Rudolph and Rudolph 1987). The state in India is a hybrid – one which diverges from the Western state "in the importance it accords to 'pre-modern' political forms... because they express different cultural values and traditions that form part of the cultural heritage." (Mitra 1990b, 6) The case study of the Indian state leads to a larger questions. Is *hybridisation* – the strategy and vision of modern political actors of *re-using* the past – the essential factor behind the resilience of the Indian state? More generally, in everyday life, is hybridity the essential reality behind the chimera of a radical disjunction between tradition and modernity?

8.1 Introduction

India's political system, which combines modern, liberal democratic institutions and elements of her pre-modern pasts in its institutional arrangement, continues to puzzle.[1] The status of the state in India as modern, and democratic, is well

---
[1] See, for example, Lijphart 2009, 36–60.

established.[2] But, while the country responds positively to most items on formal check lists of *stateness* and formal democracy, doubts persist about its authenticity because of its anomalous character in areas crucial to liberal democratic states. The authoritarian "emergency" provisions built into India's constitution, the practice of relinquishing state power to the military under the Armed Forces Act in areas such as Jammu and Kashmir and parts of the North East, considered 'disturbed', hybrid legislation that combines features of modern and religious laws, sporadic capitulation by the state to ethnic groups engaged in communal riots and, most importantly, glaring failures to protect secularism and individual rights – the ultimate symbols of high modernity – are pilloried as "functional" lapses by the defenders of the norms expected from modern democratic states.

With the state and the political system of India as the main focus, this chapter explores the components of India's hybrid state, and seeks to account for them in terms of the strategies followed by the main political actors of India. I argue in this chapter that hybridisation is part of the explanatory factor behind the resilience of the modern state. In their search for power, India's political actors transform rules and designs as they see fit. A solution where the bulk of stake-holders simultaneously reach or expect to reach their best outcomes, once achieved, yields a "lock-in" from which they would find it difficult to exit. Each hybrid institution carries a "lock-in" at its core.[3] Not all innovations or amendments work, of course, but when they do, or as Douglass North puts it, when a cluster of actors "lock-in" around a particular design or set of rules, the result – a new hybrid institution – can become enduring. This, I argue, is what gives resilience to the modern state in India.

The focus on hybrid structures generates the space for the understanding of phenomena of cultural and conceptual flow, both temporal and spatial. The hybrid state emerges as a consequence of the conflation of indigenous and alien categories and institutions. The chapter formulates the problem in terms of three questions: what are the salient hybrid features of the state in India, and what led to their incorporation into the modern state that the constitution aimed at? Is hybridisation of the state – resulting from the strategy and vision of modern political actors in re-using the past – the essential factor behind the resilience of the Indian political system? Finally, beyond the specific case of India, is hybridity the essential reality behind the chimera of a universal – 'one size fits all' – modernity, not bound by time and space (Mitra 1994, 2009, Forthcoming)?

---

[2] See Mitra and Singh 2009 for diachronic data on legitimacy and efficacy in India which shows a steady rise from 1971 to 2004, for which we have evidence from survey data. Participation in free and fair elections has gone up steadily from 1951, when the first general election with universal adult franchise was held, and has reached levels that are respectable by the standards of liberal democracies.

[3] North 1990, 94. I have drawn on North to ask why modern institutions work in South Asia, "sometimes". See Mitra 1999b, 422.

8.2 Comparative Politics of the Indian State: Analysing a Hybrid Reality Through Pure Categories

In their prescient essay – the *Modernity of Tradition,* which analysed some ambivalent aspects of modern Indian institutions[4] – Lloyd and Susanne Rudolph had laid down the groundwork for issues raised in this article. India, thanks to the mismatch between pre-conceived categories and her empirical complexity (Mitra 1999), occupies an ambiguous position in the global ranking of democracies. The empirical analysis of the features of the Indian state show, however, that rather than being merely a *diminished sub-type of liberal democracy,* the state in India is a modern state in its own right, but one which diverges from the Western state "in the importance it accords to 'pre-modern' political forms... because they express different cultural values and traditions that form part of the cultural heritage" (Mitra 1990b, 6). It is the quintessential unity in diversity, for the state is the fulcrum around with diverse ideologies, cultures, beliefs and economic regimes revolve. In the words of Lloyd and Susanne Rudolph (1987), the state in India is a manifold – an embodiment of the *"avatars* [incarnations] of Vishnu".

The hybrid elements in the modern state of India are the outcome of the historical genealogy of the state tradition and its discontinuities, cultural and geographic diversity, and the deep class conflict that underpins Indian society. Before we analyse these conditions that have affected the emergence of the state, we need to consider the theoretical bridge that connects the process of state formation to its ultimate product, namely the institutional structure of the state.

The anomalous character of India in terms of the comparative politics of democracy helps link a debate specific to comparative politics with the larger issue of hybridisation and strategic "re-use" (cf. Hegewald and Mitra Forthcoming; Hegewald Forthcoming) that has dominated critical theory and post-colonial literature. We shall make a brief foray into the larger theoretical landscape which will help us to establish a course for the empirical analysis of the Indian case. This will form the basis of an analytical toolkit that extends the conventional, rational choice, neo-institutional model of the state by drawing on trans-lingual, trans-cultural and trans-disciplinary aspects of state formation. On the basis of this heuristic model, this essay will analyse the underlying process that has made the state in India what it is, and explain why the state has become a key element in the resilience of India's political system. The conclusion returns to the issue of the relationship of the pure and the hybrid in Political Science, and opens it up for a general, cross-disciplinary debate.

---

[4] For a succinct analysis of how modernity and tradition "infiltrate and transform each other", see Rudolph and Rudolph 1967, 3.

8.3 The Post-colonial Condition and Hybrid State-Making

Post-colonial states, which often start their independent career with a deep commitment to modernity in its revolutionary or liberal avatar, soon come up with a deep hiatus between the ideology of the state and the life-world of the traditional society in which it is ensconced. Their ability to overcome the consequent deficit of legitimacy is contingent on the strategic manoeuvres of the elites. However, a brief perusal of the field of comparative politics shows that the theoretical deficiency of the discipline rises to this challenge. In its search for pure categories in terms of which to compare the diversity of states, contemporary comparative politics has left behind the pragmatic empiricism of Aristotle, which saw experience (and as such, actors' preferences) rather than superior knowledge as the basis of legitimacy.[5] Instead, the inspiration of Plato and Weberian ideal types has dominated the field. Examples of the ever-present search for pure categories, and the failure to fit the world into them are plentiful. A seminal attempt to classify contemporary political regimes (192 of them, to be precise) into democratic and authoritarian categories found 38% belonging to the pure class of liberal democracy. The rest were distributed over 'electoral democracy' (16%), ambiguous regimes (8.9%), competitive authoritarian (10.9%), hegemonic electoral authoritarian (13%), politically closed authoritarian (13%) (Diamond 2002, 26). A subsequent attempt at a similar classification came up with a deeply pessimistic conclusion with regard to the tendency of transitional regimes to move firmly away from the lure of authoritarianism, smuggled into the structure of pure democratic institutions by the way of hybridisation.[6] These unfruitful attempts to bring errant hybrid regimes into the net of neat classification hold out the portents of hope for trans-disciplinary analysis and a wider model encompassing insights gained from the new research on cultural flow[7] that can take in "pure" as well as hybrid cases.

In terms of its origin in the biological sciences, hybridity is an attempt to overcome binary opposites through the creation of a third species that combines some characteristics of the two. Critical theorists find a positive appreciation of syncretism in this phenomenon (Fludernik 1998a, 10). Hybridisation is a

---

[5] Aristotle felt that "too great a departure from common experience probably has a fallacy in it somewhere, even though it appears to be irreproachably logical" (Sabine [1973] 1975, 99).

[6] "[However] empirical evidence increasingly suggests that to a significant extent the third wave of democratization could become less of a triumph of political liberalism and liberal democracy than a success story for "hybrid" or "ambiguous" regimes, "delegative", "defective", "semi-" or "illiberal" democracies, "competitive authoritarianism". These political systems include the "Potemkin democracies" where a democratic façade conceals an authoritarian leadership and those that are "ethnocratic", "plebiscite-populist", often even with sultanistic components, and which therefore may be identified as "false democracies"" (Croissant and Merkel 2004, 2).

[7] See below for the concepts of trans-lingual and trans-cultural research. Students of comparative politics engaged in classificatory analysis have much to learn from similar attempts in history, particularly the research on "histoire croisee" (cf. Werner and Zimmermann 2006).

motivating factor – an attempt to devise a "third space" (e.g., between coloniser and the colonised or dominance of race and nationalism) which combines elements of the original duality, but folds them together in a functional, coherent way. Bhabha, to whom we own this seminal concept, transforms hybridity by adding the concept of the imaginary from Fanon, Lacan and Bakhtin.[8] Fludernik comments, "The term hybridity, from its moorings in sexual cross-fertilisation, racial intermixture and intermarriage, has now drifted free to connote (rather than denote) a variety of interstitial and antagonistic set-ups which are clearly linked to a "subaltern' (Gramsci, Spivak) perspective and a positive re-evaluation of hybridity" (Fludernik 1998b, 21–22).

The research on hybridity runs parallel to the concept of *re-use*, emanating from art history, which has gradually found its way into the larger field of social and political investigation (Hegewald and Mitra, forthcoming). Referring to the presence of the past in the interstices of the present, Morris-Jones, a leading early chronicler of politics in India says, "The political systems of modern states are usually developments from earlier, sometimes much earlier, times. The systems undergo change in response to changes in other aspects of human behaviour and thought; they also have the capacity to exert independent influence on these other aspects. If, in haste, we speak of a political system 'reflecting' social conditions, we would recognize that the process of reflection is one which changes both the instrument and the subject" (Morris-Jones 1964, 13). Further, "India's political leaders inherited under this heading of government still more than the accumulated sum of psychological capital; they received the more tangible equipment and machinery of government. These may be considered first as organization, structure and procedures, and, secondly, as personnel" (ibid., 17).

The availability of some new concepts has considerably enriched the toolkit of comparative politics in its attempt to bring post-colonial regimes under the domain of political analysis. The first of these concepts, *transculturality* (*Cultural flow*) asserts that even the seemingly most local phenomena are part of trans-cultural flows of concepts and things. Cultures are not "social groups or geographies, but social imaginaries that express or create distinctions and asymmetrical flows."[9] *Translinguality,* the second of these core concepts indicates that cultural flow "transgresses" boundaries and that rather than passive consumers of alien concepts, local societies imbue them with meaning in the process of using them. Words shed

---

[8] "Bhabha himself has complicated the notion of hybridity even further by resorting to the Lacanian category of the imaginary, a move which hearkens back to Franz Fanon's work. For Bhabha the colonizer and the colonial subject both undergo a splitting of their identity positions, a splitting that occurs through their mutual imaginary identification (pictured in terms of mimicry)." Bhabha's model also relies on Derrida and Bakhtin, bringing together a variety of poststructuralist concepts which are then applied and juxtaposed in a variety of contexts and settings. I refrain at this point from a more detailed explication of Bhabha's *The Location of Culture* (2007) since his model is discussed in great detail in the essays of Fludernik and Ray. (Fludernik 1998a, 14).

[9] cf. Home Page Cluster of Excellence *Asia and Europe in a Global Context-Shifting Asymmetries in Cultural Flows*, http://www.asia-europe.uni-heidelberg.de (2010).

or acquire meaning even as they travel. Hybridisation is the natural consequence of the real world process of institution making, and the adaptation of alien institutions into the native medium.

The very fact that societies and cultures were imagined as fixed entities restricted research to choose between either assuming a global homogenisation or a "clash of civilisations" as the most likely outcome of globalisation. Mike Featherstone (2005) and Bernd Wagner (2001) have, however, pointed out that the image of "authentic" cultures was from the beginning an illusion and therefore flawed. The main reason why cultural hybridity and "glocalisation" should indeed be regarded as relevant to premodern as well as modern contexts has to do with the agency of social actors. In combination with the structure of the social space of a society, this agency must have at all times ensured that impulses arriving from the outside world were transformed by merging them with existing values and world views.

The hybrid institutions and practices are empirical evidence of what Bhabha calls the "third space". Hybrid institutions are necessarily a part of a larger political project, one where elites and counter-elites seek to amend the rules to produce new designs and imbue them with a new spirit, geared to a political goal. The flow diagram in Fig. 8.1 depicts how elites might seek to do this in the context of a changing or challenged society through the combination of three tactics, namely, the political management of identity, strategic reform of laws, and the constitutional incorporation of core social values. (Fig. 8.1, below)

In their solicitude to gain legitimacy and enhance governance, elites look broadly across the social spectrum, and deeply into local, regional and national history, to identify useful resources for governance and legitimacy, and bring them into the mainstream. Not bound by doctrine or ideology, India's colonial rulers, the nationalist leaders, and subsequently, the leaders of the post-colonial state could afford to be "trans-lingual, trans-cultural and trans-disciplinary" in the sense that

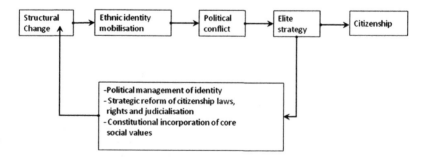

Fig. 8.1 Culture, context and strategy in turning subjects into citizens: a dynamic neo-institutional model

there was no political or scientific taboo against the search for things that would work.[10] These huge experiments in colonial dominance, anti-colonial resistance, nation-building, democratic transition, economic growth and justice, governance and legitimacy produced a whole new range of hybrid political institutions and practices. The empirical analysis below will focus on colonial hybridisation as an act of imperial domination of the Indian population; Gandhian counter-hybridisation as an act of resistance; and post-colonial hybridisation as a project of nation-building and legitimacy in the context of a deeply divided and diverse society that takes democracy seriously.

8.4 Legitimising Power Through Accommodation and Hybridisation

The British, masters at indirect rule, innovated a number of hybrid institutions to rule India in an orderly manner, with a great economy of overt force. While this sustained the British Raj over two centuries – never in history have so few ruled so many with such little use of overt force – this came at the cost of arrested growth, and the severing of India's colonial present from the pre-modern past.

We learn from scholarly accounts of everyday life in classical India that the society, polity and the economy evolved in continuous symbiosis in the course of the millennia of its early, settled existence (see Auboyer 1965 and Edwardes 1965). While self-contained, India was not insulated from outside inspiration because there were various forms of conceptual flow that continuously enriched Indian life. There were pilgrims and visitors from abroad, some international trade and military invasions that acted as a catalyst for change. However, society had mastered the art of accommodation of difference, and of re-using the past to construct new, hybrid structures that could cope with changing times.[11] With the loss of political autonomy and the destruction of the knowledge-generating universities and scholarly communities around temples through the Islamic invasions that began in the eighth century, India started to lose this capacity for endogenous self-renewal. There were local instances of fusion and innovation in art and architecture between Islam and Hinduism, Jainism and Buddhism, a process which reached a national scale under the rule of the Great Mughals.[12] But society as a whole had lost the vibrant capacity for efficient, endogenous evolution. The *coup de grace* to this

---

[10] The Chinese came to the same conclusion – "it does not matter what colour the cat is, as long as it catches mice!", as Deng Xiaoping put it three decades after the Great Proletarian Revolution.

[11] This spirit of renewal, essential to the conservative dynamism of pre-modern India, is summed up in an oft-repeated sloka from the Gita: *Whenever, scion of Bharatas! righteousness declines and unrighteousness prevails, I manifest Myself. (Bhagavadgītā 4.7).*

[12] For examples of re-use during the period of the decline of India's political autonomy, see Hegewald 2006 and Hegewald 2007.

moribund structure was dealt by the colonial intrusion from Europe, starting in the eighteenth century. By 1858, with the defeat of the Sepoy Mutiny, the victorious British proclaimed the ultimate intellectual, moral and political subjugation of the Indians at the Delhi Durbar.

While India has been no stranger to invasions through the Northwest passes in the high Himalayas, British rule was special in terms of its representation of the Indian past. Up to the arrival of the British, in India the past and the present had lived in a complex and dynamic symbiosis. But under the British, the past really became the *past*.[13] The point is made by Metcalf (1998) in a seminal article on aesthetics and power under colonial rule.

While the British continued the tradition of "appropriating the politically charged forms of their predecessors as a way of legitimising their own regime" (Metcalf 1998, 14), their method of depicting the past differed radically from their predecessors. Previous rulers of India had added their visions and symbols to existing designs so that the past and present could appear as part of a continuous flow. However, in British public buildings and political institutions, the past was depicted definitely as the "past" whose only function was to serve as a foil on which the British present could shine brighter, while staying aloof and distant. In a memorable passage, Metcalf recounts how the British *durbar* was traditional in form but thoroughly modern in content.

In his 1903 *durbar*... Curzon sought to utilise the "familiar" and even sacred form of "the East". As he proudly proclaimed, the entire arena was "built and decorated exclusively in the Mogul, or Indo-Saracenic style". Yet Curzon refused to sanction an exchange of presents, or *nazrs* which had formed the central binding element of pre-colonial durbars. Instead, he had each prince in their turn mount the dais and offer a message of congratulation to the King-Emperor. Curzon then simply shook hands with the chief as he passed by. Incorporation and inclusion, so powerfully symbolised by *khillat* and *nazr*, had given way, despite the Mughal scenery and pretence, to a wholly colonial ritual.[14]

In aesthetics as in politics, the colonial strategy consisted in the incorporation of the past – Indian tradition in this case – within the present in a subsidiary capacity. Nandy adds in the same vein "Modern colonialism won its great victories not so much through its military and technological prowess as through its ability to create

---

[13] Metcalf 1998 makes this point in his interpretation of the decorative role of past artefacts in the modern architecture of Lutyens.

[14] Metcalf 1998, 17 sums up the reciprocal relationship between Orientalism and Empire in the following passage. "Perhaps Curzon's lamp [which he had designed in Egypt and arranged to be placed on the grave of Mumtaz in the Taj Mahal] might be taken to represent the colonial aesthetic. It is an aesthetic of difference, of distance, of substantiation, of control – an aesthetic in which the Taj Mahal, the mosque of Cairo, even the *Arabian Nights*, all merge and become indistinguishable, and hence are available for use however the colonial ruler chooses. It is an aesthetic in which the past, though ordered with scrupulous attention to detail, stays firmly in the past. It is an aesthetic Shah Jahan [the Mughal emperor who built the Taj Mahal as a memorium to Mumtaz Mahal, his deceased Queen] could never have comprehended" (Metcalf 1998, 24).

secular hierarchies incompatible with the traditional order" (Nandy 1983, 9). The British told Indians that their past was truly a past: the way forward consisted in learning new, modern ways from European science, technology, institutions and morals. The *hybridisation of the Mughal Durbar* in this case was part of the colonial strategy to seal off the vital links of the colonial present from the pre-colonial past. A cluster of European publicists combined forces to teach the "childlike" Indians new, better, modern ways, and to punish them when they were "childish", refusing to learn. (Nandy 1983).

The hybridisation of the Mughal Durbar was part of the successful strategy of ruling the Empire through native intermediaries with very little use of overt force. The successful experiment spawned its variations in many other areas of administration, architectural design and city planning, and in public life. The examples of the re-use of colonial institutions in post-independence politics are plentiful. Although not always so clearly visible to those who are unfamiliar with India's colonial interlude, specialists recognise the British derivation of the rules, procedures and rituals of the Indian Parliament.[15] The *Devaswam Boards* in South India and their equivalents in other parts of the vast country – departments of religious property, also set up during the British rule – are in charge of administrating both old temples as well as the new. Government ministers of democratic India hold court – much like their colonial and pre-colonial predecessors held *durbar* – and transact state business with a motley crowd of visitors, with the same display of power, privilege and pomp. Independent India has clearly moved on, and shown, once again, the country's capacity to achieve change without revolution.

8.5 Genealogy of the Post-colonial State: The Conflation of Modernity and Tradition in Gandhi's *Satyagraha*

This trend of uninterrupted and unhindered conceptual flow from Europe to India was challenged once Gandhi got to centre stage in India's politics, fresh from the successful application of *satyagraha* as a novel, hybrid form of peaceful political resistance. Under his moral and political leadership, Indian freedom fighters learnt to gain new insights on their home ground. The process of introspection and selective re-use intervened during the process of the writing of the Indian constitution. The defining moment came with the celebrated Nehru speech "Freedom at

---

[15] The signs of the lingering British presence – Sunday as the official holiday of the week, left-hand-drive for Indian traffic, and the ubiquitous Ambassador car, a hybrid British Austin Rover adapted to Indian roads which has become the sturdy emblem of Indian officialdom, are everywhere. The *dak* bungalows, outposts of the British Raj out in the country, temporary homes for the British civilian officers on tour, are tended with the same attention to details by the PWD – the Public Works Department, also of British vintage – as are the post-independence guest houses of the national and State governments.

Midnight" in which he announced to a sceptical world the birth of a nation when he said, "when the soul of a nation, long suppressed, finds utterance". Today, the Indian state – cutting edge of the process of self-assertion of Indian society – is both structure and agency of the indigenous evolution and resilience of the political and social systems.

The Congress party, at the height of colonial rule, had become the vehicle of the synthesis of the two main strands of Indian nationalism – the liberal constitutionalists like the 'moderate' Gopal Krishna Gokhale – and the radical "extremists" led by Bal Gangadhar Tilak. Following its foundation in 1885 by a retired British civil servant – Sir Alan Octavian Hume – the Indian National Congress gradually acquired a complex, hybrid character – of collaborator and competitor, movement and party, purveyor of modern rules, committee meetings, minute taking and sporting the *khadi, charka and satyagraha* as its main political instruments – combining participation and protest action as a two-track strategy of power (Rudolph and Rudolph 1987). After Independence, when its rival Muslim League left India for Pakistan, the Congress, complete with its party organisation, Nehru as Prime-Minister-in-waiting, its core ideas about planning, foreign policy and nation-building already shaped, was more than ready for the succession to power.

Mahatma Gandhi, the most outstanding leader in India's struggle for independence and a continued source of moral inspiration, was trained as a barrister in England. He developed the method of *satyagraha* – a quintessentially hybrid concept that re-used a Jaina ritual, turning it into a tool of non-violent resistance – while he was in South Africa working for an Indian law firm. The South African experience also taught Gandhi the importance of cross-community coalitions, a theme that he subsequently transformed into "Hindu-Muslim unity". This became a salient feature of Gandhi's politics upon his return to India in 1915, and a hallmark of the politics of the Congress Party which found it useful as a political instrument to fend off its challengers – the Hindu Right, the Muslim League and their British patrons. Under his leadership, the Indian National Congress became increasingly sensitive to the gap between the predominantly urban middle-class Congress Party and the Indian masses, and shifted its attention to the Indian peasantry. Under Gandhi's leadership, the Indian National Congress steadily broadened its reach both in terms of social class and geography. To mobilise mass support, Gandhi also introduced a number of indigenous political practices like fasting and general strikes or *hartal* (a form of boycott accompanied by a work stoppage). He combined the techniques of political negotiation with more coercive direct action (such as *hartal, satyagraha* etc.) and derived both the political resources and the methods from within Indian culture and history.

The distinct character of Indian politics derives in no small measure from the trickling down of the norms of British constitutionalism and hybrid colonial institutions, and the 'trickling up' of Indian custom, and hybrid forms of cooperation and contest. The most important of the legacies consists of the modern political institutions and the process of parties, interest groups as well as the quintessential Indian political strategy that combines institutional participation and political protest. The main legacy of pre-independence politics to post-independence practice is the effort on all sides to bring political competition into the ambit of the rule of law, moderate politics and political institutions. When rules appear too restrictive or not sufficiently legitimate and the game threatens to get out of hand, the state intervenes with its own mixed strategy of suppression and accommodation, in a manner akin to that of its British predecessor. With some exceptions such as the continuing conflict in Kashmir, and the North East, this strategy has worked out successfully, adding layers of new elites and political arenas into the political system. The modest origin of decentralisation has matured into a full-fledged federal system, comparable to the now defunct Soviet federal system in its institutional complexity but endowed with far more vitality, as one can see from its resilience.

8.6 The Hybrid Post-colonial State as Both Structure *and* Agency

With the coming of independence, the state emerged both as the structure within which nation-building and development were to take place, and as the main agency for these projects. Just like their British predecessors, the leaders of independent India put the institutions of the state to task to achieve these political objectives. But democracy made the difference; the national agenda got taken over by the subaltern social groups who increasingly moved on to the offices of power and prestige. The new kids on the block came up from lower levels of the traditional society, empowered by the instruments of modern politics. They systematically transformed their traditional networks into *caste associations*[16] and found their path to power in new arenas such as *village panchayats* – village councils that combined the traditional rural leadership and modern democratic politics. In the process, the state in its larger sense – constitution, institutions, rules, leaders and the public sphere that bound them together – became both the structure of hybridization and its agent, gathering momentum as it unfolded. Across the border, the failure to do this stymied the deepening of modern politics in Sri Lanka and destroyed the state of Pakistan altogether.

The model of state-society interaction depicted above (Fig. 8.2) shows how the modern state engages society through a series of interventions such as the constitution, strategic reform through legislation, and modern bureaucratic implementation, and how society responds by sending up ideas, support and new social elites. In this dialectic of tradition and modernity, both evolve and take on something of one another. The game, initiated by the independence generation, has continued to be played on the rules laid down by the founders of the Republic. In the following diagram, these new elites – people with ambition and skills emerging from lower

---

[16] For an elaboration on the concept of caste associations see Rudolph and Rudolph 1987.

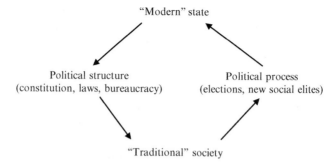

Fig. 8.2 State-society interaction as the dialectic of tradition and modernity

social orders – became the vital link between modern and traditional India, and, as a hinge group in Indian society charged with the task of acting as culture-brokers, innovated new political practices that were implemented through hybrid institutions. This section illustrates the core argument by drawing some examples from the structure of the modern state in India and the process of its interaction with the traditional society. The section below discusses why and how the post-colonial state has come to play a catalytic role in reviving the interrupted links of the present to the past, and through it, to restore the vital process of self-reflexive and authentic evolution through its hybridisation.

8.6.1 Ontology of the State: Individualist and Communitarian

Although the constitution of India was greatly influenced by its British origin (two thirds of the written constitution came from the Government of India Act, 1935, passed by the British Parliament), it nevertheless established its departure from colonial practice by conflating the individual and the community, modernity and tradition, the exogenous cultural flow and the indigenous tradition in a novel manner. Article 1 of the constitution announced: (1) *India*, that is *Bharat*, shall be a Union of States, thus affirming the dual origin of the Indian political system from the cultural flow from Europe through the conduit of colonial rule, and the resurrection of the ruptured links with Bharat – the mythical kingdom of pre-modern India. The hybrid constitution, part liberal, part communitarian, provides a third space between the rational, utility maximizing individual and the collectivity, keen on solidarity and policing the common bonds.

The Indian state moved beyond the canon of its liberal namesake and ascribed to itself a variable space between the ideals of the neutral enforcer of norms – the essential feature of Weberian, bureaucratic modernity – and the partisan defender of the traditional, marginal and the patrimonial. "Like Hindu conceptions of the divine, the state in India is polymorphous, a creature of manifold forms and orientations. One is the third actor whose scale and power contribute to the marginality of class politics. Another is a liberal or citizens' state, a juridical body whose legislative reach is limited by a written constitution, judicial review, and fundamental rights. Still another is a capitalist state that guards the boundaries of the mixed economy by protecting the rights and promoting the interests of property in agriculture, commerce, and industry. Finally, a socialist state is concerned to use public power to eradicate poverty and privilege and tame private power. Which combination prevails in a particular historical setting is a matter of inquiry". (Rudolph and Rudolph 1987, 400f.)

8.6.2 The Congress "System": Bridging Colonial Rule and Competitive Politics

The transition from colonial rule to competitive party politics within a democratic framework was facilitated by a conglomerate of interests, personalities and beliefs that drew as much on the indigenous idiom as on liberal democratic politics. With Jawaharlal Nehru at the helm of affairs, the Indian National Congress, located at the fulcrum of national politics, constituted the core of a one-dominant-party system. For about two decades, the INC ruled from Delhi and practically in all the Indian federal states. Elections were free and held regularly but the Congress, which never won a majority of votes thanks to the first past the post voting system, regularly won a majority of seats, and came to be known as the party of governance. The opposition parties, scattered around it, practically never held office but exercised power and influence in implicit coalition with factions within the Congress Party. This made it possible for India to reinforce a political culture of bargaining, reform and orderly social change without party alternation. This unique constellation of forces came to be known as the Congress System, which in retrospect was the vital link between despotic and democratic rule.

In the diagrammatic representation of the Congress System (Fig. 8.3), the axes represent major issues facing the country, at the centre of which stood the Congress Party. On each issue, left and right wing opinions were arrayed on either side of the Congress represented by the dark inner circle. The next circle stands for the opposition parties. The Congress System held the Indian National Congress in legislative power – but it was a power that could not swing the country in a clear political direction.

8.6.3 The Economy: Modern, Traditional, Liberal, Socialist and Gandhian, All at the Same Time

The "Mixed" economy, combining features of Soviet style planning and the free market, became the main frame of India's economic life. The "Indian" model of

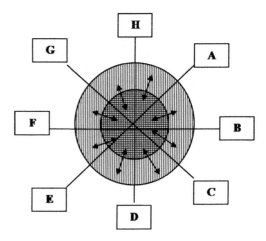

Fig. 8.3 The "Congress System" of India.

democratic development emerged from a series of strategic choices made during the early years after independence. These choices, in turn, were based on a set of compromises that attempted to blend the experience of wartime planning and controls, domestic pressures for a policy of economic nationalism, and the liberal, Gandhian and socialist ideological crosscurrents that existed within the nationalist movement. The model that grew out of these strategic choices evolved incrementally into a set of policies that became the basis of India's development consensus. It called for a system of centralised planning and a mixed economy in which a government-owned public sector would dominate basic industry and the state would control, regulate, and protect the private sector from foreign competition. Foreign capital would be permitted, but only under highly controlled and restricted circumstances. The objectives of India's development were to achieve rapid economic growth, self-reliance, full employment and social justice.

These key concepts were understood in much the same sense as during the period of rapid change in European social history which witnessed the rapid transformation of traditional agricultural society into the modern industrial society. The former was characterised by the predominance of ascription, multiplex social relations where one individual would play a variety of roles, and a deferential stratification system ensconced within primordial kin networks. A modern society, on the other hand, was seen as one based on the predominance of universalistic, specific and achievement norms, on a high degree of social mobility, specialisation and occupational differentiation, an egalitarian class system based on generalised patterns of occupational achievement, and the prevalence of association of specific groups not based on ascription.

The mixed economy gave an institutional shape to the liberal, socialist and communitarian values that constituted the three main strands of the Freedom Movement and dominated the proceedings of the Constituent Assembly. The liberal values were given a clear and incontrovertible shape in the fundamental right to the freedom of trade, occupation and ownership, Article 19 of the Constitution. The socialist values were less explicit, but nevertheless clearly discernible. Instead of the concept of due process – open to judicial interpretation – the Constitution settled for the concept of "procedure established by law" which made "national" interest more compelling than the interest of the individual, a doctrine that paved the way for land reforms, and laws aimed at curbing the full play of capitalist enterprise. Articles 39, 41, 43, 46 of the Directive Principles of state policy recommended that the state pursue policies aimed at bringing about the right to an adequate means of livelihood, the distribution of the ownership and control of material resources of the community in a manner that best serves the common good, and the avoidance of the concentration of wealth, a living wage, decent standards of living and full enjoyment of leisure and social and cultural opportunities for the entire population. Finally, even though there was no staunch "Gandhian lobby" in the Constituent Assembly, communitarian values such as welfare of Harijans, backward classes, women and children, village and cottage industries, educational and economic interests of weaker sections, cattle welfare, banning slaughter of *milch cattle* found their way into the body of this elaborate text.

8.6.4 Self Rule and Shared Rule: Combining Cultural Diversity and the Federal Structure

Apart from academic disputation about the nature and even the "authenticity" of India's federal system as defined in the constitution (Mitra 2000), lies the reality of an enormous country whose cultural heterogeneity is expressed in the federal organization of power. Since state reorganization in 1953 and 1956, state boundaries have roughly coincided with historically rooted linguistic and cultural regions. The differences reinforce the effects of size and continue in the federal system the tensions between regional kingdoms and subcontinental empire that have characterized the history of the state in India. Federalisation – the subject of numerous studies, conferences, and commissions – beginning in the early seventies with the Rajamannar Committee (1971) in Tamil Nadu (Government of Tamil Nadu 1971) and continuing to this day – reflects the crucial role it plays in national politics. The fact of the matter is that Indian federalism is very much a hybrid Indian creation, combining imported concepts of power-sharing with indigenous methods of consensus and accommodation. During the dominance of the Congress party the "Union" government (a sign of hybridity – for the constitution recognized the federal government simply as the Union) and most state governments were ruled by the same party and conflict resolution could take place informally within party channels, causing some specialists to question the purity of the Indian brand as authentically federal. However, federalism Indian style has gained endurance and legitimacy; and it has gained a new lease of life by developing an intricate set of informal channels and formal mechanisms to continue effective conflict resolution. The territorial state has seen many changes, particularly at the level of the regions. New regions have been created to give more salience to regional identity, language and economic needs. But, unlike in neighbouring Pakistan, which mainly as a result of regional imbalance split into two in 1971, the territorial integrity of India continues to be stable.

8.6.5 Indian Personal Law: Conflating the Secular State and Sacred Beliefs

India's Personal Law, governing family, marriage, divorce, adoption and succession is a unique blend of the double commitment of the state to the rights of the individual and commitment to group identities. Ironically, the collective rights and group identities were rooted in the history of representation under British rule. The British, who at home conceived of the political community in terms of equal citizens, saw it in India in terms of distinctive groups, which was taken to be a unique feature of Indian society. The same held also for the leaders of India's freedom movement who sought to achieve a political community composed of equal citizens, but early on realized that they could not build a nationalist movement without recognizing cultural and territorial communities. Political safeguards to minorities were a key element of British efforts to represent groups in Indian society. They were first elaborated in the Morley-Minto constitutional reforms of 1906, then in the Montagu-Chelmsford scheme of 1919, and finally in the constitutional framework that received the royal assent in 1935.[17]

The constitutional design and the structure of institutions that were intended to give concrete shape to the idealistic goals of the Republic, enshrined in the preamble, adopted methodological individualism as the cutting edge of social change. However, such principles as individual rights, representation based not on group identities but individual interests and structured along the lines of political majorities, seen in the context of a society based on hierarchy and tightly-knit social groups, could only lead to conflicts based on values and interests of everyday politics. Free and fair elections, universal adult franchise and the extension of the electoral principle into all realms of social power were intended to articulate, aggregate and eventually incorporate endogenous political norms and alien political institutions within the structure of the political system of the post-colonial state.

The fuzzy, hybrid practice of combining individual rights and group identity came to a sore test in the Shah Bano case, in which the Supreme Court upheld the appeal of a divorced Muslim woman for her individual right to alimony against the practice prevailing in the Muslim community of India of leaving such matters to the community. However, in the face of strong opposition to the extension of a "pure" construction of individual rights to the Muslim community, Prime Minister Rajiv Gandhi introduced the Muslim Women (Protection of Rights on Divorce) Bill

---

[17] See Coupland 1944, 147, 128, 134, 151, for the evolution of statutory communalism.

in 1986, and restored the hybrid solution to the complicated relationship of Islam and the secular state.

8.6.6 The Modern State and Cultural Diversity: India's "Three Language Formula"

Many post-colonial states, following independence, set up a single national identity – one state, one legal system, one national language and one state religion – as the basis of their statehood. Pakistan – the land of the pure – became an advocate of this form of purity whereas India stood for a more inclusive identity. In its solicitude to distinguish itself from secular and diverse India, Pakistan opted for Urdu as the national language, refusing to dilute this unity through official recognition of other major languages like Bengali. India, on the other hand, after a brief spell of disorder on the issue of national language, devised a formula in the course of the States Reorganisation Commission to encourage large sections of the people to learn a language other than their mother tongue. The idea of hybridity has found a hospitable corner.

8.6.7 Social Hierarchy and Rational Bureaucracy

The modern men and women to whom the British transferred power in 1947 had their task cut out for them. Echoing the spirit of the times, India's first Prime Minister Jawaharlal Nehru outlined his vision of the future of the Indian state, society and economy in a famous oration that has since become a landmark on modern India. Nehru, a quintessential renaissance man, had presented this modernist agenda on the background of the carnage that followed the Partition of British India into Pakistan, carved out as a homeland for India's Muslims, and the Indian republic that chose to remain a secular state. As India's first Prime Minister, Nehru, a social democrat by temperament, intensely aware of the urgency of a concerted effort to remove mass poverty and ignorance, sought legitimacy through the promotion of general welfare. Democracy, a sense of community and modernisation were values that were to lead the way into the promised future. The fact that these principles were of alien provenance did not matter at that moment of euphoria.

The modern message of Nehru and his generation of leaders was carefully wrapped in traditional Indian symbols, and conveyed through the hybrid institutions that formed part and parcel of the Indian political system. Nehru's generation of leaders who took over the mantle of hybrid modernity from their predecessors have been able to institutionalise the genre of the *Neta* – typically Indian leaders (Fig. 8.4). At the crucial nodes of this complex system, one increasingly found the quintessential Indian *neta* – Hindi for leader – who became a two-way culture

Fig. 8.4 Laloo P. Yadav

broker, constantly conflating the modern and traditional idioms of Indian politics. As much in their rhetoric as in their person, these *netas* represented a quintessential Indian genre. The picture of charismatic Laloo Prasad Yadav below shows how these political entrepreneurs combined traditional symbols and modern institutions and technology to produce a superb conduit for the flow of power, communication and legitimacy.

8.6.8 Public Buildings and Images of the Hybrid State

The architecture of public buildings in India, together with its city planning provide the final evidence of hybrid modernity. In the two images below one can see how the British colonial rulers laid down the plans of capital buildings with broad avenues (optimal for military marches as much as for showcasing the street plans of modernity) but nevertheless, adorned with symbols of traditional India (in this case, the Mughal water garden, the Buddhist *stupa*, the Islamic minarets and the Hindu *chhatris*) that would make the native feel comfortable in the modern set up. The "traditional" designs and architectural forms that the British drew on were themselves hybrid in nature, based on a re-use of local and regional forms as well as conceptual and cultural flow from outside the country.[18]

The British strategy of domination – which took into account the enormous gain in legitimacy accrued through the re-use of the institutions and sacred symbols of those defeated by it – consisted of selected incorporation of some elements of the Indian past and conspicuous rejection of the rest. Imperial design and utilitarian ideology converged in the *Anglo-Indian style* – in architectural as much as institutional design. The sole opportunity for colonised Indians to advance, as they saw it, consisted in the acceptance of modern (i.e. European) science, technology and values. The coming of Gandhi, and subsequently, India's independence, challenged it, opening in the process the flood-gates to India's pre-modern past for those fighting for freedom from colonial rule.

Colonial aesthetic and colonial politics were all of a piece. The architecture of colonial rule worked to one common purpose – of selective incorporation, de-linking traditional elites from their ancestral moorings, and justifying their power in terms of the common goal of Progress, of which colonial rule was but an instrument. The Archaeological Survey of India preserved India's monuments – both sacred and administrative – in a state of "arrested decay" (Metcalf 1998, 18) isolated and distanced from the community of which they used to be an integral part. So did the new political and administrative institutions established by the British, which presented the Indian past as inferior to the British present, and by the same analogy, the modernity symbolised by colonial rule as the superior future.

The two images below (Figs. 8.5 and 8.6)[19] show how the designers of India's capital and public buildings drew on the designs and symbols of modernity, as well as traditional symbols of India – the Hindu *chhatri*, the Islamic *minars*, Buddhist *stupas* and the Islamic water garden (Hegewald forthcoming). The intention here was to make the subject feel comfortable in his new abode, and generate legitimacy for British rule in the process. The Transfer of Power passed on this hybrid structure to the successor regime of Nehru, who found in it a useful tool of order and legitimacy, and re-used it to the extent of making minimal changes in the inner architecture of space.

---

[18] Tillotson (2008) comments: "The visual culture of the Mughals, so distinctive and instantly recognizable, was not conjured out of nothing. Its success was the product of the skilful blending together of the many different traditions that were available to the artists to draw on, including the Mughal's own central Asian heritage and the expertise and many long-established styles of India itself. The empire's greatest legacy is perhaps this composite culture; and that culture's most outstanding masterpiece is the building [Taj Mahal]" (p. 44). The architectural designs "drew inspiration from three related traditions: the architecture of the Mughals' central Asian homeland; the buildings erected by earlier Muslim rulers of India, especially in the Delhi region; and the much older architectural expertise of India itself" (p. 46).

[19] The permission of Professor Julia Hegewald to use these two images is gratefully acknowledged.

Fig. 8.5 Lutyen's Delhi (Courtesy: Julia Hegewald)

Fig. 8.6 Rashtrapati Bhavan (Courtesy: Julia Hegewald)

8.7 Conclusion: Hybrid Modernity as a Solution to Post-colonial Legitimacy Deficit

Looking back at the Indian past through hybrid eyes yields surprises. One comes to realise that modern institutions of India, nationalist sentiments notwithstanding, are a true British legacy. In the second place, a critical analysis of British rule and Indian resistance to it helps explain why democratic institutions have worked more effectively in India as compared to her neighbours.[20] That the synthesis of British

---

[20] Purists like Jinnah and Bandaranaike, following their pure visions of Islam and Buddhism respectively, have run their states – Pakistan, the land of the pure, and Sri Lanka, the sacred land of Sirindip – to political dead ends.

constitutional norms and political forms with India's indigenous political tradition led to a different outcome than the other successor states ensues from India's tradition of re-use, where the past often continues within the present by deliberate design. In the hands of British architects and designers of political institutions, the British tradition of re-use met its Indian equivalent, leading to the creation of new capital cities and an array of legislation. Avid re-users, post-independent India's leaders have appropriated many of the symbols and institutions of their predecessors, and cloaked them in Indian garb. This blending of indigenous tradition and imported institutions explains both the ability of the British to rule for so long with little recourse to overt force, as well as the smooth transition from colonial rule to multi-party democracy.

Effective accommodation of the past within the structure of the present is not necessarily a problem of mechanical accumulation. It also entails the need for leaders to strategically pick and choose; the process is marked by violence and leaves behind a trail of bitterness and anxiety. This helps to explain the juxtaposition of successful state formation and persistence of inter-community conflict and regional secession movements in India.[21]

Seen in this light, the claim of high modernity in its Orientalist avatar to the "pure" and its use of the resultant power to authenticate its claim to the high moral ground, while fending off any claims to familiarity by the subaltern (in the sense of the *hybrid, polluted, metisse, miscegenic, mimic...*), comes across as theory playing the handmaiden to politics. It is about time that the students of the modern state re-read Elias, Foucault, Nandy and Metcalf (1989) to decide for themselves how much there is to un-learn so that they might learn properly how the modern state in India has acquired its European resilience without the benefit of European history.

This is of course not to deny the historical importance that pure categories have had both for science and religion. Purity, in fact, is the transcendental goal that underpins all religions, customs and rituals.[22] It is also the norm of science. Clear concepts, precise measurements, and causal models constitute the essential toolkit of the modern scientist. The systematic study of politics is no exception to this canon. Just as apprentice physicists must learn to define and measure atoms and even smaller particles, chemists the periodic table and biologists genes and chromosomes, so must the beginners in comparative politics learn to distinguish between democracy and dictatorship, and power and legitimacy, as "pure"

---

[21] "Two salient areas of Indian politics that call for critical attention and possible re-evaluation are the relations of the state and the market, and the attitudes of the state towards religion. The former has attracted some attention already. The Indian economy has belatedly come to terms with the necessity of taking painful decisions about restructuring and accepted the need for internal and international competition. But considerable confusion and outmoded assumptions still dominate the attitudes of the state towards religion" (Mitra 1990a, 92). "For its survival and growth, the state in India will need to go beyond simple accommodation and to transcend some contentious interests – religious, social, economic and political – when the occasion so demands" (Mitra 1990a, 93).

[22] See Douglas 1966 [reprinted 1996], 1 for a lucid and "universal analysis of the rules of purity which applies equally to secular and religious life as to primitive and modern societies".

categories, and to measure them with the quantitative, qualitative or discursive methods. Bodies in charge of policing purity – the Pope and his equivalents, caste *panchayats* (literally, rule of the five), university faculties, examination boards and peer review – are expected to detect, punish and eliminate conceptual confusion, and measurement error.

Closer home to modern politics and political science, purity is seen as essential to order. In the iconography of political purity, Danton, Robespierre and the unfailing guillotine, meting out revolutionary terror to the "un-citizen" and the impure, remain the quintessential symbols of the Jacobin state, and defenders of its single-minded quest for virtue and perfect citizenship.[23]

However, whereas politics and public morality remain committed to upholding the virtues of purity, the world seen through the lens of comparative politics based on pure categories sometimes produces unsatisfactory results. The catch from this kind of trawling in terms of *pure* categories is often difficult to classify; and some big empirical fish escape the net of theory altogether (Diamond 2002). In the era of globalisation and trans-cultural, border-crossing citizenship, the political landscape of post-colonial societies and vast pockets of the Western world bear witness to the existence of hybrid structures – of institutions, practices and artistic design – that are fence-sitters, straddling different worlds, and difficult to classify in terms of the canon on comparative politics. "Caste *associations*", "fixers (culture *brokers*)", "*mixed* economies", "*satyagraha*" (the concept of mass civil disobedience coined by Gandhi in South Africa, and subsequently introduced to India) and "*gram panchayats*" (modern, elected village councils that are based on a classical concept of village self-governance) – each carrying a tenuous link to their original (root) concepts to which new impulses and experiences have been strategically added – are part and parcel of the vigorous political life in these countries.

Left to their own devices, people connected to these hybrid institutions do not necessarily see them as aberrations, or diminished forms of the real thing. Despite their stretched, mixed or altered forms, or, perhaps, because of them, hybrid political structures have a real life, full of vitality, social significance and the capacity for self-regeneration. Rather than being merely transient, many flourish over long stretches of time and space. Not all are treated kindly by different scientific disciplines; their academic standing varies from one discipline to another. The intellectual indulgence that critical theory, post-colonial literature, cultural anthropology and social history have shown to hybrid structures, concepts and institutions is missing in comparative politics. In its Jacobin mode, comparative

---

[23] [On the wake of the Revolution] "Suddenly, subjects were told they had become Citizens; an aggregate of subjects held in place by injustice and intimidation had become a Nation. From this new thing, this Nation of Citizens, justice, freedom and plenty could be not only expected but required. By the same token, should it not materialise, only those who had spurned their citizenship, or who were by their birth or unrepentant beliefs incapable of exercising it, could be held responsible. Before the promise of 1789 could be realised, it was necessary to root out Uncitizens" (Schama 1989, 859).

politics usually approaches the political process of post-colonial states with "pure" categories of European provenance, thus running the risk of parts of the empirical world escaping the classificatory project altogether, or worse, the analyst, having failed to classify or explain, out of sheer desperation, turning into a moralist (Mitra 1988, 318–37; 1999, 39–86)! Little does one realise, however, that concepts – when they travel beyond their place of origin – still carry their birth marks of cultural and contextual assumptions built into them. The mechanical application of "pure" concepts of European origin to alien soil can lead to "conceptual stretching"[24] or violent retribution by the way of radical rejection of all that goes under the banner of such concepts, leading to violent post-revolutionary frenzy.[25]

The research on hybridity questions the dominance of one society over another in the name of modernity. "Whereas for Hegel, Marx and Weber there appeared to be but one race and the West had strung the tape at the finish line for others to break, for us it has become apparent that there are multiple races and many finish lines, and the tapes are manufactured also in Tokyo and Beijing" (Rudolph 1987, 732). The symbolic presence of the past constitutes a link of modernity with collective memory. Susanne Rudolph generalises from these observations to the need to look at the universal claims of a particular variant of modernity afresh.[26]

Where, then, does comparative politics go from here? A number of theoretical developments in the social sciences and humanities since the halcyon days of structural functionalism – conceptual stretching, bounded rationality, two-level games, entangled history, re-use, and the flow of culture and concepts – point in the direction of new pastures that one can visit in order to enrich the basis of comparison that is relevant to our times.[27] The biggest challenge is to bring the two worlds – of comparative politics and conceptual flow – together and make it

---

[24] Conceptual stretching takes the shape of hybrid categories such as "people's democracy", "guided democracy", "Islamic democracy" etc. "When scholars extend their models and hypotheses to encompass additional cases, they commonly need to adapt their analytic categories to fit the next contexts. . . . [However] the overly strict application of a classical framework can lead to abandoning a category prematurely or to modifying it inappropriately" (Collier and Mahon 1993, 845–855).

[25] The motley crowd of resisters, united to fight the "intrusive Other", come together under hybrid categories such as "the Church" or Islam in contemporary Afghanistan.

[26] "When empiricists, structuralists or political economists look at what they consider the mere flimflam of the symbolic realm, they want to know where the real stuff is: the village, the irrigation network, the coalition between king and noble, the extractive mechanism. They ask, "how many divisions does the pope have?" I also want to answer those questions. But as we address the state in Asia, we must treat the symbolic as a phenomenon. We must try to create theoretical frameworks that combine a demystified, rationalist worldview with an understanding of the phenomenology of the symbolic in societies where the gods have not yet died. And we must combine it with the understanding that we too construct and act within cosmologies and that we only deny the myths we live by because we cannot see or articulate them" (Rudolph 1987, 742).

[27] Several articles point in the direction of the wider dimensions of this project. These include: Gallie 1955–56; Sartori 1970; Collier and Mahon 1993; Collier and Levitsky 1997, 430–451; Diamond 2002; Lindberg 2007; Stepan 2008.

methodologically possible for them to draw strength from one another. Even as we celebrate the value added character of hybridity for conventional research on the state and modernity, one should, nevertheless be wary of too hasty a rejection of the rigour of logical positivism at the core of comparative politics. Hybridity research stands to gain enormously from retaining the epistemological links with the historical development of comparative politics as a distinctive field. Re-use rather than replacement is the best scientific way forward, because, important as the heuristic value of hybridity is, progress in the field of research on modernity and the state is contingent on rigorous fieldwork that is the most valuable legacy of structural-functionalism. To measure the length, breadth, depth and stability of hybrid substances, we still need categories and tools that are themselves not hybrid. The alternative is to bring in a form of radical relativism that denies any possibility of inter-personal communication or replication.

The crucial issue is not to lose sight of the fact that political concepts and institutions – pure as well as hybrid – are political constructions, and as such, contingent on a cluster of interests, stakeholders, and their contextual setting. Hybridisation is not a teleological process, being pushed forward by some mystical urge emerging from the deeper recesses of culture. Indeed, it is a political phenomenon which is propelled by a sense of strategy and optimisation on the part of the agents of the process. It happens only when the underlying causal parameters are present in an optimal constellation. As long as the values, beliefs, and interests of the stakeholders are served well, and the world at large leaves it alone, an institution and its underlying concept can remain stable over long periods of time. However, today, in the age of trans-national citizenship and global communication, they are as much subject to the inward flow of concepts as to the outward. Most of all, thanks to the new research on hybridity, the ontological status of the "pure" has become contested. Hybrids do not necessarily think of themselves as impure, and it is quite conceivable that the "pure" is actually a special case of the hybrid. Noticing as one does the helpless search for a way to accommodate Islam on European soil, one looks wistfully at the success of the hybrid Indian Personal Law that has kept the divisive issues of the sacred and the secular within the bounds of the rule of law.

Acknowledgment I would like to thank the Excellence Cluster "Asia and Europe in a Global Context: Shifting Asymmetries in Cultural Flows" Heidelberg, supported by the DFG for financial support, and Lion Koenig for valuable assistance with the research on which this paper is based.

References

Auboyer, Jeannine. 1965. *Daily Life in Ancient India from 200 BC to 700AD*. London: Weidenfeld and Nicolson.
Bhabha, Homi K. 2007. *The Location of Culture*. London: Routledge.
Cluster of Excellence *Asia and Europe in a Global Context-Shifting Asymmetries in Cultural Flows*. 2010. Accessed March 3. http://www.asia-europe.uni-heidelberg.de.

Collier, David, and James E. Mahon, Jr. 1993. "Conceptual "stretching" revisited: Adapting categories in comparative analysis." *American Political Science Review* 87 (4): 845–855.

Collier, David, and Steven Levitsky. 1997. "Democracy with Adjectives: Conceptual Innovation in Comparative Research." *World Politics* 49: 430–451.

Coupland, Reginald. 1944. *The Indian Problem: Report on the Constitutional Problem in India*. Oxford: Oxford University Press.

Croissant, Aurel, and Wolfgang Merkel. 2004. "Introduction: Democratization in the Early Twenty-first Century." *Democratization* 11(5): 1–9.

Diamond, Larry. 2002. "Thinking about hybrid regimes." *Journal of Democracy* 13 (2): 22–35.

Douglas, Mary. (1966) 1996. *Purity and Danger: An analysis of the concepts of pollution and taboo*. London: Routledge.

Edwardes, Michael. 1965. *Everyday Life in Early India*. London: BT Batsford.

Featherstone, Simon. 2005. Postcolonial Cultures. Edinburgh: Edinburgh University Press.

Fludernik, Monika. 1998a. *Hybridity and Postcolonialism: Twentieth-Century Indian Literature*. Tuebingen: Stauffenburg-Verlag.

Fludernik, Monika. 1998b. "The Constitution of Hybridity: Postcolonial Interventions." In *Hybridity and Postcolonialism: Twentieth-Century Indian Literature*, edited by Monika Fludernik, 21–22. Tuebingen: Stauffenburg-Verlag.

Gallie, Walter B. 1955–56. "Essentially contested concepts." *Proceedings of the Aristotelian Society, New Series* 56: 167–198.

Government of Tamil Nadu. 1971. *Report of the Centre-State Relations Inquiry Committee*. Madras.

Hegewald, Julia A. B. 2006. "From Siva to Parshvanatha: The Appropriation of a Hindu Temple for Jaina Worship." In *South Asian Archaeology 2001. 2 volumes*, edited by Catherine Jarrige and Vincent Lefèvre, 517–523. Paris: Editions Recherches sur les Civilisations.

Hegewald, Julia A. B. 2007. "Domes, Tombs and Minarets: Islamic Influences on Jaina Architecture." In *The Temple in South Asia. Volume 2 of the proceedings of the 18th conference of the European Association of South Asian Archaeologists, London 2005*, edited by Adam Hardy, 179–190. London: British Association for South Asian Studies and the British Academy.

Hegewald, Julia A. B. Forthcoming. "Building Citizenship: The Agency of Public Buildings and Urban Planning in the Making of the Indian Citizen." In *Citizenship in the Era of Globalisation: Culture, Power and the Flow of Ideas*, edited by Subrata K. Mitra.

Hegewald, Julia and Subrata K. Mitra. Forthcoming. *Re-use: the Art and Politics of Integration and Anxiety*. Delhi: Sage.

Lijphart, Arendt. 2009. "The Puzzle of India's Democracy." In *Politics of Modern South Asia*. Critical Issues in Modern Politics 1, edited by Subrata K. Mitra, 36–60. London: Routledge.

Lindberg, Staffan. 2007. "Institutionalization of Party Systems? Stability and Fluidity among Legislative Parties in Africa's Democracies." *Government and Opposition* 42(2): 215–241.

Metcalf, Thomas R. 1989. *An Imperial Vision: Indian Architecture and Britain's Raj*. Berkeley: University of California Press.

Metcalf, Thomas R. 1998. *Ideologies of the Raj*. Cambridge: Cambridge University Press.

Mitra, Subrata K. 1988. "Paradoxes of Power: Political Science as Morality Play." *Commonwealth and Comparative Politics* 26 (3): 18–37.

Mitra, Subrata K. 1990a. "Between Transaction and Transcendence: The State and the Institutionalisation of Power in India." In *The Postcolonial state in Asia: Dialectics of Politics and Culture*, edited by Subrata K. Mitra. London: Harvester.

Mitra, Subrata K. 1990b. *The Post-Colonial State in Asia: Dialectics of Politics and Culture*. New York: Harvester Wheatsheaf.

Mitra, Subrata K. 1994. "Flawed Paradigms: Some "Western" Models of Indian Politics." In *State and Nation in the Context of Social Change*. Social Change and Political Discourse in India: Structures of Power, Movements of Resistance 1, edited by T. V. Sathyamurthy, 219–45. Delhi: Oxford University Press. (Repr. In *Culture and Rationality: The Politics of Social Change in Post-Colonial India* (1999), edited by Subrata K. Mitra, 39–86. Delhi: Sage.)

Mitra, Subrata K. 1999. "Effects of Institutional Arrangements on Political Stability in South Asia." *Annual Review of Political Science* 2 (1): 405–28.

Mitra, Subrata K. 2000. "The Nation, State and the Federal Process in India." In *Federalism and Political Performance*, edited by Ute Wachendorfer-Schmidt. London: Routledge.

Mitra, Subrata K. 2009. *Politics of Modern South Asia, Critical Issues in Modern Politics*, volumes. I-V. London: Routledge.

Mitra, Subrata K., and V.B. Singh. 2009. *When Rebels Become Stakeholders: Democracy, Agency and Social change in India*. Los Angeles: Sage.

Mitra, Subrata K. Forthcoming. *Citizenship in the Era of Globalisation: Culture, Power and the Flow of Ideas*.

Morris-Jones, Wyndreath H. 1964. *The Government and Politics of India*. London: Hutchinson University Library.

Nandy, Ashis. 1983. *The Intimate Enemy: Loss and Recovery of Self under Colonialism*. Delhi: Oxford University Press.

North, Douglass C. 1990. *Institutions, Institutional Change and Economic Performance* Cambridge: Cambridge University Press.

Rudolph, Lloyd, and Susanne Hoeber Rudolph. 1987. *In Pursuit of Lakshmi: The Political Economy of the Indian State*. Chicago: The University of Chicago Press.

Rudolph, Lloyd, and Susanne Hoeber Rudolph. 1967. *The Modernity of Tradition: Political Development in India*. Chicago: The University of Chicago Press.

Rudolph, Susanne H. 1987. "Presidential Address: State Formation in Asia – Prolegomenon to a Comparative Study." *The Journal of Asian Studies* 46 (4): 732.

Sabine, George. (1973)1975. *A History of Political Theory*. New York: Holt, Rinehart and Winston. Reprint, Delhi: Oxford and IBH.

Sartori, Giovanni. 1970. "Concept Misformation in Comparative Politics", *The American Political Science Review* LXIV (4).

Schama, Simon. 1989. *Citizens: A Chronicle of the French Revolution*. London: Penguin.

Stepan, Alfred. 2008. "Comparative Theory and Political Practice: Do We Need a "State-nation" Model as well as a "Nation-State" Model?" *Government and Opposition* 43(1): 1–25.

Tillotson, Giles. 2008. *Taj Mahal*. London: Profile Books.

Wagner, Bernd, and Elisabeth Beck-Gernsheim. 2001. *Kulturelle Globalisierung; Zwischen Weltkultur und kultureller Fragmentierung*. Essen: Klartext Verlag.

Werner, Michael, and Bénédicte Zimmermann. 2006. "Beyond Comparison: Histoire Croiseé and the Challenge of Reflexivity." *History and Theory* 45 (1): 30–50.

Chapter 9
Hybridization in Language

Christina Sanchez-Stockhammer

Abstract Hybridization is a phenomenon that can be observed in many cultural domains – not least in language. After a consideration of the term's origins, *hybridization* is defined as a process whereby separate and disparate entities or processes generate another entity or process (the hybrid), which shares certain features with each of its sources but which is not purely compositional. The paper then considers possible instances of hybridity – the basis for hybridization – on different levels of language, such as speech sounds, words and texts. It posits that hybridization is possible on all levels of language, from the most basic to the most abstract, but with regard to different aspects, namely formal, semantic, functional, etymological and communicative hybridity. The frequently used metaphor of language as an organism may explain the closeness of linguistic hybridity to the original biological concept – though particular features of the system language, such as the distinction between the levels of *langue* and *parole* (cf. de Saussure 1916/2005, 30–31), give hybridization in language a special character.

9.1 Is Hybridisation Hybrid?

At first, the question above seems to make little or no sense – at least not if it is encoded orthographically the way it is. However, if we follow the conventions which are usually adhered to in linguistics and italicize *hybridization*, the question starts to make sense indeed, since it does not refer to the process of hybridization anymore, but to the word itself. From being a question about the world it has come to be a question about language, a metalinguistic question – whose answer will need to be postponed because it first requires a definition of what is understood by a *hybrid*.

Originally, the term *hybridization* comes from the domain of biology. Since the middle of the nineteenth century, it has designated the production of hybrids, i.e. of animals or plants which are "the offspring of individuals of different kinds (usually, different species)" (SOED, i.e. Shorter Oxford English Dictionary, s.v. *hybrid*). A typical example would be the mule, which is neither a horse like its mother nor a donkey like its father (SOED s.v. *mule*).

According to Ackermann (2004, 141), the term *hybrid* (which was coined in the early seventeenth century; cf. SOED s.v. *hybrid*) was rarely used before the nineteenth century – during which it was loaded with very negative connotations, based on the assumption that this process was detrimental to a supposed original state of purity and authenticity, and mainly with reference to the biological context of mixed breeding (Fludernik 2005, 227). One reason for this negative view may lie in the fact that hybrid organisms are often (though not always) infertile (Weißköppel 2005, 317); another in the assumption, propagated by Gobineau and other racist theorists, that whenever there was interbreeding, the inferior genes would prevail over the superior genes (cf. Nederveen Pieterse 1999, 177). In addition, hybridization clearly opposed the nineteenth-century and structuralist obsession with taxonomies (Bucakli and Reuter 2004, 174) because hybridity, by its very existence, blurs the distinctions among categories (Nederveen Pieterse 1995, 56). Since the development of Mendelian genetics in the 1860s (Blech et al. 2005, 140) and particularly since the twentieth century, however, a re-evaluation has taken place which regards cross-breeding and polygenetic inheritance as valuable enrichments of the gene pool (Nederveen Pieterse 1995, 55; Ackermann 2004, 141). The concept of hybridity theory was then applied to language by the Russian literary and linguistic scholar Mikhail Bakhtin and later extended to refer to many different domains – first in linguistics, and subsequently it was turned into "a positive label of multiculturalist racial intermixing, syncretism, and transnationality" (cf. Fludernik et al. 2005, 228) by post-colonial critics. Weißköppel (2005, 334) differentiates between the terms *hybridization, syncretism* and *creolization*. According to her, the defining feature of syncretism is the idea of blending, whereas creolisation is dominated by the observation of coexistence and combinations of different weighting. In Weißköppel's terminology, hybridity emphasizes the status quo in the contact situation, the unfinished and the parallel. However, not everyone would subscribe to this distinction. According to Nederveen Pieterse (1999, 178 and 2001, 237), the term *hybridization* is more common today in humanities as a general term than its possible alternatives *bastardization, mixing, blending, melding, merging, syncretization, creolization, métissage, mestizaje, cross-over* etc. Even so, as the idea of combining disparate, seemingly pure entities to form a new, different one still seems to be widely regarded as fairly negative – for instance, *bastard* is used as an insult in different languages (e.g. English and German), and the corresponding verb *bastardize* means 'cause to deteriorate' or 'stigmatize as illegitimate' (SOED s.v. *bastardize*), – it may not be long before *hybrid* acquires the same connotations, so that a new, more fashionable term will have to be coined to designate this increasingly important process in our globalizing world once again in a neutral way.

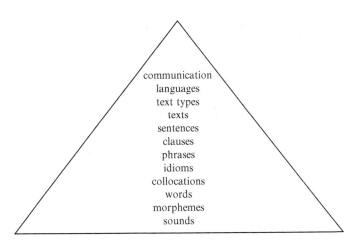

Fig. 9.1 The levels of language

9.2 Hybridity and Hybridization in Language

Before the concept of hybridization can be applied to the domain of language, we need a definition of *hybridization*: it will be understood here to be a process whereby separate and disparate entities or processes generate another entity or process (the hybrid), which shares certain features with each of its sources but which is not purely compositional. By the introduction of non-compositionality, we avoid treating entities as hybrids which are produced by an additive relationship, e.g. in the sense that three is two plus one. Not only does this definition represent a synthesis of the definitions of hybridization one encounters in linguistics but it is general enough to be applicable to a wide range of phenomena as well. It builds very much upon the original, biological concept of hybridization, just like most linguistic definitions of the concept seem to do.

The next step in the consideration of hybridization in relation to language is necessarily the contemplation of the levels of language which may be affected by hybridization processes. The triangle in Fig. 9.1 provides an overview of these levels, with the smallest elements at the bottom and the largest ones at the top.[1]

By its very nature, the definition of *hybridization* relies to a very large extent on what is understood by a hybrid. For this reason, we will now search for linguistic

---

[1] It will be noted that though hierarchical, this overview of language is characterized by a certain degree of overlap (e.g. idioms, collocations and phrases may be of varying size), and that communication on the highest level is a process rather than a tangible constituent. This is due to the fact that the higher we move up in the stratification of language – particularly beyond the sentence level –, the more difficult it is to decide what the structure is supposed to be (cf. Bolinger 1975, 16).

hybrids on all levels of language. The examples will be taken from English – but they could also be taken from any other language.

9.2.1 The Level of Speech Sounds

Speech sounds represent the most basic level of language. Since they are by definition the smallest units that language is composed of on the formal acoustic level, it is hard to see how a concept like hybridity, which involves a combinatory process, should be applicable at all. Although originally foreign speech sounds may be included into a native system, this merely involves the addition of new items to a pre-existing entity, so that no parenting relation such as that required for hybridization can be recognized.[2] However, as soon as we leave the level of individual sounds in the strictest sense and consider phenomena of connected speech, we may encounter hybridization.

Assimilation is the process whereby more or less neighbouring sounds become more similar to each other in order to make articulation easier (Gut 2009, 35). Thus when pronouncing the word *unkind*, speakers often realize the second sound as [ŋ] instead of [n] because of the following [k]. The sound [ŋ] thus shares features of both [n] and [k]: [k] is a velar plosive, [n] an alveolar nasal – and [ŋ] a velar nasal. In other contexts, though, the sound [ŋ] must be regarded as a single, basic sound – e.g. when it occurs as the last sound in *sing*. It would make little sense to speak of a hybrid there. Otherwise, practically all speech sounds would need to be considered hybrids on the basis of similarities of their articulatory features to other sounds. Nonetheless, new phonemes may eventually emerge from continued assimilation: thus the palato-alveolar English fricative /ʒ/ is the result of a combination of the alveolar fricative /z/ and the palatal approximant /j/, which emerged in contexts such *fusion* as (Scheler 1977, 79). This means that we must differentiate between two ideas of hybridization, namely first a context-independent one, which refers to the makeup of linguistic entities, and second a context-dependent one, which refers to their use in particular contexts.

This initial example also raises some further questions. For instance, how important is it that the sources should be recognizable in a hybrid in order to define it as such? The velar nasal can obviously be traced back to its two "parents" in an articulatory-feature analysis, but the relationship will presumably be unnoticeable to an uninitiated listener. As a logical consequence, an entity for which it is impossible to detect different sources by any means can never be called a hybrid because a very important prerequisite is missing. However, the parenting relationship need not be immediately recognizable, and any proof – be it visible to the

---

[2] Note, however, that this does not preclude the existence of hybrid pronunciation systems according to Wawra (this volume, for New Zealand English).

naked eye or only after an analysis by experts using special instruments – will suffice.

Careful observers will have noticed that the example above still poses another problem. If the definition requires entities to jointly give rise to a new one, does that involve any implications that the sources must remain untouched, or is it acceptable if one of them ceases to exist and is transformed into the hybrid, as the /n/ in *unkind*, whose place is filled by the newly-emerged /ŋ/, while the /k/ remains in its usual place? One may argue in favour of such a view because language is a very special system by its twofold nature, which consists of the *langue* (the system) and the *parole* (the actual use of language) (cf. de Saussure 1916/2005, 30–31). Even if the source is transformed in a process of hybridization in this particular case, it therefore still exists on another level.

9.2.2 The Level of Words: Morphemes and Words

Hybridization being a process, the question to consider on the lexical level is by which processes new words come into a language. Basically, there are three possible alternatives: either new words are formed from scratch, or new words are formed on the basis of previously existing material, or they are borrowed from other languages. In the first case, hybridization is definitely not possible: if there are no separate sources, we cannot speak of hybridization. Thus the English word *bed* is reasonably short, cannot be subdivided any further and must have been the result of a creative formation from scratch at some time in the very remote past. By contrast, in the case of word-formation processes, basic linguistic units – the so-called *morphemes*, which are the smallest units of a language with lexical or grammatical meaning (cf. Lipka 2002, 3) – are combined into larger sequences, namely words. Thus *waterbed* is a compound formed from the combination of *water* and *bed*.

9.2.2.1 Meaning

At first sight, this does not seem to be any more than an additive relation: *waterbed* = *water* + *bed*, but there is actually more to it. For instance, a determining relation holds between the two constituents, with *water* describing *bed* more precisely. While this could still be captured by language-immanent rules of the type "When two nouns are juxtaposed, there may hold a relation in which the first acts as a modification on the second", what no generally applicable rule can grasp is the precise relation between the two constituents. There are certainly a number of very typical relations between constituents of compounds – e.g. 'a kind of', 'a part of' etc. (cf. e.g. Levi 1978, 76–77) –, but it is not possible to formulate a rule that would encompass any reasons for a selection from a predetermined amount of relations. In the case of *waterbed*, the constructed meaning 'a bed made of water' comes fairly close to the word's usual meaning in the language, but is still not precise enough. In other instances, the relations between the constituents are even more idiosyncratic. For this reason, we are actually dealing with semantic hybrids here, as the rule-supported addition of the parts is not enough to arrive at the lexicalised result of the word-formational process (cf. Bauer 1983, 48–50). This is not only true of compounding but also of other processes such as suffixation, e.g. in the case of *drawer*. One of the meanings of *to draw* is 'to pull'. The suffix *-er* is typically used to convert verbs into nouns; in this particular case we can recognize the meaning 'a thing suitable for' (cf. SOED s.v. *-er^1*), so that a drawer is 'a thing suitable for pulling'. Nonetheless, it is still a certain step from here to the usual meaning of the word, which involves the meaning component 'part of a piece of furniture'. We can therefore argue that whenever an idiomatic component is involved in the formation of a new word, we are dealing with semantic hybridization.

But does that mean that all words consisting of several morphemes should be defined as hybrids because there is always some kind of semantic change, i.e. a change in meaning, when morphemes come together? No; whenever it is possible to capture the new meaning by the application of rules, we should not speak of hybrids. For instance, if we add the regular plural morpheme {S} to the word *bed*, it attains a plural meaning: *beds*. If we add this morpheme to *car*, we get *cars* – the same word, only in the plural. This is an entirely regular process. Of course one may object that this is no word-formation but only the addition of grammatical meaning by means of a grammatical morpheme, {S}. Still, this regularity also occurs with certain lexical morphemes, e.g. with the prefix *un-*.[3] When attached to an adjective, it negates its meaning in a fairly regular fashion, e.g. *reasonable* to *unreasonable*. Yet even so, there may be certain changes: the *Longman Dictionary of Contemporary English* gives more than ten meanings of the word *clear*, e.g. 'easy to understand', 'impossible to doubt', 'sure about something', 'easy to see or hear', 'clean and fresh'. *Unclear*, by contrast, is reduced to a single meaning involving difficulty in understanding. For this reason, a person's complexion can be clear but not unclear (though there are a number of hits for this collocation on the internet, too). Nonetheless, *unclear* is still compositional, if only with regard to one of the lexical units of *clear* (Cruse 1986, 80), and thus not hybrid.

Though hybrid word formation may be based on the precise number of two sources, it is of course possible that more than two morphemes are involved in the creation of new words with a semantically hybrid meaning. However, their combination usually follows a particular order, so that the process can be considered as a combination of binary steps, in which the so-called *immediate constituents* (cf. Kastovsky 1982, 170) are combined: thus *ice cream cone* consists of *ice cream + cone*, the first of which is a hybrid that can be analyzed into the hybrid

---

[3] Gauger's (1971, 133) *verschiebend* ('shifting') and *variierend* ('varying') *durchsichtige Wörter* are word pairs such as French *tendresse* 'tenderness'/*tendre* 'tender', which have the same meaning except for the fact that they differ in their part of speech, and *maisonnette* 'small house' vs. *maison* 'house', where the complex word only represents a specific variation of the base.

ice + *cream*. A reversal of this order (*ice* + *cream cone*) usually produces nonsense due to the default rule of English word formation according to which the first part of a compound determines the second part (cf. Lipka 2002, 96; though there are of course some exceptions). A similar binary order can be observed in affixations.

From a semantic point of view, polysemy and homonymy may also initially seem good candidates for semantic hybrids. By polysemy we understand that one lexical item has several, related meanings (cf. Lipka 2002, 92), e.g. *lay* 'put down into a flat position' and 'produce an egg'. Homonymous words, by contrast, have the same form but very different meanings, e.g. *ear* is not only used to designate a part of the body but also a head of corn (Lipka 2002, 154). However, a closer look at these phenomena reveals that they have one thing in common which distinguishes them from hybridity, namely the fact that the elements are not fused but merely alternatives, which can still be kept apart and may be actualized in different contexts. A hybrid, by contrast, is fed from different sources but clearly a single entity. Whenever different meanings share an identical form in the widest sense, we should therefore not speak of hybridity.

9.2.2.2 Form

This leads us directly to the formal side of words. In compounding, the two chains of sounds/letters representing the formal side of the morphemes involved usually remain untouched. Affixation will sometimes result in fairly regular formal changes, e.g. the deletion of the verb-final <e> in *drive* in the noun *driving*, but this should not be regarded as an instance of hybridization because of its rule-like character. Some other word-formational processes, though, result in more unpredictable shapes. Blends as non-morphematic word formations (Fandrych 2008, 109) are a particularly interesting case in point. Thus a *brunch* is neither breakfast nor lunch; though it does involve food typically associated with either, it is usually consumed at a time starting between the two and typically in other social contexts (the corpus sentences in the LDOCE suggest that brunch is usually consumed outside the home, and typically during holidays). Not only do blends combine more or less random parts of their source lexemes' form,[4] but their meaning also combines semantic features of both sources, so that they can be considered iconic in that their forms reflect their referents (Fandrych 2008, 113). This type of word-formation is particularly convenient in the naming of hybrid plants or animals (cf. Meredith 1948) because it can be considered hybrid itself.

---

[4] There are certain rules that are applied when words with particular properties are combined with each other (cf. Plag 2003, 122–126).

9.2.2.3 Etymology

But let us come back to the issue of how new words enter a language. The third way is represented by borrowing from other languages. The reasons for such processes of borrowing are manifold (Scheler 1977, 86–88): thus words may be taken over at the same time as a foreign concept, process or entity, e.g. English *sauerkraut* from German. Furthermore, it may be that an existing loanword in a language opens the way for related borrowings from the same word family, as is the case with the Middle English French borrowing *judge*, which is complemented by the French borrowing *just* in late Middle English (SOED s.v. *judge, just*; Scheler 1977, 87).

Sometimes the foreign origin is still obvious, as in British *bureau* (which is a large desk, just like in French), and whose borrowed spelling <eau> strikes the eye. Its quasi-synonym *desk*, by contrast, may be less easily recognizable as ultimately going back to Latin *discus* (SOED s.v. *desk*) – which means that this word has undergone massive changes in both its form and meaning. As both words were borrowed as a whole, they cannot be considered hybrid in the sense discussed before, though – in spite of the fact that the foreign word *discus* (or its medieval Latin form *desca*; cf. SOED s.v. *desk*) was modified by generations of usage on the British Isles before becoming modern *desk*: the Latin and English elements which combined to yield this modern English word are of very different types, one of them being an entity (the word) and the other one representing a process. Though it is conceivable that two different processes may engender another, hybrid, process, just as two entities can engender a hybrid entity, it is highly questionable whether the interaction of an entity and a process should be regarded as resulting in hybridity – otherwise almost everything would have to be considered hybrid in a certain way.

Similar problems arise when we consider the morphological changes arising when foreign words are integrated into a language and become loan words through this process (Scheler 1977, 89). For instance, verbs may be stripped of their inflections and/or get new ones from the target language system. While we have seen before that the rule-based addition of grammatical morphemes to word stems cannot be considered an instance of hybridization, the picture becomes somewhat different when the two sources come from distinct languages. Thus, unlike French *présenter*, English *present* no longer has an explicit infinitive ending – however, it forms the past tense with *-ed* (*presented*), the continuous form with *-ing* (*presenting*) etc. As these grammatical morphemes are of Germanic ancestry (cf. SOED), *presenting* can therefore be considered hybrid from an etymological point of view. However, this raises yet another question: the original French word had an infinitive ending and the English one does not. Can *present* in its bare form then also be considered a hybrid? As we have stated before, the stripping of the suffixes is a rule-based process in contrast to the entity-like character of the word. For the reasons outlined above, we should consequently not consider this a hybrid.[5]

---

[5] The only way to do this would be by postulating a morpheme that goes one step beyond the zero morpheme (cf. Lipka 2002, 3), which we may call a *negative morpheme* {−X}. This morpheme is

9 Hybridization in Language

Still, the interaction between different languages may result in hybridity when new words are formed on the basis of previously existing material from different etymological sources. This is a use of *hybrid* that we find very commonly – and also very early – in the linguistic literature (e.g. in McKnight 1923; Wehrle 1935). As these hybrids are formed by speakers who will usually belong more to one linguistic community than to another, the results of such processes will presumably be integrated into the stronger language.

The ultimate example for etymological hybridization in English is given by McKnight (1923, 161): *remacadamizing* consists of the following constituents:[6]

• *re-*	Latin
• *Mac*	Celtic
• *Adam*	Hebrew
• *-ize*	French < Latin < ultimately Greek
• *-ing*	Germanic/native English.

McKnight's example also demonstrates very clearly that from an etymological perspective, linguistic hybrids may have more than two sources without any problem. Etymologically hybrid word formations are attested to in different languages and varieties (cf. e.g. Schach 1948 for Pennsylvania German and Irwin 2005 for Japanese) but seem to be particularly frequent in English (Wehrle 1935, 60–61) due to its external language history: in 1066, the French-speaking Normans invaded the isles and had a strong impact on the language for several centuries (Crystal 1995, 30–31). This paved the way for a massive influx of Romance words into the language. Such integration is possible in different ways of word formation, such as compounding (*doubletalk* < French *double*, Germanic *talk*), prefixation (*besiege* < Germanic *be-*, French *siege*; *dislike* < Romance *dis-*, Germanic *like*) and suffixation (*priesthood* < Latin *priest*, Germanic *-hood*; *husbandry* < Old Norse *husband*, French *-ry*). Nonetheless, Wehrle (1935, 5) reports that there are relatively few etymologically hybrid words in English before the late thirteenth century. The first attested hybrid affixation is *sotship* – around 1050 –, which later died out (Wehrle 1935, 17). Apart from formations in *-ship*, only very few other Germanic suffixes, such as *-hood*, *-ness* or *-ful*, combined with French bases before 1300 (Wehrle 1935, 20). The first Germanic prefix to combine with a French base was *be-*, in *bespouse* (Wehrle 1935, 20–21). Up until about 1300, hybrid affixations consisted exclusively of French loan words and native English affixes (Wehrle 1935, 57–58) – a process that Wehrle regards as organic and subconscious.

---

similar to the zero morpheme in that it serves to complete inflectional paradigms and has no form but a meaning. In the example above, it stands in place of foreign infinitive endings, thereby causing their deletion – which explains its name.

[6] Though this is a nonce word, cf. the SOED for the meaning of its constituent *macadamize*: "Make or repair (a road) according to McAdam's system, by laying down successive layers of broken stone of nearly uniform size, each layer being consolidated by pressure before the next is laid."

Schönfelder's (1956, 65) explanation for the fact that we do not find the reverse pattern (Germanic base and French affix) at the same time already is that affixes are not borrowed directly from one language into another but that they enter a language by the analysis of loan-words and analogical formations.

The so-called *loan formations* (Lehnbildungen) are a very special case of etymological hybridity: though their form is native, their structure and meaning come from another language (Scheler 1977, 92–95). For example, English *folk song* was created in complete analogy to German *Volkslied*. Scheler (1977, 93) calls this subcategory of loan formation *Lehnübersetzung* (loan translation), in contrast to the slightly less literal *Lehnübertragung* (loan transfer), such as *wishful thinking*, whose German source *Wunschdenken* has the literal translation 'wish thinking'. *Lehnschöpfung* (loan creation), the third subcategory, is even freer, in that a word in a foreign language stimulates the creation of a new word with an identical meaning but a different form (e.g. German *vollklimatisiert* < English *air-conditioned*) (Scheler 1977, 93–94). Consequently, the loan translations are etymologically hybrid but in an unusual way, since the etymologically alien element may either be semantic only or refer to the structure to a greater or lesser degree. The so-called *Mischlehnwörter* (mixed loan words; Scheler 1977, 90) cross even more boundaries: while they borrow the meaning, structure and one of their components from a foreign language, the other component is native (e.g. German *Grapefrucht* for *grapefruit*; *Frucht = fruit*). The opposite trend can be observed in the *Lehnbedeutung* (loan meaning): here, only a foreign word's meaning is added to an already existing native word, e.g. German *füttern* 'feed' was extended to mean 'insert data into a computer' in analogy to English *feed* (Scheler 1977, 95).

So far we have unquestioningly accepted the common assumption that words may be etymological hybrids. However, this idea can be questioned by arguing that if an English word-formation element combines with a French one, for example the result is still an English word. The word may be hybrid in different ways (e.g. with regard to its form, meaning, and the fact that it comes from two sources), but it does not constitute an instance of a new language. However, we may counter that this reverses the perspective: the combination of word a from language A with word b from language B has to yield word c – but not necessarily in a new language, C. This can be regarded in analogy to biological hybrids: a mother with feature A and a father with feature B will yield a hybrid offspring – but still either male or female (at least usually).

According to Nederveen Pieterse (1995, 55–56), "hybridity concerns the mixture of phenomena which are held to be different, separate; hybridization then refers to a *cross-category* process." This engenders the question how distinct the sources actually have to be, so that another way of questioning the English hybrids would consist in enforcing stricter rules regarding the issue of proximate vs. original language. Thus French and Latin are different languages, but ultimately French goes back to Latin; similarly, English and French are both ultimately Indo-European. We may therefore argue that in a very broad sense, English-French compounds are not really etymologically hybrid if we wanted to restrict the term to combinations transgressing larger language families.

9.2.3 The Level of Fixed Constructions: Collocations and Idioms

Several levels lie between the level of words and that of sentences. Since these overlap to a certain extent, we shall first consider the level consisting of more or less fixed combinations of words, namely collocations and idioms. Collocations are words that typically occur together, such as *to take a shower* (and not *to *do a shower* (cf. Hausmann 2004, 309 for German examples). There are two approaches towards collocation, one of them considering a significantly high statistical frequency of co-occurrence (cf. Bartsch 2004, 91), and the other implying that a special relationship obtains between two words (cf. Hausmann 2004, 320–321; Hausmann 1985, 118). Be that as it may, words that typically occur together – and make language sound "right" to native speakers – very often contain some idiomatic component. This is even stronger in the case of idioms, whose meaning cannot usually be guessed from the meaning of their parts: e.g. *to kick the bucket* means 'to die' (Flavell and Flavell 1992, 117). In contrast to words, idioms and collocations are therefore never hybrid on the formal level (because they represent combinations of whole words) – but idioms (and to a certain degree collocations) are necessarily semantically hybrid.

In addition, the most suitable and most frequent collocation of a particular word may have a very different etymological source from the word itself: *table* is Romance, but the process of preparing a table for a meal is not expressed by the equally Romance verbs *prepare* or *decorate*; instead, we say either *lay the table* or *set the table* (cf. Hausmann 2004, 309 and SOED s.v. *table*), thereby generally combining the Romance noun with a Germanic verb. Such collocations, of which there are presumably many more, show how intricately the Germanic and Romance elements interact in English. For this reason, we may even speak of a very weak form of etymological hybridity here.

9.2.4 The Level of Syntax: Phrases, Clauses and Sentences

The same seems superficially to be true of phrases, as one can speak of *a red car* or *an orange car* without any restrictions, even though the word *car* is Romance but ultimately of Celtic origin, while *red* is a Germanic word and *orange* has entered English from Sanskrit via Persian, Arab and Old French (cf. SOED). We can use words with different etymologies freely within phrases, clauses and sentences. Syntactic rules are thus entirely blind towards etymological origin. But should this be considered a form of hybridity? No. Due to the mainly rule-based, quasi-compositional nature of syntax, this level has little to offer in terms of hybridization – as long as there is no overlap with collocations or idioms, which may take different syntactic shapes, from the combination of premodifying adjectives within a noun phrase to sentence-length proverbs such as "When in Rome do as the Romans do", to practically anything in between.

Still, this does not mean that functional hybridity – as an alternative to semantic hybridity in the realm of grammatical structure – is impossible. For instance, the construction traditionally called a *gerund* combines both verbal and nominal characteristics (Quirk et al. 1985, 1290–1292 and Herbst et al. 1991, 107–108): the word *building* in *They admired his quickly building the tower* is like a verb in that it is premodified by an adverb and followed by a direct object but like a noun in that it is preceded by a possessive determiner. Other gerunds – such as *writing* in *the art of writing poetry* – may display the additional nominal characteristic of being the head of a prepositional phrase. As these two functions of the gerund are inseparably linked with each other, we can consider it a functional hybrid.

There are even more such examples. Thus English grammar recognizes two verbs *dare* (Quirk et al. 1985, 136–139): one main verb with full inflection and *do*-support (*He doesn't dare to escape.*) and one auxiliary verb with bare infinitive and no *do*-support (*He daren't escape.*). Still, Quirk et al. (1985, 138) point out that blends between these two constructions occur and are widely acceptable, e.g. *They do not dare ask for more* – which combines the *do*-support of the main verb use with the bare infinitive typical of the auxiliary. Thus features of both categories are present in such a construction, without it belonging to either of the two. Not only is this an instance of functional hybridity but also of gradience (cf. Quirk et al. 1985, 90), i.e. the fact that an item does not clearly belong to one category or another but is situated in between. Instances of functional hybridity are thus always gradient – but in the special sense that they are situated at a more or less equal distance to the two ends of the scale (while gradients that are closer to one particular end would rather be regarded as being atypical instances of that particular type). As grammatical categories are always a matter of definition (cf. the different categorization of parts of speech in different grammars), the determination of functional hybridity will be particularly dependent on the grammatical model used as the basis for categorization.

9.2.5 The Level of Text: Texts, Text Types and Genres

If we move yet another step higher, etymological hybridity may also seem to be observable to a certain degree in texts. However, one must question whether words may be considered as directly generating hybrid texts – after all, phrases, clauses and sentences function as intermediate steps, and the definition of hybridization does not provide for the omission of the parent generation and the jump from the grandparents to the grandchildren. In addition, we must not forget that the intermediate syntactic steps between words and texts are rule-based (unless we are dealing with fixed expressions, which are usually idiomatic to a certain extent; cf. above) and therefore not really of interest to hybridization, whereas it is not really possible to ascribe a particular etymology to individual sentences.

However, we can observe a new kind of hybridization on the level of texts, namely the emergence of new text types from the combination of existing ones. Galster (2005, 227) uses the term *hybrid genre* to designate "works of art which transgress genre boundaries by combining characteristic traits and elements of diverse literary and non-literary genres". This might result in the re-classification of more traditional text types as hybrid genres, but more usually in the description of new text types in which elements of one genre appear in another, e.g. when a laudatory speech is blended with an appeal (Jamieson and Campbell 1982, 147), or when talk show elements are introduced in political interviews (Lauerbach 2004). Promotional news represents a mixture of journalism and advertising, which is reflected in the blend *advertorial* (Erjavec 2004, 554). Hybrid novels may break down the boundaries between fiction, poetry and drama (Galster 2005, 227). Some genres have exerted such a strong influence on the structure of particular novels that the emerging novel-types were named after them, e.g. the confession, the diary etc. (Bakhtin 1981, 321).[7]

9.2.6 The Level of Individual Languages

In narrative studies, as opposed to linguistic usage, the term *hybrid novel* is used with reference to "novels in which Western and post-colonial (native) writing traditions creatively interact" (Fludernik et al. 2005, 227). This usage of the term *hybrid* thus refers not so much to an intermixing of genre but rather to the merging of cultures. It is one step further away from the linguistic use of the term, which relies more on the original, biological definition. But this is no surprise, because language, the subject of linguistic study, is often – particularly in the later nineteenth century, and modelled on Darwin's ideas – likened to an organism, which evolves, dies etc. (cf. Gut 2009, 7). This is still recognisable in the fact that linguists have for a long time been talking about language families (cf. Bolinger 1975, 457), i.e. languages that are "genetically" related to each other (Bußmann 1990 s.v. *Sprachfamilie*), and which may be depicted in family trees, in analogy to human families (e.g. Bußmann 1990, 277). This may be the reason why the idea of hybrid languages is one that is fairly frequently used, even in the older linguistic literature. In this context, it is interesting to note that hybridity in language differs from hybridity in biological organisms in that there seems to be no restriction on the possible combination of languages, whereas biological organisms need to be structurally relatively similar to produce offspring (Croft 2000: 209). Even though English is certainly not the only hybrid language (cf. e.g. Wurm 1995), English is often considered "the standard example of a hybrid language" (Roberts 1939, 23).[8]

---

[7] While the former are either written texts – or at least may be written –, we can apply the concept of hybridity to spoken texts as well: thus, Kamberelis' (2001, 86) *hybrid discourse practice* involves "teachers and children juxtaposing forms of talk, social interaction, and material practices from many different social and cultural worlds to constitute interactional spaces that are intertextually complex, interactionally dynamic, locally situated accomplishments", while Duff's (2003) *hybrid discourse* refers to the interweaving of non-academic and academic texts in a classroom situation.

[8] Bayer (1999, 233), in an alternative definition, considers as hybrid those languages that "show a mix of final and initial heads" with regard to their phrase structure. As this simply implies a choice between alternatives it would not be considered an instance of hybridity in the model followed here.

As we have seen before, the originally English lexicon has undergone a massive influence from Romance vocabulary. While Old English is still a clearly Germanic language, Middle English is traditionally delimited by the Norman Conquest as the starting date for the Romance loans, and Modern English is characterized by its mixed character (cf. Leisi and Mair 1999, 41–46). This is evidenced particularly nicely in the following sentence from *Decline and Fall of the Roman Empire*, in which the few native elements – all of them grammatical – are italicized (Roberts 1939, 37):

> *The* indissoluble connection *of* civil *and* ecclesiastical affairs *has* compell*ed and* encourag*ed me to* relate *the* progress, *the* persecution*s, the* establishment, *the* division*s, the* final triumph, *and the* gradual corruption *of* Christianity.

According to Scheler (1977, 74), the proportion of loan words in English constitutes more than 70% of all words. It is only a small step from this extreme intermingling of two different languages which marked a new period in the history of the English language to a contact situation that results in a new language spoken by a particular group, namely to pidgins and creoles, which typically evolve in colonial situations (cf. Holm 2000, 4–9). A pidgin represents the intermediate step between two distinct source languages and the creole that develops out of them, which can be regarded as a language in its own right.[9] This constitutes etymological hybridity *par excellence*.

When two languages blend to form a new, third one, one of them usually contributes its grammar (in the case of English, this was the Germanic Anglo-Saxon), whereas the other contributes its vocabulary (in the case of English, the Anglo-Norman vocabulary was taken over and many Old English words fell out of use) (Roberts 1939, 28). Hybrid languages thus do not take over 50% of the vocabulary and grammar from language A and B each, but they split up the possible domains of influence (though there may be the occasional A-influence in a B-domain and vice versa). This raises the question of how important each source's contribution to the resulting hybrid language needs to be. Roberts (1939, 28) considers that the language which contributes its grammar "must be considered the victorious tongue from the genealogical point of view" and even goes so far as to call it the "surviving language" (Roberts 1939, 31) at the end of a bilingual situation, which is "colored in greater or less [sic] degree by the perishing language" (Roberts 1939, 31).[10] Even if one may believe that the contribution of the new language's lexicon, for example, should be considered of equal importance to that of its grammar, the question remains whether the source languages' contributions necessarily need to have equal weight, as would be the case in a hybrid organism inheriting 50% of each parent's genetic material. The English lexicon, for instance, contains a considerable amount of Germanic words, the Romance influence thus being further diminished in comparison to the Germanic element that also dominates grammar. Still, English is classified as a hybrid language. But what if the influence of the second language is even smaller? While it seems obvious that the existence of a few foreign words in a language are not

---

[9] But cf. Görlach 1986, according to whom not every mixed language is a creole.

[10] These metaphors can presumably be regarded as closely linked to their time of utterance.

enough to consider it hybrid – otherwise all languages would need to be considered hybrid, so that the concept would no longer be useful – it is still difficult to determine where to draw the line. For this reason, it makes sense to posit that hybridity ideally requires an equal contribution of the sources (i.e. 50% for two sources, 33.3% for three sources etc.), while a process with an extreme imbalance between the sources' contribution should not be classified as hybrid. Where the line should be drawn, however, is a matter of dispute and will have to be decided individually.

Furthermore, we must ask ourselves whether the existence of a few individual foreign words in a language already results in something new. Maybe we should rather consider this an instance of addition. In this respect, Roberts' (1939) gradations of mixture are very convenient: when the two languages are equally strong, and virtually the entire vocabulary of the grammar-providing language is swallowed up by the other's, he speaks of *intermixture*; where one of the two languages retains both its grammatical and lexical integrity, and where only a portion of the other is added, he speaks of *admixture* (Roberts 1939, 31). Note, though, that even in these cases, Roberts speaks of *hybridness*.

This leads to the question of whether the opposite exists, whether there is actually such a thing as a "pure" language. The generally agreed-upon answer is no (Roberts 1939, 23). Scheler (1977, 85) believes that there has always been mixing between different languages due to the contact between different people and peoples. Still, it is not only on the level of individual languages that we are confronted with the question of purity. Most categories are gradient and have fuzzy boundaries. To give but one very basic example, the speech sounds that are discussed in linguistic analyses represent an abstraction from a whole "cloud" of sounds whose articulation is similar enough to qualify as the same. Similarly, there are better and worse examples of hybrid entities such as individual hybrid genres – which is sometimes reflected in the existence of a more or less common designation for the one but not for the other. The idiosyncrasy of the hybrids seems to prevent strict categorization; they seem to be better suited for a description by prototype theory. No-one expresses this dilemma better than Nederveen Pieterse (1995, 55):

> A theory of hybridity would be attractive. We are so used to theories that are concerned with establishing boundaries and demarcations among phenomena – units or processes that are as neatly as possible set apart from other units or processes – that a theory which instead would focus on fuzziness and mélange, cut-and-mix, crisscross and crossover, might well be a relief in itself. Yet, ironically, of course, it would have to prove itself by giving as neat as possible a version of messiness, or an unhybrid categorization of hybridities.

The opposite of liminal space is thus situated at the centre of the prototype. Prototypically, hybridization combines two very different, pure entities – but of course this does not prevent the (presumably far more frequent) case that several entities that are hybrid themselves generate a new hybrid. In contrast to cultural hybridity issues, which often seem to revolve around the problematic idea of purity (cf. Stockhammer, this volume), linguistic hybridity need not determine whether the sources are actually pure; one need only determine which features are mixed. For this reason, from a linguistic point of view nothing prevents hybridization from hybrids and other entities, e.g. in decreolization processes: when creoles come into contact with the source language of the creole's vocabulary (e.g. in Guyana), intermediate hybrid varieties may be created from the combination of the hybrid creole and the creole's lexical source language (Croft 2000: 213).

Languages also influence each other in the case of code-switching, which society often seems to regard as a defective and inferior language use (cf. Räthzel 1999, 213 with regard to Turkish teenagers in Germany). While code-switching may be used as a stylistic means to demonstrate linguistic skills or to play with language, learners of a foreign language who have not yet achieved full command of it sometimes fill gaps in the L2 system (vocabulary or grammar) with elements from their L1 (or other languages). The result of this process, the so-called *interlanguage* (cf. Selinker 1972), is a hybrid form of language, too. However, the hybrid languages resulting from such individual shortcomings are to a certain degree idiosyncratic, and the interlanguage may progress towards a more standard version of the L2 within a fairly short period of time (or decay, conversely, if there is not enough training). This points towards another feature of hybridization in language: typically, we would want to consider not idiosyncratic, ephemeral phenomena but rather those that achieve a more durable status within the language (and thus the linguistic community).

So far we have considered languages in the sense of (inter)national means for communication, but not only these may be affected by hybridization processes. The same phenomena can be observed where dialects of one particular language meet in a geographical area. This will lead to an overlap of certain features in the local dialects of the border region[11] – and thus to hybrid varieties as well.

To sum up, we can recognize a gradience in the strength of etymological hybridity on the level of languages going from idiosyncratic code-switching at the bottom, which leaves the source languages' integrity untouched (Weißköppel 2005, 334), to the creation of whole new creole languages at the top.

9.2.7 The Level of Communication

So far, we have basically treated language like an object or an organism whose hybridity we can investigate. What one must not forget, though, is that language is no abstract entity but a means of communication, by which human subjects interact with each other via a channel. Speech events involve the following constituent factors (based on Jakobson 1985, 150 but with a slightly modified terminology): a

---

[11] Cf. de Saussure (1916/2005, 277–280): where many isoglosses – i.e. geographical borderlines between dialectal features – coincide, the two areas that are separated constitute different dialects. However, not all neighbouring languages/dialects are separated by hybrid intermediate varieties. Thus, there is no intermediate step between the Germanic and the Slavic languages (de Saussure 1916/2005, 280). This is in line with the idea reported above, that languages behave to a certain extent like biological organisms, so that no hybrid offspring are possible at all between individuals of very different species (such as dogs and bears).

sender sends a message with a particular subject, written in a particular code, to a receiver via a channel in a particular communicative situation. These various factors involved in communication are all potentially hybrid. Some of these we have already considered. Thus, the *code* refers to language (in terms of sounds, words, syntax etc.), while the *message* covers the level of text and text types. As the subject refers to extra-linguistic events and entities, it is not of interest in the scope of the present paper – in contrast to sender, receiver and channel.

9.2.7.1 Sender and Receiver

Both sender and receiver of speech are (usually) humans. This means that as soon as we move away from the level of language as a code, a vast range of options for hybridity opens up: for instance, we may argue that the linguistic proficiency of each speaker constitutes a hybrid entity. After all, many micro-systems are mixed in it; systems that are appropriate for particular communicative situations such as a written scientific journal article or an intimate spoken conversation among friends. This does not represent a choice between different alternatives, but rather an intricately interwoven system, in which the parts influence each other. The sender may also have a hybrid identity – either because of a mixed cultural background or simply in the wider sense because every person takes on different social roles in different situations. This hybrid identity may have an effect on that person's particular style of speaking or writing etc. If a multifaceted linguistic background, e.g. knowledge of several languages or dialects, is added, this may influence the pronunciation, vocabulary etc., too. Consequently, it is not surprising that Croft (2000: 209) should regard bi- or multilngual individuals as hybrids. In a very artificial situation, it is even possible to combine the recorded voices of several speakers and thus to achieve hybrid spoken syllables (cf. Whiteside and Rixon 2000, 935).

Sometimes, the identity of the sender may be unclear, namely when another's speech is introduced in the discourse of a novel's author without any formal markers (Bakhtin 1981, 303). This *double-voiced discourse* or *heteroglossia*, according to Bakhtin (1981, 324), is created by *hybrid constructions*, which are "an utterance that belongs, by its grammatical (syntactic) and compositional markers, to a single speaker, but that actually contains mixed within it two utterances, two speech manners, two styles, two 'languages,' two semantic and axiological belief systems" (Bakhtin 1981, 304). Even one and the same word may thus simultaneously belong to two different utterances (Bakhtin 1981, 305). Consider the sentence

> It began to be widely understood that one who had done society the admirable service of making so much money out of it, could not be suffered to remain a commoner

from Charles Dickens' *Little Dorrit*: it contains a very typical hybrid construction, in which the subordinate clause "of making so much money out of it" is in direct authorial speech, while the main clause reflects a different and more general opinion about the person referred to (Bakhtin 1981, 306). We thus read a second story, the author's story, behind the narrator's story at each moment (Bakhtin 1981, 314).

The two voices constantly interact with each other as if in a dialogue (Bakhtin 1981, 324). This "mixture of two social languages within the limits of a single utterance, an encounter, within the arena of an utterance, between two different linguistic consciousnesses, separated from one another by epoch, by social differentiation or by some other factor" are called (deliberate, conscious) *hybridization* by Bakhtin (1981, 358). He sets off this fairly narrow definition against unintentional, unconscious hybridization, which he believes to be "one of the most important modes in the historical life and evolution of all languages" (Bakhtin 1981, 358). This latter concept of hybridization seems closer to the one discussed here – though it is highly questionable whether the hybridization that results in language changes is always unconscious –, but it is difficult to compare the two more closely, as Bakhtin does not define the concept in more detail.

In addition, more than one individual may actually be involved in a text's creation: if several people jointly write a text with which they all agree and in which the individual contributions cannot be distinguished from each other, we can speak of a hybrid sender, a form of communicative hybridity. When a translator translates a text, we may even ask ourselves whether we are dealing with two senders (or with only one – plus the translator as an intermediary black box; cf. Reiß and Vermeer 1991, 41) – and if so, whether this is an instance of a hybrid sender, too.

Another aspect to consider are quotations or the transmission of others' ideas in everyday conversation. Bakhtin (1981, 338–339) believes that the modified reproduction of other's talk constitutes an extremely large proportion of every person's utterances and that "re-telling a text in one's own words is to a certain extent a double-voiced narration of another's words" (Bakhtin 1981, 341). Following this view would mean that half of spoken discourse is hybrid from a communicative point of view.

As soon as we include the receiver as well, it gets even more complex: Weißköppel (2005, 325–326) points out that meaning in speech acts always emerges from the interaction between the participants. To take this one step further, we may even posit more sources of meaning in communicative situations, among them the context, the speaker's intention, the hearer's interpretation etc. Thus, the emergence of meaning in communicative situations is extremely hybrid. This is expressed by Bhabha (1994, 36) in his concept of the so-called "third space":

> The pact of interpretation is never simply an act of communication between the I and the You designated in the statement. The production of meaning requires that these two places be mobilized in a passage through a Third Space, which represents both the general conditions of language and the specific implication of the utterance in a performative and institutional strategy of which it cannot 'in itself' be conscious. What this unconscious relation introduces is an ambivalence in the act of interpretation.

A similar argument is advanced by Bakhtin (1981, 279):

> On all its various routes toward the object, in all its directions, the word encounters an alien word and cannot help encountering it in a living, tension-filled interaction.

He speaks of the "internal dialogism of the word" (Bakhtin 1981, 279) and stresses that words should not be looked at in isolation. Bakhtin (1981, 279) also emphasizes the role of the listener (and his answer), at whom (and at whose conceptual system) the word is directed – and basically the intra- and extralinguistic context in which words attain their meaning (Bakhtin 1981, 281–282). If we thus consider that many different sources contribute to a word's meaning, we may even argue that words are always hybrid. However, as their meanings are disambiguated by the context, they are not hybrid from a semantic point of view.[12] Instead, we have to recognize yet another type of hybridity, namely communicative hybridity.

9.2.7.2 Channel

The communicative channel can be hybrid, too. Thus, spoken and written Japanese used to be so different from each other that they could be considered separate systems. Toward the end of the nineteenth century, a new written language, which adapted spoken elements, emerged from the *gembunitchi* movement.[13] In recent years, new electronic means of communication have been blurring the traditional dichotomy between the spoken and the written modality not only in English but presumably in all languages making use of them (cf. Brown and Yule 1983, 12–19): thus Fandrych (2007, 148) advocates regarding electronic forms of communication (such as text messages, e-mail or chatrooms) as a new medium between the traditional two media – or, to apply the terminology of the present paper, as a hybrid medium. Crystal (2001, 48), however, would oppose this view because, among other things, electronic texts are simultaneously available on an indefinite number of machines, because they do not degrade when copied, and because they have permeable boundaries as far as links to others etc. are concerned. In the approach followed here, though, these other, additional characteristics do not prevent hybridity. We therefore agree with Fandrych (2007, 152), who suggests that we should consider media as a scale or cline: spoken – electronic – written – and not as a separate medium, like Crystal (2001, 238).

There are also certain text types/art forms that transgress media boundaries (cf. Hansen-Löve 1983). A case in point are comics, in which language and pictures interact in such a way that one is very often needed for the interpretation of the other. Internet pages may consist of a video and text that refers back to the video; in this case, the page as a whole is also a hybrid kind of text. Harpold (2005, 110) points out that some texts are crafted with one medium in mind and consumed in another – e.g. digital versions of printed texts – whereas others are created with multiple media in

---

[12] According to Bakhtin (1981, 305), it is a frequent phenomenon "that even one and the same word will belong simultaneously to two languages, two belief systems that intersect in a hybrid construction – and, consequently, the word has two different meanings, two accents...". If a word has different meanings, this does not yet make it hybrid – but if two or more of these meanings are simultaneously realized in a particular communicative situation, this is hybrid indeed.

[13] I would like to thank Noriyo Hoozawa-Arkenau (Heidelberg University) for pointing this out to me.

mind, e.g. magazine articles that appear both in print and on the magazine's website. Even more extreme in this respect are modern dictionaries – which are now crafted in a format that can be used in the form of digital applications for computers, mobile phones etc. Yet I would not consider these examples of hybridity but rather argue that such texts are underdetermined with respect to their medium.

9.2.8 The Level of Abstraction: Models of Language

We have now covered the various levels of language – but there is still another level beyond language itself, which is related to it: the abstract level. Linguists attempt to explain how language works, both in a general sense and with relation to how humans learn and understand language. The models devised to this end often fail to take into account certain features, which are then pointed out by subsequent research. This means that there are usually several competing models which all have their shortcomings. In order to overcome these drawbacks, there is a tendency to combine existing models into new models in the next step of the research (cf. e.g. Stevenson 1994 for syntactic disambiguation, Shen 1999 for metaphor interpretation and Caillies and Butcher 2007 for the processing of idiomatic expressions). Since additive models are unlikely to exist, the new models are usually hybrid, so that there is a lot of language-related hybridization on this level.[14]

9.3 Summary and Conclusion

To sum up, language and linguistic elements may be hybrid with regard to the following variables:

- Formal hybridity (e.g. blends)
- Semantic hybridity (e.g. idioms)
- Functional hybridity (e.g. syntax)
- Etymological hybridity (e.g. languages)
- Communicative hybridity (e.g. double voice in the novel).

This overview of hybridisation phenomena within language is of course not exhaustive. Even if it had attempted to cover all relevant areas, it is highly probable that many other language-related issues will be found to be legitimate instances of hybridity or hybridization, depending on the precise definition that is chosen.

---

[14] Sometimes, though, *hybrid* is not defined in articles whose title contains this term. In such cases, it is usually doubtful whether we are actually dealing with hybrid phenomena, and one may argue that Meskill and Anthony's (2005) "hybrid" language class is simply instructed with a mixture of different methods, and that the elements in Watson et al.'s (2003) "hybrid" lists do not interact to create something other than an additive entity.

What we have not considered so far is why hybridization happens in the first place and who is responsible for it. For even if we have mainly considered language as a structure, the changes in language are brought about by its speakers, and we can assume that more often than not, they have a reason why they apply processes of hybridization. For instance, hybrids may be formed in order to enlarge the range of options: new words meet the demand to express a newly-emerged concept (and may be etymologically hybrid if one of the bases has been borrowed from another language); a new genre meets the demand of a particular author's wish to express themselves in a particular way etc. Particularly where the mixed character of the linguistic entity is very evident, hybridization can also serve as a stylistic means, e.g. to create a poetic effect. Thus, Dadaist artists such as Hans Arp, Walter Serner and Tristan Tzara switched between different languages to create a poetic multilingual text (Mersmann 2002). The combination of very disparate constituents may also result in a comic effect, e.g. in the so-called macaronic texts, which usually integrate native (e.g. English) words into a Latin system of grammar and inflection, as in "Boyibus kissibus sweet girliorum, girlibus likibus, askum for morum" (Hansen 1961, 56). This comic effect can also be achieved with creative word formations in an otherwise English text, as long as the disparity between the constituents is felt, e.g. in *trade-ocracy* or *weatherology* (cf. Hansen 1961).

While these last examples may evoke the impression that hybridizations are typically produced by artists, writers, journalists and other creative language users, this is not entirely true. Even if formal hybrids such as new blends are presumably formed mainly by these groups, new words in general, particularly compounds, are often created very spontaneously by all kinds of speaker, so that semantic hybrids are actually very common among very different acting subjects. Once originally foreign linguistic elements have become part of the vocabulary of a language, they may enter these word-formation processes very naturally as well, so that etymological hybrids may be formed by the unaware language user.[15]

Nonetheless, it seems that hybridization in language very often refers to deliberate new creations rather than to instances of incomplete appropriation, as is frequently the case in other cultural domains (cf. Werbner 1997, 5, who speaks of "routine cultural borrowings and appropriations"). Similarly – and in contrast to cultural hybrids –, the number and amount of influence of the sources of linguistic hybrids can usually be determined quite clearly, at least on the lower levels of the pyramid (cf. Fig. 9.1).[16] This may explain a certain tendency for linguistic hybridity

---

[15] However, as long as there is still an exotic element about them, only certain groups of language users may produce new hybrids. Wehrle (1935, 6) believes that at least the early etymological hybrids will have been formed in written language (because of their learned character) and entered the spoken language from there.

[16] By contrast, hybrids in language can often not be unique in the sense that they are in other disciplines because of the distinction between *langue* and *parole* (cf. de Saussure 1916/2005, 30–31). Thus the hybrid, e.g. an etymologically mixed word, may be unique on the level of the system of *langue*, but not on the level of *parole*, because it may be used many times by different speakers in different situations.

Table 9.1 The etymology of *hybridization*

Constituent	*Hybrid*	*-ize*	*-ation*
Etymology	Latin	French < Latin < Greek	French < Latin
Meaning	'X'	'turn into'	'result of'

to be likened to biological hybridity.[17] The higher we move up, the more complex it gets, because language functions as a means of communication within culture – so that culture may even be added as an additional level at the top of Fig. 9.1.

But let us return to the initial question: is *hybridization* hybrid? Let us consider the etymology first (cf. the etymological information from the *Shorter Oxford English Dictionary* summarized in Table 9.1):

One constituent comes directly from Latin and the other two have a French origin. As they all involve Latin at one stage in their history, all three components could be categorized as having a classical origin. If we decide to look at the parent generation only, though, we do find a certain degree of etymological hybridity (Latin and French). From a formal point of view, the final <e> of the second constituent is deleted – but since this is rule-driven, we do not regard this as an instance of formal hybridization. Let us therefore consider semantics, which usually involves some idiomatic element: as long as we determine precisely what is meant by a *hybrid*, the derivation itself is fairly regular, with *-ize* contributing 'bring or come into some specified state' and *-ation* forming a noun 'denoting verbal action or an instance of it, or a resulting state or thing' (cf. SOED). *Hybridization* is thus not a semantically hybrid word either – and therefore only a very weak instance of hybridization if we consider all levels jointly.

However, as we have seen, hybridization as a phenomenon occurs on all levels of language. Therefore, if we consider all the instances of hybridization introduced above, we must necessarily come to the conclusion that language is a hybrid system *par excellence*.

Acknowledgements I would like to thank Philipp Stockhammer and Ingrid Fandrych for our valuable and stimulating discussions about hybridization.

References

Ackermann, Andreas. 2004. "Das Eigene und das Fremde: Hybridität, Vielfalt und Kulturtransfers." In *Handbuch der Kulturwissenschaften*, 3rd vol. *Themen und Tendenzen*, edited by Friedrich Jaeger and Jörn Rüsen, 139–154. Stuttgart: Metzler.
Bakhtin, Mikhail. 1981. *The Dialogic Imagination. Four Essays*. Austin: University of Texas Press.
Bartsch, Sabine. 2004. *Structural and Functional Properties of Collocations in English*. Tübingen: Narr.

---

[17] Note, though, that linguistic hybrids are often fertile, e.g. hybrid words that engender new word formations.

Bauer, Laurie. 1983. *English Word-Formation*. Cambridge: Cambridge University Press.
Bayer, Josef. 1999. "Final complementizers in hybrid languages." *Journal of Linguistics* 35: 233–271.
Bhabha, Homi. 1994. *The Location of Culture*. London: Routledge.
Blech, Jörg, Rafaela von Bredow, and Johann Grolle. 2005. "Darwins Werk, Gottes Beitrag." *Der Spiegel* 52/2005: 136–147.
Bolinger, Dwight. 1975. *Aspects of Language*. 2nd ed. New York: Harcourt Brace Jovanovich.
Brown, Gillian, and George Yule. 1983. *Discourse Analysis*. Cambridge: Cambridge University Press.
Bucakli, Özkan, and Julia Reuter. 2004. "Bedingungen und Grenzen der Hybridisierung." In *PostModerne Dekonstruktionen. Ethik, Politik und Kultur*, edited by Susanne Kollmann and Kathrin Schödel, 171–182. Münster: LIT Verlag.
Bußmann, Hadumod. 1990. *Lexikon der Sprachwissenschaft*. 2nd ed. Stuttgart: Kröner.
Caillies, Stéphanie, and Kirsten Butcher. 2007. "Processing of idiomatic expressions: Evidence for a new hybrid view." *Metaphor and Symbol* 22: 79–108.
Croft, William. 2000. Explaining Language Change: *An Evolutionary Approach*. Harlow: Pearson.
Cruse, David A. 1986. *Lexical Semantics*. Cambridge: Cambridge University Press.
Crystal, David. 1995. *The Cambridge Encyclopedia of the English Language*. Cambridge: Cambridge University Press.
Crystal, David. 2001. *Language and the Internet*. Cambridge: Cambridge University Press.
Duff, Patricia. 2003. "Intertextuality and hybrid discourses: The infusion of pop culture in educational discourse." *Linguistics and Education: An International Research Journal* 14: 231–276.
Erjavec, Karmen. 2004. "Beyond advertising and journalism: Hybrid promotional news discourse." *Discourse & Society: An International Journal for the Study of Discourse and Communication in Their Social, Political and Cultural Contexts* 15: 553–578.
Fandrych, Ingrid. 2007. "Electronic communication and technical terminology: A rapprochement?" *NAWA Journal of Language and Communication* 1: 147–158.
Fandrych, Ingrid. 2008. "Submorphemic elements in the formation of acronyms, blends and clippings." *Lexis – E-Journal in English Lexicology* 2: 105–123.
Flavell, Linda, and Roger Flavell. 1992. Dictionary of Idioms and Their Origins. London: Kyle Cathie.
Fludernik, Monika. 2005. "Hybridity." In *Routledge Encyclopedia of Narrative Theory*, edited by David Herman, Manfred Jahn, and Marie-Laure Ryan, 227–228. London: Routledge.
Galster, Christin. 2005. "Hybrid genres." In *Routledge Encyclopedia of Narrative Theory*, edited by David Herman, Manfred Jahn, and Marie-Laure Ryan, 226–227. London: Routledge.
Gauger, Hans-Martin. 1971. *Durchsichtige Wörter: Zur Theorie der Wortbildung*. Heidelberg: Winter.
Görlach, Manfred. 1986. "Middle English – a creole?" In *Linguistics Across Historical and Geographical Boundaries* 1, edited by Dieter Kastovsky and Aleksander Szwedek, 329–344. Berlin: de Gruyter.
Gut, Ulrike. 2009. *Introduction to English Phonetics and Phonology*. Frankfurt/Main: Lang.
Hansen, Klaus. 1961. "Makkaronische Sprachformen – hybride Wortbildungen." *Zeitschrift für Anglistik und Amerikanistik* 9: 49–64.
Hansen-Löve, Aage A. 1983. "Intermedialität und Intertextualität: Probleme der Korrelation von Wort- und Bildkunst: Am Beispiel der russischen Moderne." In *Dialog der Texte: Hamburger Kolloquium zur Intertextualität*, edited by Wolf Schmid and Wolf-Dieter Stempel, 291–360. Vienna: Gesellschaft zur Förderung slawistischer Studien.
Harpold, Terry. 2005. "Digital narrative." In *Routledge Encyclopedia of Narrative Theory*, edited by David Herman, Manfred Jahn, and Marie-Laure Ryan, 108–112. London: Routledge.
Hausmann, Franz Josef. 1985. "Kollokation im deutschen Wörterbuch. Ein Beitrag zur Theorie des lexikographischen Beispiels." In *Lexikographie und Grammatik*, edited by Henning Bergenholtz and Joachim Mugdan, 118–129. Tübingen: Niemeyer.

Hausmann, Franz Josef. 2004. Was sind eigentlich Kollokationen? In *Wortverbindungen – mehr oder weniger fest*, edited by Kathrin Steyer, 309–334. Berlin: deGruyter.
Herbst, Thomas, Rita Stoll, and Rudolf Westermayr. 1991. *Terminologie der Sprachbeschreibung. Ein Lernwörterbuch für das Anglistikstudium*. Ismaning: Hueber.
Holm, John. 2000. *An Introduction to Pidgins and Creoles*. Cambridge: Cambridge University Press.
Irwin, Mark. 2005. "Rendaku-based lexical hierarchies in Japanese: The behaviour of Sino-Japanese mononoms in hybrid noun compounds." *Journal of East Asian Linguistics* 14: 121–153.
Jamieson, Kathleen Hall, and Karlyn Kohrs Campbell. 1982. "Rhetorical hybrids: Fusions of generic elements." *Quarterly Journal of Speech* 68: 146–157.
Jakobson, Roman. 1985. "Closing statement: Linguistics and poetics." In *Semiotics: An Introductory Anthology*, edited by Robert E. Innis, 147–175. Bloomington: Indiana University Press.
Kamberelis, George. 2001. Producing heteroglossic classroom (micro)cultures through hybrid discourse practice. *Linguistics and Education: An International Research Journal* 12: 85–125.
Kastovsky, Dieter. 1982. *Wortbildung und Semantik*. Düsseldorf: Schwann-Bagel.
Lauerbach, Gerda. 2004. Political interviews as a hybrid genre. *Text: An Interdisciplinary Journal for the Study of Discourse* 24: 353–397.
Leisi, Ernst, and Christian Mair. 1999. *Das heutige Englisch: Wesenszüge und Probleme*. Heidelberg: Winter.
Levi, Judith N. 1978. *The Syntax and Semantics of Complex Nominals*. New York: Academic Press.
Lipka, Leonhard. 2002. *English Lexicology: Lexical Structure, Word Semantics & Word-Formation*. Tübingen: Narr.
McKnight, George Harley. 1923. *Words and their Background*. New York: Appleton.
Meredith, Mamie J. 1948. "Hybrids." *American Speech: A Quarterly of Linguistic Usage* 23: 302–303.
Mersmann, Birgit. 2002. "Weltanschauungen sind Vokabelmischungen. Deterritorialisierung und Hybridisierung als Entgrenzungsstrategien der Avantgarde." *TRANS. Internet-Zeitschrift für Kulturwissenschaften* 13. Accessed 30 December, 2010. http://www.inst.at/trans/13Nr/mersmann13.htm.
Meskill, Carla, and Natasha Anthony. 2005. "Foreign language learning with CMC: Forms of online instructional discourse in a hybrid Russian class." *System: An International Journal of Educational Technology and Applied Linguistics* 33: 89–105.
Nederveen Pieterse, Jan. 1995. "Globalization as hybridization." In *Global Modernities*, edited by Mike Featherstone, Scott Lash, and Roland Robertson, 45–68. London: Sage.
Nederveen Pieterse, Jan. 1999. "Globale/lokale Melange: Globalisierung und Kultur – Drei Paradigmen." In *Gegen-Rassismen*, edited by Brigitte Kossek, 167–185. Hamburg: Argument.
Nederveen Pieterse, Jan. 2001. "Hybridity, so what? The anti-hybridity backlash and the riddles of recognition." *Theory, Culture & Society* 18: 219–245.
Plag, Ingo. 2003. *Word-Formation in English*. Cambridge: Cambridge University Press.
Quirk, Randolph, et al. 1985. A Comprehensive Grammar of the English Language. Harlow: Longman.
Räthzel, Nora. 1999. "Hybridität ist die Antwort, aber was war noch mal die Frage?" In *Gegen-Rassismen*, edited by Brigitte Kossek, 204–219. Hamburg: Argument.
Reiß, Katharina and Hans J. Vermeer. 1991. *Grundlegung einer allgemeinen Translationstheorie*. 2nd ed. Tübingen: Niemeyer.
Roberts, Murat H. 1939. "The problem of the hybrid language." *Journal of English and Germanic Philology* 38: 23–41.
Saussure, Ferdinand de. 1916/2005. *Cours de linguistique générale*. Paris: Payot.
Schach, Paul. 1948. "Hybrid compounds in Pennsylvania German." *American Speech: A Quarterly of Linguistic Usage* 23: 121–134.
Scheler, Manfred. 1977. *Der englische Wortschatz*. Berlin: Erich Schmidt.
Schönfelder, Karl-Heinz. 1956. *Probleme der Völker- und Sprachmischung*. Halle: Niemeyer.
Selinker, Larry. 1972. "Interlanguage." *International Review of Applied Linguistics* 10: 209–241.

Shen, Yeshayahu. 1999. "Principles of metaphor interpretation and the notion of 'domain': A proposal for a hybrid model." *Journal of Pragmatics: An Interdisciplinary Journal of Language Studies* 31: 1631–1653.

The Shorter Oxford English Dictionary on CD-ROM. 2002. 5th ed., version 2.0. Oxford: Oxford University Press.

Stevenson, Suzanne. 1994. "Competition and recency in a hybrid network model of syntactic disambiguation." *Journal of Psycholinguistic Research* 23: 295–322.

Watson, Jason M. et al. 2003. "Creating false memories with hybrid lists of semantic and phonological associates: Over-additive false memories produced by converging associative networks." *Journal of Memory and Language* 49: 95–118.

Wehrle, Otto. 1935. *Die hybriden Wortbildungen des Mittelenglischen (1050–1400): Ein Beitrag zur englischen Wortgeschichte.* Freiburg: Weis, Mühlhans & Räpple.

Weißköppel, Cordula. 2005. ""Hybridität" – die ethnografische Annäherung an ein theoretisches Konzept." In *Globalisierung im lokalen Kontext: Perspektiven und Konzepte von Handeln in Afrika,* edited by Roman Loimeier, Dieter Neubert, and Cordula Weißköppel, 311–347. Hamburg: LIT.

Werbner, Pnina. 1997. "Introduction: The dialectics of cultural hybridity." In *Debating Cultural Hybridity: Multi-Cultural Identities and the Politics of Anti-Racism,* edited by Pnina Werbner, and Tariq Modood, 1–26. London: Zed Books.

Whiteside, Sandra P., and E. Rixon. 2000. "Identification of twins from pure (single speaker) and hybrid (fused) syllables: An acoustic and perceptual case study." *Perceptual and Motor Skills* 91: 933–947.

Wurm, S. A. 1995. "The Silk Road and hybridized languages in North-Western China." *Diogenes* 43: 53–62.

Chapter 10
New Zealand English: A History of Hybridization

Daniela Wawra

Abstract The aim of this paper is to reconstruct the history of New Zealand English. New Zealand English today has some special features in its lexicon and grammar and particularly in its phonetics and phonology, when we compare it to other varieties of English. Therefore it is the accent that reveals most about the origins of New Zealand English. Theories about the development of the New Zealand accent can mainly be divided into three categories: Lay, single origin and multiple origin. This study will discuss and evaluate different hypotheses against the background of New Zealand's cultural history and in the light of linguistic theories about the development of varieties of English. Arguing for a multiple origin theory as the likeliest scenario, the paper will show that the New Zealand English accent is the result of a mixture of other English accents. Thus, the history of this variety of English is a classic case of hybridization.

10.1 Introduction

"Aotearoa" – land of the long white cloud – was the name that the Polynesians of the Maori tribe gave their country – two islands in the Pacific Ocean they had inhabited since the middle of the twelfth century. Five hundred years later, on 13 December, 1642, two ships from the Dutch East-India Company reached the South Island. The Dutchman Abel Tasman was in command. A few men of the crew were sent ashore in longboats. On their way, they were attacked by the aborigines and four of the crew members were killed. After this incident, Tasman gave orders to leave. In a sketch of the West coast of the island he marked the place as "Murderers' Bay", and he called the islands "Statenland" in honor of the Dutch general states. The islands were soon renamed New Zealand, after Tasman's home state (cf. Gaertner 1994, 15, 33; Crystal 1997, 37; Gordon and Deverson 1998, 9–13).

In 1769, New Zealand was "rediscovered". It was the country's first contact with the English language: Captain James Cook landed on the East coast of the North

Island. He charted the islands and claimed them for the British crown in 1770. From the 1790s until 1841 New Zealand was a dependency of the Australian colony New South Wales. It had no government of its own and no legal system. The first smaller settlements, of mainly English speaking immigrants, were founded. Many of these early settlers came from Australia, mainly because of the "strong trading links" between the countries (Bauer and Warren 2008, 39). In 1840 the Treaty of Waitangi was signed, which Captain William Hobson had negotiated with the Maori to acquire their land for the British crown. One year later, New Zealand was a crown colony (cf. Gaertner 1994, 15, 33; Crystal 1997, 37; Gordon and Deverson 1998, 9–13).

This is when the history of English in New Zealand starts. It is the history of a new variety of English: New Zealand English.[1] It has some special features in its lexicon (cf. e.g. Orsman 1997; Kennedy and Yamazaki 1999; Deverson and Kennedy 2005) and its grammar (cf. e.g. Bauer 1994, 399–401; Hundt 1998) – but above all in its phonetics and phonology (cf. e.g. Bauer 1986; Bell and Holmes 1990). And so it is the accent of New Zealand English that reveals most when we want to reconstruct the history of this variety of English. Unfortunately, this is the area that is the most difficult to study as we do not have any evidence for pronunciations "in the time before" spoken language could be recorded (Gordon and Deverson 1998, 21). Let me therefore make a few remarks on the methods that are applied to reconstruct earlier pronunciations.

10.2 Methods

As we do not have any nineteenth century recordings of New Zealand English, we have to rely on written sources such as personal letters, newspaper articles, letters to the editor, and reports of teachers, school inspectors and professors who comment on the New Zealand accent (cf. Gordon and Deverson 1998, 21–25). In addition, there is a corpus of spoken New Zealand English that comprises the speech of 325 people who were born in New Zealand in the nineteenth and early twentieth century. The recordings were made for the National Broadcasting Corporation of New Zealand between 1946 and 1948. The data were then digitalized and transcribed by the department of linguistics at Christchurch as part of the "Origins of New Zealand English" (ONZE) project. This project started in 1989. The recordings give us a unique insight into the speech of first generation New Zealanders (cf. Trudgill 2004, x). Finally, another important source is demographic data: Where did the settlers in New Zealand come from?

---

[1] For overviews of New Zealand English see also Turner (1966) as an early work as well as Burridge and Mulder (1998) and Burridge and Kortmann (2008).

But at what point in time exactly should we start with our investigation? Since when can we call the English language in New Zealand a separate variety of English?

10.3 The Beginnings of New Zealand English as a Variety in Its Own Right

The first English speaking settlers came to New Zealand between 1780 and 1800. More and bigger groups of immigrants arrived after the treaty of Waitangi. The decisive phase of the rise of New Zealand English took place between 1840 and 1890. This was because, for the first time, more Europeans were born in New Zealand than there were European immigrants (cf. Trudgill 2004, 25, 129). Between 1900 and 1912 certain aspects of the pronunciation of English in New Zealand were mentioned in written sources for the first time. We can deduce that there was already a distinct New Zealand accent at the beginning of the twentieth (cf. Gordon and Deverson 1998, 24–25; Trudgill 2004, 25). In 1910, for example, Mr. Andrews of Napier Boy's High School commented: "I am just now observing that a dialect, and that not a defensible one, is becoming fixed in the Dominion among the children and the younger adults" (Gordon and Deverson 1998, 28).

10.4 Special Features of the New Zealand Accent Today in Comparison to Received Pronunciation

What does the New Zealand standard accent sound like today?[2] The following tables summarize its most characteristic peculiarities in comparison to Received Pronunciation (RP), the standard accent of British English. Differences between RP and the New Zealand English accent can mainly (although not exclusively, cf. also Bauer 1986; Kuiper and Bell 1999; Burridge and Kortmann 2008) be found in the vowel systems on which I am to concentrate here. Before continuing to an overview

---

[2] The following discussion refers to the standard accent of New Zealand English. There is little regional and social variation in comparison to other varieties like American or Australian English: "The surprising thing about regional variation in New Zealand English is how little of it there is (...). In this sense, New Zealand is dialectally homogeneous (...)" (Bauer 1994, 411). Still, New Zealand English is sometimes classified into broad, general and cultivated New Zealand English, variably with RP on top as the accent with the highest prestige in the country (cf. Bauer 1994, 411; Hansen et al. 1996, 169). At any rate, there are fewer and less marked differences between the strata of New Zealand English than there are between the strata of other varieties like American, Australian or British English.

of characteristic New Zealand English vowels the following RP vowel chart provides orientation (Fig. 10.1, Table 10.1–10.3):

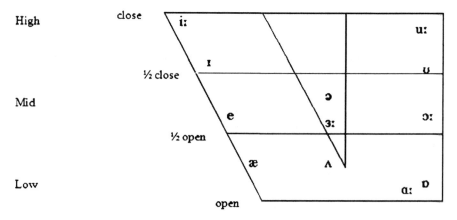

Fig. 10.1 RP vowel chart

Table 10.1 New Zealand accent today in comparison to RP – **short monophthongs**

KIT	Centralized
DRESS	Closer
TRAP	Closer
STRUT	More front
LOT	Slightly more centralized
FOOT	More central

Extracted from Bauer and Warren (2008, 46–49)

Table 10.2 New Zealand accent today in comparison to RP – **long monophthongs**

FLEECE	Slightly diphthongized
BATH	More front
THOUGHT	Closer
GOOSE	More front
NURSE	Closer

Extracted from Bauer and Warren (2008, 49–50)

Table 10.3 New Zealand accent today in comparison to received pronunciation – **diphthongs**

FACE	First element more open
PRICE	First element more back
CHOICE	First element closer
GOAT	First element more open, second more front
MOUTH	First element closer
NEAR, SQUARE	Merger; first element closer
CURE	First element more front, second element more open

Extracted from Bauer and Warren (2008, 51–2)

10.5 Theories About the Development of the New Zealand Accent

Theories about the development of the New Zealand accent can be divided into three categories:

1. Lay theories
2. Single origin theories and
3. Multiple origin theories.

10.5.1 Lay Theories

One lay theory, for instance, says that the climate is responsible for the New Zealand accent. The argument goes like this: Pollination in New Zealand regularly causes hay fever, an infection of the nose. That is why a particularly nasal pronunciation has developed in New Zealand (cf. Hornadge 1980, 15). According to another lay theory the New Zealand accent imitates the sounds of the many sheep in the country (cf. Gordon and Deverson 1998, 36). Yet another theory claims that the New Zealand accent is based on the huge percentage of people in the country whose third teeth do not fit properly. This prevents people from opening their mouths wide enough to speak proper English – because they are afraid that their teeth might fall out (cf. Gordon and Deverson 1998, 25). This seems partly to reflect the linguistic fact that, as Bauer and Warren put it, "[l]ip-rounding and spreading is never strong in New Zealand English" (Bauer and Warren 2008, 42).

Let us have a look at the linguistic research into the origins of the standard New Zealand English accent.

10.5.2 Single Origin Theories

According to single origin theories, New Zealand English is a pure import from another country. There are three possibilities for the source of the import (cf. Gordon and Deverson 1998, 26–29):

1. New Zealand English is based on Australian English.
2. New Zealand English is based on Cockney English.
3. New Zealand English is based on South-Eastern English.

10.5.2.1 Is New Zealand English Based on Australian English?

What is there to be said in favor of the hypothesis that New Zealand English is based on Australian English? When we look at the cultural history of the country it is obvious that many settlers came from Australia to New Zealand. Especially between the 1850s and the 1870s a high percentage of immigrants came from Australia. In some years, there were more settlers from Australia than from Great Britain: Between 1854 and 1856, for example, 1451 immigrants came from Great Britain and 1841 from Australia (cf. table in Gordon and Deverson 1998, 27). Not all immigrants from Australia were born in Australia, but a considerable part of them spoke Australian English. In addition, the contact between New Zealand and Australia intensified in the second half of the nineteenth century and at the turn of the century. Finally, New Zealand English and Australian English are closely related phonologically (cf. Gordon and Deverson 1998, 18). There are many comments about this fact from the early twentieth century onwards (cf. Gordon et al. 2004, 73). The lawyer Louis Cohen wrote in 1912: "I think it is beyond controversy that the English spoken in the Dominion of New Zealand has become characteristically colonial. It fortunately has not reached the despairing depths of what we in New Zealand call 'Orstreilian', but it is in grave danger of touching that point" (Gordon and Deverson 1998, 28).

Recordings that were made in the 1940s of people born in New Zealand at the turn of the nineteenth century show that many of them pronounce "chance" and "dance" for example as in Australian English, not as in British English. This is also the standard pronunciation of modern New Zealand English. Even today, New Zealand speakers are often thought to be Australians. Even people from New Zealand do not always recognize an Australian accent and Australians do not always recognize a New Zealand accent (cf. Bauer 1994, 425; Gordon et al. 2004, 73).

The conclusion we can infer from this is that it is very likely that New Zealand English has been influenced by Australian English to a greater or lesser degree. Gordon et al. (2004) reach the same conclusion: "(...) the (...) weight of the evidence indicates that New Zealand English owes some of its character to Australian input" (Gordon et al. 2004, 257). Let us now turn to the second single-origin theory.

10.5.2.2 Is New Zealand English Based on Cockney English?

What is the evidence for New Zealand English being based on Cockney English? There are three hypotheses about the importing of the Cockney accent to New Zealand (cf. Gordon et al. 2004, 219–23):

1. The Cockney accent was imported via Australia.
2. It was imported directly from the British Isles.
3. It was imported from *both* countries.

First of all, what is meant by "Cockney accent"? Some typical features of Cockney are (cf. Gordon et al. 2004, 219–20):

10 New Zealand English: A History of Hybridization

1. "h"-dropping (i.e. not articulating the <h-> at the beginning of words like "hear", "her", "him" etc.),
2. Shifts of diphthongs ("today" for example would sound like "to die" (cf. Bauer 1986, 240)),
3. The drawling (i.e. lengthening) of vowels,
4. The "clipping" of the suffix <–ing>, resulting in the pronunciation /ın/ in words like "singing", "walking" etc..

All of these features are documented in early New Zealand English, particularly in the reports of school inspectors (cf. Gordon and Deverson 1998, 166f) and some of the diphthong shifts have become the standard pronunciation (see table above).

However, we must be careful when defining "Cockney". There are two definitions. According to a narrow definition, the accent of the London working class has been imported to New Zealand. However, this assumption seems implausible. The number of immigrants from London was simply too small. However, there is every indication of an influence of the Cockney accent according to a second, broader definition: The majority of immigrants to New Zealand came from the South-East of England, and most of them were lower class people (cf. Gaertner 1994, 36). Charles Darwin visited New Zealand in 1835 and he even spoke of the "scum" of British society that immigrated to New Zealand (cf. Gaertner 1994, 34). In 1939 Arnold Wall estimated that about 80% of the population of New Zealand spoke more or less distinct Cockney-English (cf. Wall 1939, 8). This claim is only plausible when we assume an influence of the Cockney-accent according to the broader definition. Finally, let us take a closer look at the third single origin theory.

10.5.2.3 Is New Zealand English Based on South-Eastern English?

The third single origin theory is that New Zealand English originates in the standard South-Eastern accent of England. Lass promulgates that all the colonial varieties of English are dialects from England's South. He claims that "this simple characterization is true without exception: There is no extra-territorial English that is *not* a variety of Southern English" (Lass 1990, 247). Which arguments support this hypothesis?

First of all, the phonetics and the phonology of New Zealand English have always been very similar to South-Eastern English pronunciation. Bauer for example emphasizes: "Phonologically, New Zealand English is a variant of the South-East-English system" (Bauer 1994, 388, 391; cf. also Bauer 1999, 298, 300). Gordon et al. also come to the conclusion that features of the South-Eastern English accent are clearly dominant in New Zealand English (cf. Gordon et al. 2004, 231). When looking at the vowel systems today, it is apparent that the majority of monophthongs and diphthongs are very similar to the South-Eastern vowels. In addition, it is an undisputed fact that most immigrants to New Zealand came from the South-Eastern part of England (cf. Gordon et al. 2004, 256).

10.5.2.4 Discussion

How plausible is it then to assume that there is one single origin of the New Zealand accent? Adherents of single origin theories agree in one respect: The starting point for the development of New Zealand English is one single imported variety, be it Australian English, Cockney English or South-Eastern English. The hypothesis is that while people with different accents met in New Zealand, all of them sooner or later adapted their pronunciation to one single variety. Is this homogenization scenario plausible? In the early variety of New Zealand English, and still today, we find features of all three varieties, albeit with a clear dominance of South-Eastern English features. Therefore, South-Eastern English is the most likely candidate for a single-origin theory. But if this single origin theory were correct, why do we still find features of Cockney and Australian English in standard New Zealand English today? Could it be that those features developed independently, by chance? To be able to properly weigh up the likelihood of such a process against that of the three accents mixing, we first have to take a closer look at the multiple origin theories. At the core of these theories is the assumption that New Zealand English is the result of a process of hybridization.

10.5.3 Multiple Origin Theories

The New Zealand accent has features of South-Eastern English, Australian English and Cockney. How and why should these three accents have mixed? Why are most of the variants in the New Zealand accent based on the South-Eastern accent? And why are there no remnants of the Scottish and Irish accents in standard New Zealand English?[3] After all, about a quarter of the immigrants from Great Britain came from Scotland and Ireland (cf. Trudgill 2004, 13). To find answers to those questions, let us take a closer look at different theories about the development of varieties.

10.6 Theories About the Development of Varieties

There are many different theories regarding the process and result of the mixture of varieties, including their accents. The following positions are the most extreme:

---

[3] There is no trace of the Scottish or Irish accent to be found in today's standard pronunciation of New Zealand English. However, we can make out a Scottish influence on the accent of people in the south of South Island, where immigrants from Scotland outnumbered settlers from other regions (cf. Bauer 1994, 411; Bauer 1997).

1. The New Zealand accent is the result of a purely mechanistic and deterministic process.
2. Only social factors lead to the New Zealand accent.

10.6.1 Deterministic-Mechanistic Approach

10.6.1.1 The General Mechanisms of New-Dialect Formation

A prominent advocate of the deterministic-mechanistic approach is Peter Trudgill. He suggests that in colonial situations a new dialect always develops through the following mechanisms or chronological stages (cf. Trudgill 2004, 84–89). His model can be applied to dialects in general and accents in particular:[4]

1. Mixing
2. Levelling

   – Rudimentary levelling
   – Apparent levelling

3. Unmarking
4. Interdialect development
5. Reallocation
6. Focussing

1. Mixing. A necessary prerequisite for dialect mixing is that speakers of different dialects of the same language or speakers of different languages that are easily mutually intelligible come together at a certain place (cf. Trudgill 2004, 84).
2. *Levelling.* During the process of levelling the variants of minorities get lost. At the very beginning of a dialect mixing situation – for example when people start to settle in a new colony – we usually find many variants of different dialects. In due course the variants that survive in the mixture are reduced (cf. Trudgill 2004, 84f). During the process of levelling we can distinguish the following chronological stages, which can be roughly attributed to different generations following each other (cf. Trudgill 2004, 89–115):

---

[4] I am using the terms accent, dialect and variety here in the sense that Bauer (2005, 2–4) describes: "The important thing about an accent is that it is something you hear: the accent you speak with concerns purely the sound you make when you talk, your pronunciation" (Bauer 2005, 2). "What you speak with your accent is your individual version of a dialect – a kind of language which identifies you as belonging to a particular group of people. (...) Standard Southern British English (...) is just one dialect among many." (Bauer 2005, 3). "The term 'variety' is an academic term used for any kind of language production, whether we are viewing it as being determined by region, by gender, by social class, by age or by our own inimitable individual characteristics. It (...) [is] used (...) as a neutral term." (Bauer 2005, 4).

- *Rudimentary levelling.* This is the first stage of levelling when adult speakers adapt to each other in their language use. It is especially locally marked variants of a dialect that get lost in this process. This is because they hinder mutual understanding.
- *Apparent levelling.* During this stage children play the decisive role. They are confronted with a number of different linguistic models (variants) and, according to Trudgill, there is no apparent reason why they should prefer one variant over the other. Trudgill assumes that it is a purely deterministic process that "decides" which variants "win", i.e. will be part of the new variety: It is the "majority variants" that survive, i.e. demographically majority forms (Trudgill 2004, 114).

3. *Unmarking* can as well be seen as a subcategory of levelling. The variants that survive are, according to Trudgill, the unmarked and more regular forms (cf. Trudgill 2004, 85).
4. *Interdialect development.* In the course of the building of a new variety of a language, an interdialect develops (cf. Trudgill 2004, 86f). It is relatively stable for some time and still contains more variants of the input dialects than will be part of the resulting new variety. Interdialects comprise a compilation of variants that does not exist in the same form in any of the input dialects. Three kinds of interdialects can develop (cf. Trudgill 2004, 86f):

- *A simplified dialect.* The variants that make up the interdialect are simpler and more regular than the variants of the original dialects.
- *An "in-between" dialect.* The interdialect can consist of variants that are in between the variants of the original dialects phonologically, morphologically and/or syntactically.
- *A hyperadapted dialect.* The interdialect is the result of hyperadaptation(s), for example hypercorrections. Here, language users would try to use dialect variants with a higher status and apply language rules to variants to which they are not applied in the source dialect.

5. *Reallocation* happens when after the process of levelling more than one of the competing variants "wins", i.e. is used regularly, in the speech community. These will be social or stylistic variants or allophones in pronunciation.
The mechanisms 1–5 can also be subsumed under the term *koinéisation* (cf. Trudgill 2004, 89). When at last focussing takes place, the new-dialect formation is complete.
6. *Focussing* finally happens when certain variants are established and when the new dialect gains stability (cf. Trudgill 2004, 88f).

10.6.1.2 Discussion

The deterministic approach seems to bear some major traces of Keller's invisible hand theory of language evolution in that language change is described as non-teleological, cumulative and dependent on the interplay of variation and selection (cf. Keller 2003, 195). According to Trudgill, the result of a mixture of different variants of pronunciation is always a statistical composite (cf. Trudgill 2004, 123). This is in accordance with Nettle's observations of language acquisition: Unconsciously, children try to learn language as accurately as possible. For them, the optimal learning strategy is a kind of error-minimizing procedure. They minimize the discrepancy between their own speech and the speech they hear. In the end, such error-minimizing strategies result in children learning a statistical composite of the speech they hear (cf. Nettle 1999, 22). It is always the majority variants that prevails. However, a decisive point here is the question of what is meant by "majority" – the majority of speakers or the majority of tokens of a certain type of variant? According to Trudgill, the relevant category is the majority of speakers (he talks about the "loss of demographically minority forms") (Trudgill 2004, 114). He proposes that children acquire those variants in their pronunciation that they hear from the majority of people with whom they have contact. However, it seems more plausible to assume, like Gordon et al. (2004, 241), that the pronunciation variant, of which children hear the most tokens, predominates.

This can be demonstrated with an example, the rhotic and the non-rhotic "r". Rhotic "r" means that "r" is articulated in every position in a word. Non-rhotic means that "r" is only articulated when it precedes a vowel sound, i.e. non-prevocalic "r" is not pronounced. The standard British English accent, RP, is non-rhotic, so one does not articulate the "r" in "car" or "cart", for example. The standard American English accent, General American, is rhotic, so one would articulate the "r" in "car" and "cart". If Trudgill were right, children learning English who were exposed to the rhotic and non-rhotic accent would acquire the variant that the majority of speakers use. If the majority of the people that the children have contact with articulates "r" in all positions, they would acquire the rhotic accent. However, we have to take into account that there is also intraindividual variation: one and the same speaker sometimes mixes rhotic and non-rhotic pronunciations. As a consequence, children can hear both variants from one and the same speaker. Which one they adopt will depend on which is the more frequent. It will depend on the number of *tokens* of the rhotic and non-rhotic accent respectively (cf. Gordon et al. 2004, 239–241).

This hypothesis can be supported by a quantitative study by Gordon et al. (2004). It shows that 98% of first generation New Zealanders pronounced the "r" every now and then, even if it did not precede a vowel. Consequently, they would be classified as rhotic speakers. However, if we take a look at the total number of rhotic and non-rhotic tokens in the corpus, the rhotic "r" only has a share of 9% (cf. Gordon et al. 2004, 241). According to Trudgill's hypothesis, New Zealand English would have to be a rhotic accent, as the majority of speakers use the rhotic "r". However, New Zealand English is a non-rhotic accent, which is the natural consequence when we look at the number of rhotic and non-rhotic tokens: the number of rhotic tokens at 9% is clearly outnumbered by non-rhotic tokens at 91%.

I think the mechanistic approach is important and necessary, but not sufficient as an explanation for the development of new varieties. We also have to take sociolinguistic approaches into account.

10.6.2 Sociolinguistic Approaches

Sociolinguistic approaches assume that social factors, such as the prestige and status of variants, or rather their speakers, play an important role in the development of varieties. Labov, for example, has shown in his famous Martha's Vineyard study (1963) that speakers' identification with certain social groups can influence their pronunciation (cf. also Labov 2001). This is also the result of more recent studies. Eckert (2000), for example, shows that young adults in Detroit use linguistic variants of certain groups they want to be identified with. LePage and Tabouret-Keller (1985) have described such behavior as "acts of identity". According to Giles' accommodation theory (cf. Giles et al. 1991) speakers regularly change their language to better integrate in social groups or to distance themselves from others. Thus, it seems that it is not only the pure number of tokens of a certain variant a child hears that determines which will survive in a new variety like New Zealand English. In addition, the child's relationship to the person from which she hears a token influences whether she tends to use the variant or not, i.e. whether or not the child feels in some way attached or attracted to the person.

Milroy's (1980) network theory also explains why new varieties should develop through the mixture of varieties. The development of new varieties is favored and accelerated by loosely knit social networks. This is exactly the case in New Zealand, due to extended mobility of the population. The immobile, "stable" part of society is only 10% or less, according to Gordon et al. (2004, 53).

In addition, I think it is also very plausible to assume that schools had a considerable influence on the development of the New Zealand English accent. Around the turn of the century, schools worked against a New Zealand accent because it was clearly influenced by Cockney English. In 1912 a special commission was founded to examine education in New Zealand, the Cohen Commission (cf. Gordon and Deverson 1998, 23). The development of the Cockney colored New Zealand accent was not welcome and pronunciation exercises were introduced in New Zealand schools to overcome it and to teach the children correct RP. If schools had not worked against the New Zealand accent that developed at the time, I think Cockney features would feature much more prominently in the present-day New Zealand accent.

10.6.3 Cognitive-Biological Approach

Finally, a theory about the development of a variety must also take into account cognitive and biological aspects of language acquisition. A language cannot develop into a totally arbitrary variety. There are restrictions regarding the acquisition of certain variants. As Deacon puts it: "The structure of a language is under intense selection because in its reproduction from generation to generation, it must pass through a narrow bottleneck: children's minds" (Deacon 1997, 110). In other words:

which kind of language structures will be acquired in what manner depends on the biological equipment and the cognitive processing capacity of human or, more precisely, children's brains. "Language operations that can be learned quickly and easily by children will tend to get passed on to the next generation more effectively and more intact than those that are difficult to learn" (Deacon 1997, 110). Unmarked linguistic forms, those that are expectable and according to the rule, will therefore be more likely acquired by children than marked forms. Language structures that are not well adapted to children's cognition will not survive for long.

10.7 Conclusion

Many questions remain unanswered. To reconstruct the development of New Zealand English, an integrative approach seems to be the most promising. Neither a purely deterministic-mechanistic approach nor a purely sociolinguistic one is sufficient to account for the complex processes. We need both, and children's brains are the ultimate place where new varieties originate. Therefore, the more we learn about children's choices in language learning, the more we will learn about the historical development of varieties. When we look at the development of New Zealand English, the likeliest explanation is a multiple origin approach that includes an account of the hybridization processes involved. In any case, New Zealand English has developed from an "objectionable colonial dialect" (Gordon and Deverson 1998, 23), as commentators sometimes called it at the beginning of the twentieth century, into a variety in its own right.

References

Bauer, Laurie. 1986. "Notes on New Zealand English phonetics and phonology." In *English World-Wide* 7 (2): 225–258.
Bauer, Laurie. 1994. "English in New Zealand." *The Cambridge history of the English language, Vol. 5: English in Britain and overseas: Origins and development*, edited by Robert Burchfield, 382–429. Cambridge: Cambridge University Press.
Bauer, Laurie. 1997. "Attempting to trace Scottish influence on New Zealand English." *Englishes around the world 2: Studies in honour of Manfred Görlach*, edited by Edgar Schneider, 257–272. Amsterdam: Benjamins.
Bauer, Laurie. 1999. "The dialectal origins of New Zealand English." *New Zealand English*, edited by Allan Bell and Koenraad Kuiper, 40–52. Amsterdam: Benjamins.
Bauer, Laurie. 2005. *An introduction to international varieties of English*. Edinburgh: Edinburgh University Press.
Bauer, Laurie, and Paul Warren. 2008. "New Zealand English: Phonology." In *Varieties of English 3: The Pacific and Australasia*, edited by Kate Burridge and Bernd Kortmann, 39–63. Berlin: de Gruyter.
Bell, Allan, and Janet Holmes. 1990. *New Zealand ways of speaking English*. Clevedon: Multilingual Matters.
Burridge, Kate, and Jean Mulder. 1998. *English in Australia and New Zealand: An introduction to its history, structure, and use*. Oxford: Oxford University Press.

Burridge, Kate, and Bernd Kortmann. 2008. *Varieties of English 3: The Pacific and Australasia*. Berlin: de Gruyter

Crystal, David. 1997. *English as a global language*. Cambridge: Cambridge University Press.

Deacon, Terrence. 1997. *The symbolic species: The co-evolution of language and the brain*. New York: Norton.

Deverson, Tony and Graeme Kennedy. 2005. *The New Zealand Oxford Dictionary*. Oxford: Oxford University Press.

Eckert, Penelope. 2000. *Linguistic variation as social practice*. Oxford: Blackwell.

Gaertner, Hildesuse. 1994. *Neuseeland*. München: Cormoran.

Giles, Howard et al. 1991. *Contexts of accommodation: Developments in applied sociolinguistics*. Cambridge: Cambridge University Press.

Gordon, Elizabeth, and Tony Deverson. 1998. *New Zealand English and English in New Zealand*. Aukland: New House.

Gordon, Elizabeth et al. 2004. *New Zealand English: Its origins and evolution*. Cambridge: Cambridge University Press.

Hansen, Klaus et al. 1996. *Die Differenzierung des Englischen in nationale Varianten*. Berlin: Erich Schmidt.

Hornadge, Bill. 1980. *The Australian slanguage: A look at what we say and how we say it*. North Ryde: Cassell Australia.

Hundt, Marianne. 1998. *New Zealand English grammar: Fact or fiction? A corpus-based study in morphosyntactic variation*. Amsterdam: John Benjamins.

Keller, Rudi. 2003. *Sprachwandel: Von der unsichtbaren Hand in der Sprache*. Stuttgart: UTB.

Kennedy, Graham, and Shinji Yamazaki. 1999. "The Influence of Maori on the New Zealand English Lexicon." *Corpora Galore: Analyses and Techniques in Describing English*, edited by John M. Kirk, 33–44. Amsterdam: Rodopi.

Kuiper, Koenraad, and Allan Bell. 1999. "New Zealand and New Zealand English." In *New Zealand English*, edited by Allan Bell and Koenraad Kuiper, 11–22. Amsterdam: Benjamins.

Labov, William. 1963. "The social motivation of a sound change." *Word* 19: 273–309.

Labov, William. 2001. *Principles of linguistic change, vol. 2: Social factors*. Oxford: Blackwell.

Lass, Roger. 1990. "Where do extraterrestrial Englishes come from? Dialect, input, and recodification in transported Englishes." In *Papers from the 5th international conference on English historical linguistics*, edited by Sylvia Adamson et al., 245–280. Philadelphia.

Le Page, Robert, and Andrée Tabouret-Keller. 1985. *Acts of identity: Creole-based approaches to language and ethnicity*. Cambridge: Cambridge University Press.

Milroy, Lesley. 1980. *Language and social networks*. Oxford: Blackwell.

Nettle, Daniel. 1999. *Linguistic diversity*. Oxford: Oxford University Press.

Orsman, H.W. 1997. *The Dictionary of New Zealand English: A dictionary of New Zealandisms on historical principles*. Aukland: Oxford University Press.

Trudgill, Peter. 2004. *New-dialect formation: The inevitability of colonial Englishes*. Edinburgh: Edinburgh University Press.

Turner, George. 1966. *The English language in Australia and New Zealand*. London: Longman.

Wall, Arnold. 1939. *New Zealand English: A guide to the correct pronunciation of English, with special reference to New Zealand conditions and problems*. Christchurch: Whitcombe & Tombe.

Chapter 11
From Myths and Symbols to Culture as Text: Hybridity, Literature and American Studies

Carsten Schinko

Abstract Any interdisciplinary effort to conceptualize hybridity or hybridization has to take into consideration potential differences between the disciplines, and this entails not only a reflection on the term's translation from natural into social sciences, linguistics or the humanities, but also – within the humanities – a recognition of the different fields of literary and cultural studies in which the term was popularized most successfully. Thus, in the first part of my essay, I will briefly reconstruct the emergence of American studies from its inception in the myth and symbol school to the current attempts at dismantling and deconstructing static conceptualizations of "America" by the so-called New Americanists. Thriving on a strong democratic ethos from the very beginning, American studies has aimed at a progressive political function, and hybridity is among the latest entries in its critical vocabulary. Yet, how does the terminology, with its poststructuralist affiliations, fit into such an engaged scholarly agenda? Homi K. Bhabha's *The Location of Culture* (Bhabha 1993) has had, and continues to have, a strong impact on the academic understanding of American society, its contradictory epistemological and political claims, as well as its underlying aesthetic connotations. Comparing Bhabha's efforts to Wolfgang Iser's conceptualization of an aesthetic "in-between state" (Iser 1990) in theory of aesthetic response, I will tackle the widely-held critique that Bhabha offers an aesthetic perspective on culture rather than a political one.

11.1 Preliminary Remarks

It is hardly more than a truism to note that Homi K. Bhabha has become one of the leading figures of postcolonial criticism, and it can be safely assumed that by now *The Location of Culture* is standard intellectual currency in most literary departments. In this seminal contribution, as well as in his other essays, Bhabha tries to give contours to what he calls the "hybridity" of the "Third Space," or an "in-between state", terms suggesting that all too firm distinctions like West vs East, oppressor vs oppressed have ceased to live up to the complexity of a globalized modernity with its steady flows of information and migration. Given his disinclination to binary thought, Bhabha strongly distinguishes between a multicultural diversity (in which two or more camps can be distinguished as self-sufficient entities), and a far more complex transculturality.The terms he uses to describe transcultural phenomena, most notably hybridity, have strongly altered the academic understanding of national belonging.

If we set out to conceptualize hybridity or hybridization in an interdisciplinary effort, as the editor of this volume asks us to do, one of the first and obvious tasks is to pin down potential differences between the disciplines that might block the desired transfer of knowledge. Such an identification of problems will need to be concerned not only with the oft-mentioned (metaphorical) borrowing between the "two cultures" (C.P. Snow), in which a biological terminology has been transferred to the social sciences and the humanities. But even within the humanities, most notably the literary studies departments in which the term took hold most successfully, there are distinct institutional traditions and conventions leading to a remarkable variance in appropriating and embracing hybridity. My own discipline, American studies, was fertile ground for using and disseminating the term, and while the consistent reference to a work like Homi K. Bhabha's *The Location of Culture* (Bhabha 1993) is hardly a unique phenomenon, the promise of hybridity, its academic appeal, will have to be scrutinized against the background of the specific self-descriptions and patterns of expectations that are, implicitly or explicitly, at work in this distinct scholarly field. Therefore, I will begin with a rough sketch of my discipline.

Delineating the strong "democratic ethos" (Bergthaller and Schinko 2010), i.e. the regulating ideal of an engaged scholar-citizen, I will offer a brief overview of its academic history from the point of view of someone working mostly in American *literary* studies (as opposed to, say, a historian working in that field).[1] This qualification is of importance because hybridity has fared especially well in literary studies departments after the cultural turn. And there is a reason for this unique commitment, of course, as I will argue later, when comparing Homi K. Bhabha's notion of hybridity – along with its neighboring concepts – with Wolfgang Iser's literary theory in which an "in-between state" (Iser 1990, 953) is also discussed, albeit as an aesthetic element within the reader's reception. This, however, brings in a further qualification, as hybridity has been adopted in English-speaking countries with strong affinities to cultural studies, whereas in Germany these openly politicized interventions have had to compete with the more sober, disengaged form of

---

[1] Even though there are interdisciplinary departments like the John F. Kennedy-institute at the FU Berlin that bring in the expertise of different fields, offering their students a varied curricula, American studies by and large is dominated by literary and cultural studies today. Historians specializing in US American history do have a hard time qualifying for jobs in either American studies or history departments, as the former, at least in Germany, tend to focus on aesthetic communications that cannot be neatly reduced to a historical interpretations, whereas history departments seem to be skeptical about this specialization. It is institutional realities like these that will have to be kept in mind in order to not lapse into a blind celebration of interdisciplinarity.

Kulturwissenschaften. It is here, too, that aesthetic considerations have continued to influence scholarship, whereas in U.S. academia the success story of cultural studies more often than not involved a discrediting of aesthetics.[2] For a *German* scholar working in American studies, this results in a different shading to the institutional evolution of my field. And if this binarism is an all-too-neat oversimplification, it nevertheless captures what I take to be a helpful heuristics for the specific academic atmospheres in which critical vocabularies flourish.[3]

11.2 American Studies, or the Roads to Hybridity

American studies emerged in the 1930s when literary scholars and historians tried to overcome the limitations of their respective disciplines in order to tackle the assumed uniqueness of "American" culture.[4] Even in these first tentative efforts, one can spot the interdisciplinary leanings of a field which can be considered an early instance of cultural studies, not only for its aversion to ideas of aesthetic autonomy and acceptance of popular culture but, even more importantly, in its engaged mode of criticism.[5] Not only were those early scholars eager to work

---

[2] A simple indicator for this tendency is the absence of any real aesthetic criteria in the influential reader *Critical Terms for Literary Studies,* which features entries for race, class, and gender. Apart from the difficulties of defining terms like "art" or "literature", this lacuna is owed to the fact that questions of aesthetics in cultural criticism have been reduced to the normative value they seem to transport. Art, then, would be nothing but a symptom for boundary maintenance, a representation of (upper-) middle-class decorum. Instead of an aesthetic experience in its own right, there is a return to a collective expressivist line of thought. Alternatively, art and literature are seen as merely another social site of interpellation or subject-constitution. This, as Fluck (Fluck 2002, 84) explains, is the logic behind "representation" as key concept, "the most neutral, the most 'dehierachized' term one can find to describe the form in which the object (and its ideology) appear."

[3] In fact, instead of heuristically distinguishing two alternatives, one could read this fuzzy institutional atmosphere as an instance of institutional hybridization. See Schinko (2007) for further thoughts on this institutional complexity.

[4] I am well aware of the problematic notion of "America" here, when the reference is solely to the United States. The reason I stick to this politically incorrect labeling is (a) because it is maintained by scholars even when they would criticize US policies or mentalities, and (b) because it is, as semantics and iconography, part of the popular appeal. And "America" is evoked in the founding documents of the discipline, e.g. the early three-volume study *Main Currents in American Thought* (1927–30) by historian Vernon Parrington, or Constance Rourke's *American Humor. A Study of the American Character* (1931).

[5] This engaged criticism is one of the reasons cultural studies has been received with quite some delay and reservation in Germany. Here, as Aleida Assmann (1999) argues, the more sober *Kulturwissenschaften* reacted to the co-optation of scholars in the Third Reich. Seeking to "cool rather than ignite, they ward off rather than encourage political action" – a "barrier against fatal politicization" (91). Evidently, the cultivation of disengagement is a form of engagement in its own right, e.g. one that accepts functional differentiation, and the semi-autonomy of academic discourses, and thus follows a different route where processes of democratization are concerned.

towards a critical understanding of the political and social dynamics, they were, as Günter Lenz (2002) points out, also trying to combine the roles of the scholar and the citizen. According to this self-description, Americanist scholarship should not only reflect American democracy, it should contribute to the further implementation of democracy – it should be democratic in its performativity. "As students and scholars of American studies," Alice Kessler-Harris writes, "we are called on to engage in, to facilitate, the conversation that occurs in the public marketplace by ensuring the perpetuation of a processual notion of America." (Kessler-Harris 1992, 311) Here, Kessler-Harris seems to imply that Americanists should act as wardens of the public sphere; their role is not merely that of analysts of democratic culture, nor even of simple participants, but as 'facilitators' they have the responsibility to uphold the rules of the ongoing conversation that is American democracy.

Without a doubt, a lot has changed in americanists' self-understanding during the on-going institutionalization of the discipline, and still, this democratic ethos has continued to be a decisive driving force, even though one will find great variance in its manifestations, i.e. in the way society has been conceived, the way its ills have been diagnosed, and in the prescription of the right cures at different stages, from the optimistic egalitarian spirit of early instances to the ideology critical, yet still somehow inclusion-oriented reformist revisionism, to the breathtakingly dark visions of the currently dominating New Americanists. Despite the (semi-)autonomy of scholarship, these manifestations can (and have to) be contextualized. If the Vietnam War has had a great impact, the New Americanists' gloomy vision might have reached its peak with George W. Bush's second presidency.

11.2.1 Genealogies and Changing Self-descriptions

Early efforts notwithstanding, the actual institutionalization of American studies at universities such as Yale, Minnesota, Harvard, and Pennsylvania began in the 1950s with the so-called myth and symbol school. Henry Nash Smith, Leo Marx and others tried to capture what can be called the imaginary substratum of *the* American experience. The emphasis is on the one, sharable experience, and needless to say, this holistic view of "American culture, past and present, as a whole" (Smith 1957) met with severe criticism later on for its reluctance to face difference in what can be considered American culture, for its conception of culture, community and belonging, and for its imaginary investment in what Bhabha calls the "fixed horizontal nation-space" (Bhabha 1993, 142). Indeed, monographs like Smith's *The Virgin Land: The American West as Symbol and Myth* (1950), R.W.B. Lewis's *The American Adam: Innocence, Tragedy, and Tradition in the Nineteenth Century* (1955) or Marx's *The Machine in the Garden: Technology and the Pastoral Ideal in America* (1964) drew on cultural, political and most of all unifying myths, which, in their assumed integrationist drift, marginalized and excluded non-mainstream experiences. One of the consequences of this quest for key national symbols and narrations of the nation was that this scholarly effort helped to establish a canon of *classical* American literature, a set of books that today is – with mild irony by some, rather scornfully by others – labeled the canon of dead white protestant males. In their attempt to craft a public criticism that would help ameliorate American democracy, these scholars, mostly left liberals, were not really interested in a consistent theoretical framework, even though questions about the right methods of studying "America" had been discussed at an early stage (e.g. Smith 1957).

In the late 1960s, "a deep crisis" overshadowed the discipline the agenda of which was considered "intellectually bankrupt, politically reactionary, a handmaiden of American imperialism during the Cold War era" (Lenz 2002, 461). Coming into full force in the 1970s and early 1980s the reformist optimism of the myth and symbol school became the target for consistent criticism, for its idea of conflict-free consensus, for its imaginary homogeneity, for its chauvinism in the name of "America" and the perpetuation of an Exceptionalist rhetoric, a rhetoric that saw the US not merely as one nation among others but as the guiding light in its democratic potential.[6] In a nutshell, American Exceptionalism suggests that modernity reaches its peak on US American soil, and that it is here, in this Puritan version of a "New Jerusalem", that the global future can first and legitimately be glimpsed, and, as a consequence, "America" must serve as the guiding light for the rest of the world. The chauvinism of this mythic self-conception and the narrations it engenders was scrutinized by the next generation of scholars. Works like *Ideology and Classic American Literature*, a seminal contribution edited by Sacvan Bercovitch and Myra Jehlen, has "redefined myth as ideology" and paved the way for "a variety of politically oriented revisionist approaches" (Fluck 2009, 3).

Moreover, with the emergence of new social movements and political collectives, a turn to identity politics could be observed, a decisive change in the political imaginary that would soon result in the by now familiar multicultural politics of recognition (cf. Taylor 1992). The general drift towards multiculturalism impacted on the scholarly endeavors, too. The focus was now on national diversity rather than unity and on cultural dissent rather than consensus, even though dissent was regarded as part of the innate consensus-orientation in the US imaginary, the *Rites of Assent* (Bercovitch 1993) that rendered contradicting voices impotent. It is with the revisionist movement that ideology critique supplanted the absence of a coherent theoretical framework,[7] thus semantics (ideology; dissent) and the shift towards academic autonomy (theoretical reflection) signal drastic change. But still, the promise of "America" was not completely abrogated but rather multiplied, and the idea of a container-like national culture integrating its citizens continued, albeit in a pluralized, more complex sense. The canonization of formerly unheard and marginalized voices that followed the "deconstruction" of the "American" canon, gave way to a more prismatic view of United States literary culture. In other words,

---

[6] The religious overtones in this rhetoric cannot be missed, and in almost every single inauguration speech of American Presidents one of the key metaphors will re-emerge: the "City Upon a Hill" that Puritan settler John Winthrop projected.

[7] The seminal work here is Bercovitch and Jehlen (1986).

there might be different perspectives from which to assess "America" – now transformed into a *hyphen-nation* of many cultures (African-American, Asian-American etc.) – but these cultural collectivities still share a strong sense of nationhood. Formerly imagined as a melting pot, the *e pluribus unum* motto gave way to new metaphors for national cohesion with "America" now reconceived "as a cultural mosaic, of separate pieces with hard, well-defined edges." (Hannerz 1992, 218)

While much of revisionist criticism and especially multiculturalist identity politics still cling to a notion of American culture, however diversified this notion might be, the poststructuralist criticism of more recent academic factions tried to overcome the impasses of spatial metaphors of national or cultural containment. The New Americanists, dominating American studies in the US since the 1990s, took issue with the "over-integrated conceptions of culture" (Gilroy 1993, 2). These concepts are rejected because they portray people as thoroughly integrated into a culture (even if that culture might contain diversity); and culture, in turn almost unambiguously provides those who belong for orientation: culture, according to this now criticized train of thought, suggests stability as a symbolic horizon that encompasses and shapes our perceptions, our actions, our ways of world-making, and it is such a strong force for the very fact that it remains in the background of our everyday-life agency. As Armin Nassehi (2008) succinctly puts it, culture is often theorized as a kind of "invisible algorithm" (148) structuring social life. Culture, conceived as such an algorithm, is logically prior to individual or collective action "otherwise it could not serve as foundation for these actions. Therefore, one can then take everything we do [...] as a result of culture, and such a conceptualization of culture in turn points to the fact that every action takes place in a previously interpreted world, in which some possibilities are more probable than others." (148; my translation)

To some extent, poststructuralist interventions seem to share the idea of an invisible algorithm that informs and even controls our perceptions, thoughts, and actions. What sets concepts like Foucauldian panopticism or Derridean logocentrism apart from the integrationist train of thought, however, is their severe attack on the identity model of culture and the holism it necessitates. Instead of one American culture, or its mere pluralization into a neat multicultural diversity, poststructuralist scholars put emphasis on the shiftiness of concepts such as culture or nation. Highlighting the inherent difference in this (or any other) identitarian term, "America," after these critical interventions, is seen as a contested field, a discursively created label at best, a field, moreover, that has to be conceptualized transnationally. The story behind this genealogy depicts a turn from what Leo Marx has called the divide which sets a reform-oriented "Believing in America" (2003) apart from a disenchanted version of "America" increasingly denying the existence of reform potentials. New Americanists have abdicated reformism to such an extent that some of their critics have chastised their scholarly agenda as "Anti-American Studies" (Wolfe 2003), and while this charge is highly dubious because of its alarming political implications – e.g. the recent silencing of critical voices in the discussion of the "War on Terror" – it points to the almost claustrophobic vision in many of these scholarly texts. According to these interpretations, the United States is nothing but an evil force, and the possibility of real difference almost an illusion. In cultural studies fashion, the task then is to work against all odds, unearthing the last remaining sites of resistance against a hegemonial force whose nationalist containment and imperialist greed is getting worse by the day.[8] In this situation, hybridity offers a welcome perspective of minimal hope, pointing as it does to the necessary failures of (symbolic) control, the impasses in assigning fixed identities, and the agency that these imperfections of power engender. If power, as poststructuralists believe, needs to perpetually reconfirm its grasp on singularities, addressing and subjecting them into contingent forms of identity, then one of the promising models for resisting containment is playing with these assigned identities, with the semantics and iconographies circulating in society. Instead of simply adopting the labels and adhering to the patterns of expectations, a more ironic mode of crafting an identity is enabled by the need to iterate the political grasp on individuals. Hybridity, then, is both an acknowledgement of the inherent non-purity of any "culture" and, in a more political register, its inherent failure to fully control individuals. This lack, in poststructuralist thought, promises a (however vague) sense of empowerment. Seen from the side of the agents, it is also a potential strategy of self-fashioning.[9] If, as Bhabha argues, colonial governmentality and similar power structures by necessity will produce ambivalence, then a "sly civility" causes irritation in its "refusal to satisfy the colonizer's narrative demand" (99) and a potential form of resistance.

11.2.2 Aesthetic Continuities

Highlighting the discontinuities between the different stages, the account of American studies presented above might is certainly not without peers. An alternative reading of the discipline's historical development has been proposed by Winfried Fluck (2003), professor at the JFK institute in Berlin, who not only questions the rather hyperbolic political critique but, by focusing on the underlying aesthetic assumptions, is able to spot continuities within American studies in its interpretational practices. Fluck avoids the scathing commentary on the myth and symbol school, but tries to find out what these critics actually do when reading texts. Instead

---

[8] This is, of course, not to deny that imperialism and nationalism continue to be a problem that needs to be addressed. The question, however, is how to address these phenomena both on epistemological and stylistic levels. Urs Stäheli has made one of the most promising attempts, offering poststructuralist re-readings of systems theory, e.g. Stäheli (1998).

[9] I am using these terms – irony, self-fashioning – for their playful connotations; it is exactly the accusation of a certain light-heartedness that Bhabha has had to face from the beginning of his intellectual career. Obviously, it is a general charge against poststructuralist politics and ethics whose reliance on performance and textualism will have to irritate materialists and idealists alike. However, the fact that Bhabha is interested in both a description of the postcolonial situation and a more normative form of engaged criticism has raised the stakes in his writings,.

of taking scholarly self-descriptions at face value, he reads the semanticization of "American identity" against the grain by observing an aesthetic sensibility at work. It is a sensibility connected to a distinct understanding of "modernity" and America's place in it: while the texts they eagerly helped to canonize could be later read for the myths they contained, it is the aesthetic experience of reading itself that Fluck tries to recover. Modern literature enables a doubleness of aesthetic signification. A double meaning at play within the texts is scrutinized in the interpretations of the myth and symbol school, and to Fluck it is this doubling which links critics like Marx or Smith to their European counterparts, most notably the Frankfurt School, as here, too, a core of aesthetic experience is set against the grasp of modern rationality and the dialectics of enlightenment. This is an acknowledgement of the more downbeat discourses on modernity at large that are lost when the focus is solely on their conceptualization of "America" and the promises of progress it holds. It is an acknowledgement, one should add, that tries to embed the concept of "culture" in the context of a more encompassing social dynamic. Later, during the so-called cultural turn, the term will often lack this contextualization, treating "culture" more or less synonymously with "society".

American literature, formerly belittled as lacking the erudition of its European counterpart, is redefined as truly modern, Fluck argues, and while he grants that there is an implicit affirmation of the United States in times of the Cold War in the myth and symbol school's agenda, his emphasis is on a decisive "literature of negation" inherent in their criticism rather than on the self-congratulatory gestures in the name of "America". Seen from this angle, the myth and symbol school's interpretation of literature is informed by a basic logic that sets apart a surface level from a deeper level of meaning:

> "One level, the narrative surface, reflects, in its bland optimism and lack of a critical perspective, the instrumentalization of reason in modernity, while a second, underlying level of meaning provides a resource – in fact, the only remaining resource – for negating this reductionist version of progress." (Fluck 2003, 67)

The actual workings of the texts aim at – or at least include – a certain non-identity, even if one can easily detect a tendency towards "identity" in the reconstruction of binding American myths and symbols. It is an experience that has the power to subvert, counter, or irritate the putative naivety of the myths and symbols that are structuring and making coherent the narration of the nation. Fictionality in itself is the core element here, and it seems to bring into existence an in-between state of its own, as the text oscillates between surface and depth, and we, the readers, experience this phenomenon while reading fiction. Fluck, who expands Wolfgang Iser's reception theoretical arguments for American studies, insists on a recognition of aesthetic experience, and he is right to recognize consistent waning of literary sensibilities in American studies, and, more generally, in cultural studies at large. For the myth and symbol school the "heroes" of their narrative were the representative authors – though only a certain segment of American writers was considered – who would provide a complex and rich core experience in their carefully crafted literary texts. This aesthetic potentiality is already diminished in the multiculturalist scholarship to a considerable degree. Literature continues to be an important field of study, one should hasten to add, yet the texts in question are evaluated for their (multi)cultural expressivity, thus privileging identity (of a collective experience). The focus is not so much on the experience of reading, i.e. on the textual play or the way it activates and is activated by the reader, but on the work as a sign of cultural belonging. If, in other words, critics are able to reconstruct, say, a black literary tradition, their aim is less to see how the respective texts that form this tradition actually work (in a phenomenological, aesthetic, etc. sense), but rather it is a means to a different end – an important claim in the politics of recognition. The text under scrutiny is made safe, somehow, for it is approached as already read. Instead of a more contingent outcome of the communication that would highlight the experience of aesthetic otherness, its function has been predesigned: it exists either to propel a sense of belonging to a formerly suppressed group, or to dismantle the ideological suppression of marginalized identities. The "heroes" of this revisionist stage are the movements themselves, the new collective social agents that have changed political semantics.

In the ideology critique of the revisionists, aesthetic difference is questioned, and the artwork's status as potent adversary force is put into doubt, as art "can no more transcend ideology than an artist's mind can transcend psychology." (Bercovitch 1993, 360) The choice between literature and politics, between aesthetic success and ideological containment that structured the argumentation of myth and symbol scholarship, has been dismantled as ideological in itself. Even here, however, a certain privilege of literature is maintained: the ambiguities of language that allow us to read critically, to read against the grain, and that make literature a resource for such a second-order observation are embraced by the revisionists after all. Key authors like Nathaniel Hawthorne, were still attractive to them, although the interest in their works has changed, for "if there is no longer any ontological difference between art and ideology, then ambiguity might also have an ideological function, and an ideal object of demonstration must be Hawthorne, to which revisionist critics therefore returned again and again in order to show that, in the words of Bercovitch, Hawthorne uses representational modes like ambiguity to absorb and refashion 'the radical energies of history'" (Fluck 2009, 5).

With the New Americanists, this concern for aesthetic experiences has been almost cancelled. Literature (or any other aesthetic object or research) is reduced to what Fluck calls "systemic power effects" within a discursive regime that forms the paradigm of modern society. Fluck writes, "In a system, in which the manifestation of power, racism, or imperialism is everywhere, that is, both 'inside' the text and 'outside' of it, there can be no difference between text and ideological system. Instead of non-identity, the literary text is characterized by a negative identity in which an 'absent cause', pervading and marking all aspects of the system, is reproduced. As a result of this conflation of inside and outside and the radical rejection of the negating potential of literature linked with it, all fictionalizing acts and forms of aesthetic experience can function only as sources of systemic containment." (Fluck 2000, 198)

In short, what Fluck misses, and rightly so, is the recognition of the specificity of aesthetic negativity and the experiences that literary texts possibly invite and trigger. In fact, if evoked at all, questions of aesthetics in cultural studies are mostly reduced to normative ideas of beauty, and are at best criticized for their normalizing function. While these perspectives are important aspects and should continue to be elements of critical scholarship, communication through works of art might not be fully grasped by simple allegiance to "representation" and "ideology". Nor, one should add, by concepts of interpellation (Althusser 1971) or subjection (Butler 1997) that fail to recognize different modalities of in- or exclusion, different social realms and institutionalized patterns of expectations (art, politics, law, etc.), and different social situations. It does make a difference, for example, whether a cultural contact zone is based on the fleeting nature of spoken language or on a printed text; it is important to know whether the cultural management of difference emerges in momentary interactions or in an organization with attributable roles. (Huck and Schinko, forthcoming)

This, however, seems exactly what has happened to the textualization of culture as encompassing discourse, a textualization that overburdens "culture", a term lacking a conceptual other (e.g. "media" or "society") against which it could be defined. The success story of hybridity within American studies, then, can be measured against conventionalized patterns of expectations within this discipline. It reintegrates the observation of complexity. Thus, a structural equivalent to aesthetic sensibility is recovered in a different realm, culture, a now textualized field that has been de-limited in transnational, or even post-national or non-national American studies, opening up almost endless perspectives and contexts. And, as Fluck elaborates, the basic impulse to set a non-identity apart from identitarian power games in the name of "America" still holds true – a diversity conceived of as difference, a form of hybridity that opens up a Third Space that counters both cultural monocentrism and relativism. Diversity, Fluck argues,

"is designed to counter the ideological hold of the idea of America, and this hold can only be undermined by non-identity. Difference is thus of interest only if it constitutes genuine otherness. Only then can it successfully fulfill its two main promises: to open up a space outside of the ideological hold of the center and to create multiple, flexible identities – and thus, the seemingly philosophically impossible, a positive non-identity. When diversity is defined as difference and difference as unbridgeable otherness, it can become the real test for how far America is willing to go in the realization of its utopian promises. Recent developments – most notably animal studies, disability studies, and transnational studies – all provide logical extensions of this idea of diversity and its claim for a full recognition of otherness" (Fluck 2009, 6f.).

The dynamics I have described so far help understand the function of hybridity within American studies practices. The discipline's political imaginary starts out with a belief in reformism, in an attempt to ameliorate American democracy. It is story of real self-critical progress, and its main "heroes" or privileged agents for resistance are Anglo-American writers (even though this, in fact, is open to all and has been supplemented by an occasional, say, black author). This gives way to a political radicalization that is soon turned into a multicultural promise of inclusion with new privileged agents, e.g. African-American writers. Finally, a darker vision, often claustrophobic, emerges; it calls forth a hybrid America as a minimal chance of resistance against the "tenacious grasp" of American Exceptionalism (and its idea of progress, and its holistic cultural unity) the invocation of a hybrid America. Here, any notion of a national culture is at odds with the interests of the critics who seek to discredit the idea of cultural coherence or identity. Culture is now conceived of as a total force, a systemic effect that controls the individual and his capacities for reflection. Hybridity is the term best suited to meet this minimal resistance against such a total force. While the term already had a subversive function in Homi K. Bhabha's work, this political impact has been reformulated within American studies and its democratic self-description.

Hyperbolically speaking, hybridity is the answer to the institutional problem of what to do as a literary critic trained in a certain form of reading practices, which have severely fallen into discredit with the cultural turn. Ambivalence, indeterminacy, ambiguity – these terms are re-integrated into the critical register without falling under the now dubious rubric, "aesthetics." As part of a cultural enunciation, they are interesting for their promise of resistance. Whether they want to or not, scholars working in literary studies have to qualify by proving their expertise in reading complex texts, and culture, which is by now considered to be a "text", offers ample possibilities. This, of course, is an institutional argument rather than an epistemological one. I am certainly not suggesting that cultural dynamics fail to perplex us (they do not), nor that hybridity or hybridization are bad concepts (they are not), nor that culture is far less complex than current scholarship would like it to be (it is not). It does, however, remind us of the surprisingly strong ties between aesthetic concerns and the notions of hybridity, as employed in contemporary cultural studies.

11.3 The Dislocation of Culture, or Acts of Reading

11.3.1 The Politics of Poststructuralist Postcolonialism

In Bhabha's transcultural theory, the designated roles between "us" and "them" are unsettled, and this unfixing is theoretically linked to the distinction between signifier and signified in poststructuralist thought. Consequently,

> "the production of meaning requires that these two places be mobilized in the passage through a Third Space, which represents both the general condition of language and the specific implication of the utterance in a performative and institutional strategy of which it cannot 'in itself' be conscious" (Bhabha 1993, 36).

Signification, we learn, invalidates neat binarisms and the promises of spatial distance they carry, and this inherent deconstruction has repercussions on how we define identity and belonging, self and other. It is this re-reading of the postcolonial situation that sets *The Location of Culture* apart from earlier classics of the field that tend to juxtapose the West with the rest more patently, e.g. Edward Said's *Orientalism* and its interpretation of imperialism that focuses on "the practice, the theory, and the attitudes of a dominating metropolitan centre ruling a distant territory" (1978, 8). Bhabha reflects the increase in actual everyday interactions between people from different backgrounds and the protagonists of his theory are exactly those immigrants who, voluntary or not, are "in the West, not of it". Thus, by taking note of the multiple contact zones his theory recognizes the complexity of the ensuing transactions in these emergent spaces.

In Bhabha's writings, semiotics is reconceived as performance, as cultural enunciation that by necessity disqualifies authority in the postcolonial setting. If the practice of signification turns out to be ambivalent at best, then this poststructuralist re-reading of linguistics will have repercussions on claims of mastering the inherent symbolic fuzziness in a culture defined as "activity of articulation" operative "at the level of the sign." (1993, 247) As this symbolic activity is located in the multifarious postcolonial contact zones, Bhabha can conceive of politics as "a discursive event." (23) This textualization of contact allows him to model cultural performance in the same way Derrida has temporalized structuralism: "The reason a cultural text or system of meaning cannot be sufficient unto itself is that the act of cultural enunciation–'the place of utterance'–is crossed by the 'différance' of writing" (36). Following this logic of a dynamic process, cultural meanings are shifting because signifier and signified are never stable, never matching, endlessly slipping, and in the same way there is a "time-lag" (194) inherent in any articulation.

As Thomas Wägenbaur (2000) lucidly argues, Bhabha's "postcolonial poststructuralism [...] aligns theory with literature and his 'Commitment to Theory' to political practice." (113) While not necessarily unsympathetic to such an agenda, Wägenbaur sketches some of the "blind spots in Bhabha's theoretical design", and shows that *The Location of Culture* is very much indebted to a set of aesthetic key concepts: the time-lag, to him, "recalls the topos of epiphany. [...] It is the performative moment between two representations and to Bhabha it means 'enlightenment'. The Third Space is 'unrepresentable in itself'". Yet, this celebratory embrace of the moment of indecision is problematic to Wägenbaur, who correctly asks: "How is 'history' supposed to happen in a moment? If you have time-lag you only have moments, if you have history you don't have time-lag." (113) In addition, he reminds us that the "negotiation" of the "In-Between" – the moment of performativity in any given cultural situation – more than anything "recalls the rhetorics of liberalist economics" (113), a vocabulary that, given these affinities, falls strikingly short of Bhabha's goal to subvert Western idioms by identifying the differences within (the West or any other culture conceived as closed *Kulturkreis*). According to Wägenbaur, these blind spots present "the inevitable failure of discourse", e.g. the meaning production in political communication, whereas they "usually constitute the success of the literary text." (114) In literature we do not merely accept but – voluntarily experiencing the complexities of the text over and over again – hold dear the simultaneity, oscillation of meanings and references that Bhabha locates as seminal instances of postcolonial contact. Despite the diversity of aesthetic programs (e.g. realist or modernist, etc.), we negotiate the richness of metaphors and allusions when reading literature; in contrast, even though we might read political speeches against the grain, for example, its communicational logic does not seem to be identical to the ways of literary communication.[10]

11.3.2 In-Between Politics and Aesthetics

Time and again, Bhabha has insisted on the fundamentally political nature of his critical project and the ethical agenda of his writing. Then again, almost as often he has been condemned for aestheticizing urgent political issues. It is here, in the strange and difficult mix of politics and aesthetics, that a comparison between Bhabha's project and Wolfgang Iser's theory of aesthetic response might help to assess this ambivalence. Both the postcolonial critic and the literary theorist refer to an "in-between state", a Third Space where meaning is fuzzy, structures are temporalized (although in non-linear fashion), and perceptions of identity (self and other) oscillate.

To recapitulate: at the heart of Bhabha's project one will find a postcolonial semiosis in which problems of transcultural difference (strictly opposed to multi-cultural diversity) are described as translational processes. This translation is needed as we are lacking the resources to come to terms with the enigmatic state of current society. However, it is not a "successful" translation, as meaning can never be (finally) fixed. Or, to put it differently, it is successful in its failure to come to terms with the cultural enigma that is the postcolonial situation, of a self always infected with otherness. Non-translatability and unreadability, are therefore reconfigured as a form of agency. It is an agency, however, not in any intentional sense, as completely planned activity, not in a humanist sense, starting with a firm subjectivity, but rather an opening of possibilities in the realm of socio-political signification. It takes place in a hegemonial social space that seems to have established binary thought the consequences of which are strict in- and exclusions: e.g. West vs East, male vs female, etc. Here, into these structures of power ambivalence must be reinserted, if the binary order and the narratives it triggers are to be irritated. To reach this goal alternatives to the linear histories of nationhood and national culture have to be proposed. According to Bhabha, this quest for alternative temporalities disables the

---

[10] See Niklas Luhmann (2000b), who argues that the function of the political system is the production of collectively binding decisions. Even if this seems to be a narrow functional view that could be supplemented by other functions, e.g. the production of visible collectives (Nassehi 2002), one should refrain from reducing literature to politics. The very fact that there still is no convincing definition of "literature" might confirm this finding. We simply lack a meta-language for this rather unique language use, i.e. we cannot pinpoint the uniqueness of this mode of language use successfully and are at a loss when trying to grasp its social function.

reliance on traditional dialectial thought, too. There is no sublation or absorption of the particular by the general, as the critic makes clear:

> "Reconstituting the discourse of cultural difference demands more than a simple change of cultural contents and symbols, for a replacement within the same representational time frame is never adequate. This reconstitution requires a radical revision of the social temporality in which emergent histories may be written: the rearticulation of the 'sign' in which cultural identities may be inscribed. [...] Such 'indeterminism' is the mark of the conflictual yet productive space in which the arbitrariness of the sign of cultural signification emerges within the regulated boundaries of social discourse." (1992, 46–47)

Conventional sites of articulation, such as parliamentary politics or state-of-the art political commentary, are hardly appropriate for the task Bhabha assigns, and yet, it is in the regulated boundaries of social discourses that one needs to do justice to the experiences in the West, not of it. It is quite characteristic for his, at times quite opaque, style that Bhabha refrains from spelling out these boundaries. The passepartout word "culture" seems to embrace all forms of contact and communication, and this openness is keys to the accusation of aestheticization. Bhabha himself disapproves of such a reading: "The undecidability of discourse is not to be read as the 'excess of the signifier, as an aestheticization of the formal arbitrariness of the sign" (1992, 50). Aporia, ambivalence, indeterminacy – all of these concepts, as part of a culturalized politics of difference, are taken "outside *object d'art* or beyond the canonization of the 'Idea' of aesthetics"; as such these phenomena "engage with culture as an uneven, incomplete production of meaning and value, often composed of incommensurable demands and practices, and produced in the act of survival." (47)

One can happily accept Bhabha's emphasis on suffering and survival, and the necessity to come to terms with these (post)colonial perspectives. Still – and here I want to come back to literature's potential – how far does his invocation of hybridity feed on a notion of aesthetic negativity? What is the relation of culture, as conceived by Bhabha, to a theory of literature as proposed by Iser, who at times uses a quite similar terminology? Once contrasted with Iser, we can ask Bhabha about the location (and locatability) of cultural hybridity. For, if we refrain from understanding culture simply as "a symbolic textuality" (Bhabha 1992, 47) which is not further conceptually refined, we run the risk of doing what Bhabha himself does when he skips from a diagnosis of hybridity as almost empirical postcolonial phenomenon (as opposed to a contingent construction of an scholarly observer) to an invocation of "the ethical *right to signify*" (49) a bit too swiftly. Despite the legitimacy of such calls, a delimitation of culture as text-tropes – informed by media theory and sociology – seems to be a much-needed task in current scholarship, because it matters if we are talking about interactions, organizations, or function systems, about fleeting face-to-face interactions or the processing of texts that are archived and can be re-read, etc.

Literature is the name we have given to one specific way of textual communication, and it is a most nebulous term. Bhabha himself makes use of literary texts, mostly modernist or postmodernist in design. These highly complex texts force us to slow down our understanding, bringing "normal" communication to a halt, forcing us gently to experience the simultaneity and oscillation of meaning. Here, in the process of reading literature, we are "in-between", too. "The basic characteristic of this space 'in-between'" Winfried Fluck reasons, "is that it is a state between either/or positions, never identical with any of them, but, instead, always moving between them." (180f) Cited approvingly by Fluck, Wolfgang Iser further elaborates: "The resultant dynamic oscillation between the two ensures that their old meanings now become potential sources for new ones. It is such transformations that give rise to the aesthetic dimension of the text, for what had long seemed closed is now opened up again." (Iser, qtd. in Fluck 181) Taking up this lead, Fluck further refines Iser's argument, revealing striking similarities to Bhabha's reading of postcolonial enunciation: "This space in-between should not be understood as a dialectical synthesis, however, that is, as creation of a 'third' position in which the first position and its negation are reconciled. It is a halfway state that is, by definition, not a position, because it can only be conceptualized as an interplay between its constituents." (181) Or, in another quote from Iser's early reflections: "Reconciliation was not a dialectic movement toward synthesis; it was, rather, an interaction of opposites, a telescoping of incompatibles." (qtd. in Fluck 2000, 39)[11]

For all these similarities, the differences between the two thinkers should not be downplayed. The oscillation of meaning that Bhabha attributes to culture in a postcolonial context is turned into the dynamic playfulness of the literary text in Iser's theory. As with any text, however, it needs a reader to be actualized, i.e. to make its sheer potentiality come to life. Best known for his theory of aesthetic response established in seminal contributions such as *The Act of Reading* (1978), Iser is interested in a phenomenology of reading that pays tribute to both the text at hand and the reading subjectivity. Unlike the strictly response-oriented critics, he tracks an "implied reader" at this stage of his career, a reader that is generated by the blanks of the text in question, gaps of meaning the reader needs to fill in. In short, it is a virtual Third Space between text and reader that emerges in the process of reception, and it is in this process that given meanings, and, more importantly even, cultural conventions of meaning making are de-stabilized.[12] Not completely determined by the text, nor an idiosyncratic construction, the meaning of literature stems from the indeterminacy of an interaction between the textual offer and the reader, heuristically conceptualized as empty subjectivity at first, i.e. beyond cultural differences. Most importantly, however, the openness of literature has a distinct temporal dimension. Iser knows all too well that any reading will end and become a 'having-read', that the oscillation of meaning – certainly part of the thrill

---

[11] If Bhabha insists on the engaged mode of his criticism, Iser's literary theory, according to Fluck, is not "a flight from commitment, therefore, but quite the contrary, as a consequent application of the idea of negation, one that also embraces negation itself." (181)

[12] While at the same time these destabilizations are stabilized by a set of institutional patterns of expectations. We usually know when, say, picking up a "novel" that we are leaving the realm of the everyday, that there is a fictional world that might not correspond to the familiar routines in cognitive, emotional, or moral terms.

of literature – is re-stabilized by the sense-making activities of the reader who will have found a way to close the gaps (at least for this time as one can always return to the text in question). The reader will have found explanations for what the respective literary text has, by design, left unexplained. Put differently, meaning itself is a diffuse phenomenon, engendered by fiction's transitory bracketing of reality, by the 'As If' (Iser 1993, 269ff.) of literary communication that allows the actual and the possible to co-exist in a virtual or Third Space.

Bhabha, in contrast, refrains from this location of hybridity almost completely. To him, the openness of signification, the politically empowering crisis of representation, is always at stake, for culture itself is this virtuality that has to iterate its distinctions, its semantics, its addressing and forming of subjects. The enabling space of enunciation, then, emerges in the unceasing process of signification, the time it takes for a signifier to find its signified, a process that cannot be stopped, or that, once (provisionally) ended, begins anew. In such a conceptualization, the Third Space has to be unlocatable, cannot be restricted to the fictionalizing acts that Iser describes; it cannot be contained at all, for the simple fact that sense-making activities of individuals and groups will go on (or culture and society would come to an end).[13] And, given that he relies on the notion of culture as text, Bhabha's model of postcolonial criticism presents an ethics of reading more than a theory of culture.[14] It takes the ethical impulses already embedded in poststructuralist thought and their focus on moments of indecision – the undecidability, untranslatabilities etc. – and invests these strategies of indeterminacy with the new realities of postcolonial self-descriptions of society.

11.3.3 Cultural Difference and the Otherness of Literature

It would be wrong to claim that Iser gets it completely right by restricting himself to "literature", whereas Bhabha unnecessarily delimits his scope. Iser's focus, however, might be of help in pointing to a more nuanced form of criticism. It bears to mention that fictionality is not restricted to those books we find neatly stacked on the "fiction" shelves of our library and favorite bookstores, set apart from non-fiction. In fact, in his later turn "from reader response to literary anthropology", Iser

---

[13] In contrast to this basic cultural sense-making activity, our exposure to literature is, apart from the assigned reading in schools and university curricula, a voluntary act, and we could easily stop taking part in literature.

[14] This should not be taken to suggest that Bhabha has failed in his attempt to offer an interesting study of postcolonial dilemmas, or that his ethics are flawed; nor am I suggesting that one should stop reading books like *The Location of Culture*. Far from it; all I would maintain, however, is that his eager attempt to update a fundamentally Derridean poststructuralism to meet the postcolonial situation, he jumpily juxtaposes writers as different as Fanon and Foucault. One a keen observer of the psychosocial dynamics of interactions, the other the clever analyst of institutional micro-power and archival control, there is no simple link between the logic these writers respectively describe.

would insist that the selection and combination of elements that are part of fictional acts can be found anywhere in culture. What sets literature apart, however, is the fact that it happily discloses its 'As If' function, i.e. it signals that we are exposed to literary texts. Evidently, these signals are conventional rather than timeless, and, in their contingency, open to change, both historically and institutionally, but they will be, Iser insists, always an element of literary communication.

For the real reader, one will have to reflect on the diversity of backgrounds, on the reader's specific knowledge, his or her emotional ties to the themes and topics, the biases and blindness, all of which are brought to bear on the actualization of the virtuality at hand. It is here, then, that cultural differences (e.g. race and ethnicity, gender and sexuality) and social positionalities (class status) can be addressed as influences on the actual reading. For Bhabha's poststructuralist, post-humanist agenda, such a phenomenological level of empty subjectivity is hardly an option; subjectivities are produced within and through the cultural discourses and according to the cultural differences and biases buried in them. It is not reflective individuals using communication, quite the contrary; the appellation and subjection bring forth the subjects in the first place, and, as products of discourses, they are epistemologically on the same level, textualized, i.e. interwoven into the texture of culture. Yet, in order to make claims for subjection – the production of racialized, sexualized selves – there must be some element to be subjected, and this is less than a tautological argument: "Individualization can only be thought of as subjection," Fluck (2007) argues, "if, at least theoretically, a non-subjected individual is set as reference and norm for otherwise subjection could not be conceptualized as such." (74) This notion of a 'non-subjected' element within the social is certainly a most tricky thought, and the cautious formulation "at least theoretically" suggests that, at first, it is nothing more than a figure of non-identity. Yet, this non-identity, in phenomenological criticism, is more than just a figure, and in Iser and Fluck it is the site of reflexivity, a cognitive distance; it is where a potential social agent resides, one who can feed back his experiences into the social operations.

Another term might help understand the different implications of the respective notions of "in-betweenness" and the problem of subjectivity, and this is the notion of the imaginary. In order to come to terms with the driving force behind those cultural projections that refuse to accept the inherent hybridity of any identity claim, Bhabha makes an occasional nod to the psychoanalytical theory of Jacques Lacan, especially his seminal reading of the "mirror stage".

> "The Imaginary is the transformation that takes place in the subject at the formative mirror phase, when it assumes a discrete image, which allows it to postulate a series of equivalences, samenesses, identities, between the objects of the surrounding world. However, this positioning is itself problematic because the subject finds or recognizes itself through an image which is simultaneously alienating and hence potentially confrontational. This is the basis of the close relation between the two forms of identification complicit with the Imaginary – narcissism and aggression. [...] Like the mirror phase 'the fullness' of the stereotype – its image as identity – is always threatened by 'lack'." (Bhabha 1993: 77)

As part of the cultural inventory, the stereotype is characterized by a dual experience of presence and absence: celebratory self-reference and the hurtful destabilization of this self-identification induced by a necessary lack of control. Due to this duality of forces, the power of projection cannot be regulated or brought to a standstill: I see myself through the other, and I see the other. Never, however, is there a sovereign agent. And I see, e.g. as white person, the other whose otherness I have to accept as self-evident. In a predominantly white society, black skin will stand out, whereas it is easier to *not* see whiteness, an experience I want to control but cannot. Bhabha resorts to Fanon, a brilliant predecessor, who pinpointed these irritating glances in his seminal *Black Skin, White Mask* from the perspective to the addressee of projections:

> "'Look, a Negro!' It was an external stimulus that flicked over me as I passed by. I made a tight smile. 'Look, a Negro!' It was true. It amused me. 'Look, a Negro!' The circle was drawing a bit tighter. I made no secret of my amusement. 'Mama, see the Negro! I'm frightened!' Frightened! I made up my mind to laugh myself to tears, but laughter had become impossible. I could no longer laugh, because I already knew that there were legends, stories, history, and above all historicity [...]." (Fanon 1967, 114)

Fanon was a chronicler of the interactive situation, and the psychic loops these encounters cause in the victims of racism. This perspective has to be contrasted with a cultural contact through textual communication, e.g. a mode of analysis that focuses on the archives, on the texts cultivated by society. Texts invite and necessitate re-readings, and, asking for interpretation, are hardly as self-evident as the epiphanic moment sketched by Fanon. Bhabha also calls up such texts – legends, stories, history – in his critical project, yet he remains vague about these medial implications. Moreover, even though he is willing to concede that control is never complete, he fails to fully analyze how we could ever move beyond this vicious circle of racist self-affirmation. More to the point, his criticism habitually includes the interpretation of literary texts, approving these for their potential to subvert the order of discourse, at least momentarily.

In turn, Iser refuses to specify a functionalization of the imaginary in his later work on the anthropology of literature. Because he refrains from associating the concept with a distinct theory, sketching it as an oscillating phenomenon in the "in-between" of emotions, daydreaming, projections, and the whole set of moods known to human-kind, the imaginary turns into the ideal point of reference for his ideas about literary communication. Instead of relying on a neat binarism, e.g. the "distinction between a real and a fictional, imagined reality" (Luhmann 2000a, 143) Iser suggests "to replace this duality with a triad: the real, the fictive, and [...] the imaginary" and claims: "It is out of this triad that the text arises." (1993, 232) The real in this relational model is not reality as such but rather specific models of reality. Reality as pure contingency can never be the referential point for a fictional text. The category of the imaginary is especially important, a featureless, ungraspable one, "not semantic, because it is by its very nature diffuse, whereas meaning becomes meaning through its precision." (ibid.) Anteceding the text and part of the psychic operations, the imaginary, as Paul B. Armstrong succinctly summarizes, "mediates between the fictive and the real and animates their interaction, but it is knowable only through its effects. Not a faculty or an essence, it is the power of human plasticity to create forms, play with the given, and overstep limits." (2000, 213) Fiction, in turn, gives a definite *gestalt* to this incessant flow through the selections and combinations of the text. As an act, the fictive is the site of an intertwining of the real and the imaginary, de-realizing the real and concretizing the imaginary in what Iser calls the "play" of the text.

Aesthetic communication has to be attractive to Bhabha's postcolonial project, we can now infer, as it encompasses a form of negativity that "goes beyond the semantic level of negation to include an 'unformulated and unwritten dimension' of our experience of the literary text." (Fluck 2000, 185) As Fluck reminds us, Iser had already pointed to this dimension in his *Act of Reading*:

> "Blanks and negations increase the density of fictional texts, for the omissions and cancellations indicate that practically all the formulations of the text refer to an unformulated background, and so the formulated text has a kind of unformulated double. This 'double' we shall call negativity [...]. Unlike negations, negativity is not formulated by the text, but forms the unwritten base; it does not negate the formulations of the text, but – via blanks and negations – conditions them. It enables the written words to transcend their literal meaning, to assume a multiple referentiality, and to transcend their literal meaning, to assume a multiple referentiality, and so to undergo the expansion necessary to transplant them as a new experience into the mind of the reader." (qtd. in Fluck 2000, 185)

It is here, in this claim of a specific discursive reality that any conflation of literature and culture as text seems to be an impossible maneuver. Hybridity, in Bhabha's location of culture, is the oscillation of meaning in the (perpetual) moment(s) of significatory indecision. The Third Space he envisions in this postcolonial performativity disturbs the neat cultural conventions of meaning-production, and as such, makes possible acts of negation. This basically defamiliarizing pursuit might help to explain the choice of literary allusions in Bhabha, which are predominantly complex modernist or postmodernist texts. The negations of meaning the scholar finds in them are the fundament of negativity, yet the latter transcends the textually anchored distinctions and differentiations and opens up an experiential reality of its own. Consequently, Iser's attempt to sketch aesthetic dynamics redefines negativity more fundamentally "as effect of a structure of doubling which characterizes the literary text and distinguishes it from other discursive modes by definition." Although made of written language, literature implies a specific use of this medium, and even though a completely satisfying definition of literature is still missing, one can follow Iser's definition as a mode of experience that tends to challenge the stability of the reading subject, necessitating an awareness of the fundamental inaccessibility of individuals to themselves.[15] We know that we do not, cannot (finally) know ourselves. But we can try (again).

Iser convincingly argues that, in the act of reading, we are simultaneously ourselves and someone else, i.e. hybrid creatures for literature's sake. We do not simply see a character in its fictional quest but add imaginary elements to the text in the process of reception, elements that we can see as if from the outside at the same

---

[15] This basic element of aesthetic experience is not a privilege of modernist or postmodernist texts that have given up the securities of realist writing. Negativity, as Iser would argue in his later writings, is a general feature of literature, regardless of questions of aesthetic programs or distinct writing styles.

time. In short, while reading, we are creating alternative versions of ourselves. According to Iser, the reader's required activity "resembles that of an actor, who in order to perform his role must use his thoughts, his feelings and even his body as an analogue for representing something he is not." (1993, 244) If, however, our sense of self is destabilized during reception, then this irritation might well have repercussions for the perception of the Other analyzed in postcolonial studies. It is easy to see that this irritation corresponds with the ethical implications of Bhabha's writing; but one has to concede, too, that *one* possible reaction to this destabilization could be the return to the familiar, the conventional, the known, once the interval of reading has ended and we put down the book.

Although Iser admits shifting uses, his attempt to describe the functionality of fiction remains rather abstract and unspecific, as one would expect in a literary anthropology. Whatever the cultural and historical variances, it is the anthropological founding that counts, and that, according to Iser, connects human creativity with an eternal sense of loss: "Literary fictionality may therefore be regarded as an indication that human beings cannot be present to themselves – a condition which makes us creative (even in our dreams) but never allows us to identify ourselves with the products of our creativity." (1990, 948) This opacity of the psyche to itself, so central to Iser's work, may also be understood as the anthropological precondition for those processes of identity formation via habits, discourses, institutions, which are the main subject of cultural studies. In the multiculturalist politics of recognition, the ascribed identities were not only deconstructed but, as part of a general cultural politics, reconstructed, and to that end, literary texts, musical pieces, and visual arts were demarcated as cultural realms of belonging. Iser, in turn, sees "literary fictions diverge from the fictions of the ordinary world," and the reduction of aesthetic experience to a cultural (or culture-political) register would obviate the transgressive nature of literature, returning it to the realm of ordinary "assumptions, hypotheses, presuppositions." (1990, 951)

Yet, when Iser argues that literary fictions "are always accompanied by convention-governed signs that signalize the 'As If' nature of all the possibilities they adumbrate," the question of cultural difference creeps back in. For what are conventions other than culturally designed patterns of expectations, contingent dynamic structures that are, moreover, loaded with conflictuous interests? This not only opens up the debate about the nature art and aesthetic communication to cultural studies questions. It also provides an understanding of implicit aesthetic values and processes of canonization that could overcome the residual essentialisms of cultural identity discourses. Iser's anthropological model grants cultural difference only after setting up a universal model of the imaginary. Is there only one 'As If' or a whole spectrum? And, as we have learned from Bhabha, if there is diversity, the real issue might well be hybridity. Iser refers mostly to Western or, even more specifically, European literature where there is a 'printed privilege' at work, a focus on a specific segment of literature indebted to a distinct form of print culture. As a consequence, he highlights the individualizing quality of modern art forms, a tendency that was propelled by the historically contingent emergence of silent reading. Those works considered worthy of an expanded canon could well offer alternative avenues of interrogation. For example, Toni Morrison, winner of the

Nobel Prize in 1993, is lauded for her celebration of African American culture and its residuals of oral storytelling and black music styles. Simultaneously, her work is cherished for its intertextual affinities with the pantheon of literature that has up until now been dominated by the so-called canon of dead, white males. Here, scholarly efforts continue to set apart (to borrow a heuristic distinction from Hans Ulrich Gumbrecht (2004)) a presence culture from a meaning culture, the former privileging immediacy of experience, the latter distance and reflexive potentials. One is well advised to dismiss the either-or and work towards a notion of literature's hybrid ties instead; a perspective that can do justice to the political concerns of postcolonial studies by acknowledging the power-structures behind the institutionalization of literature and its complex conventions, while not losing sight of the aesthetic specificities of the literary texts.

References

Althusser, Louis. 1971. *Lenin and Philosophy and Other Essays*. New York: Monthly Review Press.
Armstrong, Paul. 2000. "The Politics of Play: The Social Implications of Iser's Aesthetic Theory." *New Literary History* 31.1: 211–223.
Assmann, Aleida. 1999. "Cultural Studies and Historical Memories." In *The Contemporary Study of Culture*, edited by Bundesministerium für Wissenschaft und Verkehr/Internationales Forschungszentrum Kulturwissenschaften, 85–99. Wien: Turia + Kant.
Bercovitch, Sacvan. 1993. *The Rites of Assent. Transformations in the Symbolic Construction of America*. New York: Routledge.
Bercovitch, Sacvan, and Myra Jehlen. 1986. *Ideology and Classic American Literature*. Cambridge: Cambridge University Press
Bergthaller, Hannes, and Carsten Schinko. 2010. "Keeping Up Appearances: The Democratic Ethos of American Studies in a Polycontextural Society." In *American Studies / Shifting Gears*, edited by Elisabeth Schäfer-Wünsche, Birte Christ, Christian Klöckner, and Michael Butter, 327–348. Heidelberg: Winter.
Bhabha, Homi K. 1992. "Freedom's Basis in the Indeterminate". *October* 61: 46–57.
Bhabha, Homi K. 1993. *The Location of Culture*. London: Routledge.
Butler, Judith. 1997. *Psychic Life of Power. Theories in Subjection*. Stanford: Stanford University Press.
Fanon, Frantz. 1967. *Black Skin, White Masks*. New York: Grove.
Fluck, Winfried. 2000. "The Search for Distance: Negation and Negativity in the Literary Theory of Wolfgang Iser." *New Literary History* 31.1: 175–210.
Fluck, Winfried. 2002. "Aesthetics and Cultural Studies." In *Aesthetics in a Multicultural Age*, edited by Emory Elliott, Louis Freitas Caton and Jeffrey Rhyne, 79–103. Oxford: Oxford University Press
Fluck, Winfried. 2003. "American Culture and Modernity: A Twice-told Tale." In *Theories of American Culture. Theories of American Studies. REAL – Yearbook of Research in English and American Literature 19*, edited by Winfried Fluck and Thomas Calviez, 65–80. Tübingen: Narr
Fluck, Winfried. 2007. "Theories of American Culture (and the Transnational Turn in American Studies)." *REAL - Yearbook of Research in English and American Literature* 23: 59–77.
Fluck, Winfried. 2009. "American Literary History and the Romance with America." In *American Literary History* 21 (1): 1–18.
Gilroy, Paul. 1993. *The Black Atlantic. Modernity and Double Consciousness*. Cambridge: Harvard University Press.

Gumbrecht, Hans Ulrich. 2004. *Production of Presence: What Meaning Cannot Convey*. Stanford: Stanford University Press.
Hannerz, Ulf. 1992. *Cultural Complexity. Studies in the Social Organization of Meaning*. New York: Columbia University Press.
Huck, Christian, and Carsten Schinko. Forthcoming. "Die Wahrnehmung der Systemtheorie: das In-Between der Interaktion." In *Differenz(theorien). (Wie) können sich Postkoloniale Theorie und Systemtheorie beobachten?* Edited by Mario Grizelj und Daniela Kirschstein. Berlin: Kadmos.
Iser, Wolfgang. 1978. *The Act of Reading: A Theory of Aesthetic Response*. Baltimore: Johns Hopkins University Press.
Iser, Wolfgang. 1990. "Fictionalizing: The Anthropological Dimension of Literary Fictions." *New Literary History* 21.4: 939–955.
Iser, Wolfgang. 1993. *Prospecting: From Reader Response to Literary Anthropology*. Baltimore: Johns Hopkins University Press.
Kessler-Harris, Alice. 1992. "Cultural Locations: Positioning American Studies in the Great Debate." *American Quarterly* 44.3: 299–313.
Lenz, Guenter. 2002. "Toward a Dialogics of International American Culture Studies. Transnationality, Border Discourses, and Public Culture(s)." In *The Future of American Studies*, edited by Donald E. Pease and Robyn Wiegman, 461–485. Durham: Duke University Press.
Lewis, Richard W. B. 1955. *The American Adam. Innocence, Tragedy, and Tradition in the Nineteenth Century*. Chicago: University of Chicago Press.
Luhmann, Niklas. 2000a. *Art as Social System*. Stanford: Stanford University Press.
Luhmann, Niklas. 2000b. *Die Politik der Gesellschaft*. Frankfurt/M.: Suhrkamp.
Marx, Leo. 1964. *The Machine in the Garden. Technology and the Pastoral Ideal in America*. New York: Oxford University Press.
Marx, Leo. 2003. "Believing in America: An intellectual project and a national ideal." *Boston Review* 28.6: 28–31.
Nassehi, Armin. 2002. "Politik des Staates oder Politik der Gesellschaft? Kollektivität als Problemformel des Politischen." In *Theorie der Politik. Niklas Luhmanns politische Soziologie*, edited by Kai-Uwe Hellmann and Rainer Schmalz-Bruns. 38–59. Frankfurt/M.: Suhrkamp.
Nassehi, Armin. 2008. *Soziologie: Zehn einführende Vorlesungen*. Wiesbaden: VS Verlag.
Parrington, Vernon Louis. 1927–1930. *Main Currents in American Thought. Vol. I-III*. New York: Harcourt, Brace, and Company.
Rourke, Constance. 1931. *American Humor. A Study of the National Character*. New York: Harcourt, Brace and Company.
Said, Edward W. 1978. *Orientalism*. New York: Vintage.
Schinko, Carsten. 2007. "America as Medium: Culture and its Others." In Transnational American Studies. REAL – Yearbook of Research in English and American Literature 23, edited by Winfried Fluck, Stefan Brandt and Ingrid Thaler, 133–162. Tübingen: Narr
Smith, Henry Nash. 1950. *Virgin Land: The American West as Symbol and Myth*. Cambridge: Harvard University Press.
Smith, Henry Nash. 1957. "Can 'American Studies' Develop a Method?" *American Quarterly* 9.2: 197–208.
Stäheli, Urs. 1998. "Politik der Entparadoxierung. Zur Artikulation von Hegemonie- und Systemtheorie. " In *Das Undarstellbare der Politik. Zur Hegemonietheorie Ernesto Laclaus*, edited by Oliver Marchart, 52–66. Wien: Turia & Kant.
Taylor, Charles. 1992. *Multiculturalism and the Politics of Recognition*. Princeton: Princeton University Press.
Wägenbaur, Thomas. 2000. "'East, West, Home's Best'. Homi K. Bhabha's and Salman Rushdie's Passage to 'Third Space'." In *Colonizer and Colonized*, edited by Theo d'Haen and Patricia Krüs, 109–122. Amsterdam: Rodopi
Wolfe, Alan. 2003. "Anti-American Studies. The Difference between Criticism and Hate." *New Republic* 10: 25–32.

Chapter 12
The Agony of the Signified: Towards a Usage-Based Theory of Meaning and Society

Remigius Bunia

Abstract The present paper proposes to accept a usage-based theory of communication, as recently advanced by developmental psychology and cognitive linguistics. With respect to semiotics, this change of theoretical design means to abandon the belief that verbal language is strongly connected to reasoning; it drops the distinction between signifier and signified; and it draws attention to the blurry difference between "ordinary things" and signs. It turns out that, in fact, only essentially hybrid objects exist whose communicative "parts" can hardly be disentangled from their non-communicative "parts." The present paper assesses a theory of communication which does not depart from language but asks what one can *do* with things. Such a question leads to an examination of the conditions governing mental representation, social interaction, and abstract analysis. Nonetheless, it finally explores why language is so important in increasing social complexity and in creating mental representations of the world – even though it cannot be equated with reasoning and abstract thought.

The distinction between signifier and signified appears to be well established; its widespread use indicates that the concept is considered quite precise. However, de Saussure's (2006 [1916]) initial idea very much differs from the vulgar, dominating terminology that identifies the signifier with the physical sound of speech or the printed word and the signified with a corresponding mental idea. This terminology is inherited from Cartesian dualism, which separates the soul from the body: the signifier is considered a solid part of tangible reality while the signified only exists in a speaker's mind. But this configuration is simplistic and cannot account for more thorough insights, such as the idea of a reality structured by communication on the one hand, and the knowledge of the material foundations of mental ideas in the brain on the other.

De Saussure's general linguistics was more refined and aware of the intricacy inherited from the body/soul model. De Saussure insists on the fact that both the signifier and the signified are only mental images. In doing so he does not overcome the Cartesian body/soul difference altogether, but locates all processes of signification on the soul side only. He denies connecting images to solid and tangible phenomena and thus tries to ignore the body side. His students and most of the formalist school did not follow him in that: they inserted the referent into semiotic theory to have a material counterpart of the signified; and many saw matter-like qualities in the signifier, which was conflated with the physical stream of sounds and with the visible words on paper. From then on, a permanent problem of semiotic theory has been to differentiate between signified and referent. The signified is considered the abstract meaning of a word (the denotation), whereas the referent is the distinct object which an expression can refer to. The late twentieth century sparked a debate over the "nature" of reference and denotation, the poststructuralist and the analytic views being the most eccentric contributions.

Doubts now arise as to whether the popular, the Saussurian or the referent-based configuration is still acceptable and in agreement with our views on reality. I am going to deepen these doubts and show that processes of signification and communication can only be understood if the inseparability of material and mental processes is accepted, that is, if the hybridity of all elements of communication is accepted. This hybridity no longer allows seeing signification and meaning as *pure* phenomena that can be detached from actual, material processes, and that can be analytically prescinded from their involvement with things. The central problem is body/soul dualism itself. In the Cartesian tradition, mental processes and communication are thought of as entirely detached from tangible reality. Theories such as analytic realism or constructivism tacitly accept this dualism and try to work around it. In the following discussion, however, I wish to emphasize the role of things and observable processes, and reject the body/soul difference altogether. In a movement of thought that has very much benefited from Latour's (2006 [1991], 2005) and Rancière's (2008 [2003]) ideas about the importance of material reality, I am going to present an understanding of communication and verbal language that drops dualism. The idea of the purity of two spheres can be overcome by recognizing that mental processes are identifiable only if they are "materially existent." I am going to attack this idea of purity by identifying the use of things within material processes.

Although Homi Bhabha's concept of hybridity is not essential to my venture, his idea of an irreducible "ambivalence of hybridity" (2000 [1994], 162) comes from observations similar to mine. Bhabha denies that it is possible to define a domain of pure and controlled signification. Although he apparently does not dismiss the concepts of signifier and signified, he shows that they presuppose moot semiotic postulations of purity. I argue that *any* assumption of semiotic purity is amiss – not only in the postcolonial context. The expression *hybridity* does not hint at objects of a specific quality but rather stresses that the acknowledged schemes of explaining cultural and meaningful phenomena are based on a strong division between the material and the mental sphere. This is the trail I will follow in this paper. Hybridity plays an essential role for my argument, even though it will not be mentioned explicitly very often.

As Bennett and Hacker state (2003, 111–114), philosophy and neuroscience have not yet abandoned body/soul dualism. In part, the Cartesian concept of mind is simply and crudely replaced by the neuroscientist's concept of brain. They explain that this is why current explanations of consciousness are inadequate. In fact, this problem has to do with conceptions of symbols and language (here, Bennett and Hacker unfortunately adhere too much to conventional notions). But they are right in pointing out that philosophy still assumes that there is an immaterial sphere. I claim that we are used to locating signifieds in this mental sphere, instead of scrutinizing material processes of symbol use. This also includes the social which also "takes place" in the material world. As Latour puts it: "When any state of affairs is split into one material component to which is added as an appendix a social one, one thing is sure: this is an artificial division imposed by the disciplinary disputes, not by any empirical requirement" (2005, 83).

Although I do not believe in the suitability of the concepts, of signifying and signified, I would readily admit that a difference between "bringing forth signification" and "relating to knowledge" can be made. It would be a folly to assume that there is no difference whatsoever between using the word "trees" and thinking of trees, yet some ambiguities should be borne in mind: when one thinks of either the word "tree" or of a tree in the park, in both cases a mental image and a relation to real-world phenomena (such as a sound in the case of the word) are involved; to bring forth signification can add to knowledge or even produce knowledge; and signification not only points to existing or emerging knowledge, but also presupposes it. The task is to describe signification without relying on the subjective and "merely" psychical concepts of image and mental ideas.

The overall purpose of the final section of this paper is to explain to what extent language plays an important role in creating a complex society (which includes complex communication), even if the claim is correct that language is neither essential for human reasoning nor a means to represent reality. This claim is directed against a strong tradition in Western philosophy. However, it does not imply that "exact meaning" is an illusion, but it states that precision is rather a rare case, strictly confined to particular fields of social interaction and a product of a long and complicated cultural evolution. In order to show *why* language does play such an important role in society, I must first of all explain to what extent language does *not* so much differ from other "things" that are used as a means of communication.

12.1 Towards a Theory of Communication

12.1.1 *Some Remarks on the History of Semiotics*

When one is thinking of a tree, there is an image of a tree, the knowledge of how the tree behaves, and some ideas about what one can do with the tree. However, when one is bringing to one's mind the word "tree," there is an image of "tree," the knowledge of how "tree" behaves, and some options of what one can do with "tree." Both tree and "tree" have solid or physical realizations such as wooden things in the park or plastic things made of Lego on the one hand, and ink on paper or sound waves on the other. Both also have rather abstract or mental instances such as family trees or memorized sound images. Then what is the difference between tree and "tree"?

The starting point of my argument is the rather basic insight that words are things in the world.[1] Since the rationalistic period (the 17th century) we have become used to keeping things and words strictly apart from each other. In antiquity, this was different: words and things (*res* and *verba*) occupied the same topical space. Even though Quintilian distinguished the signifying ("quae significant," 2001 [~80]: 3.5.1) from the signified ("quae significantur," *ibid.*), thus using the diathesis and the lexical stem Saussure would pick out more than 1,800 years later, both were related to each other in the topical matrix where things, arguments, processes, words, and whole phrases had their own place and could move between places (in metaphorical speech, for instance). The rationalists, however, claimed that language is in perfect accordance with thought, and thought was considered a sphere completely detached from tangible things. Descartes famously distinguished the *res cogitans* from the *res extensa* (Descartes 2005 [1641], 118). Reasoning expressed itself in language. A precise and logical language was deemed possible even if this meant to purge vague expressions. Arnauld's and Nicole's *Logic of Port-Royal* (1964 [1683]) provided rules governing such a clarified speech. They defined a sign as an object that represents another object: "Mais quand on ne regarde un certain objet que comme en représentant un autre, l'idée qu'on en a est une idée de signe, & ce premier objet s'appelle signe" (1964 [1683], 55).[2] The sign is here barely seen as an object (even if it is called so), for it is an object which hides itself as to make another object visible. It conveys the idea of the original object, and hence the sign (as an object) practically disappears. The rationalistic model of a sign cannot look at the solid, matter-like aspect of a sign, but, metaphorically speaking, sees through the sign to look at the original object (see Wellbery 1984).

Despite the many differences in detail, the school of empiricism followed the same line: it questioned the possibility of a precise verbal description and, in doing so, dismissed anything based on language as artificial and unreal. As for the details, the empiricists differed from the rationalists in that they did not equate reasoning and language – which is why until today some natural scientists deny that the humanities are of any use because they only deal with words. Nevertheless, they

---

[1] This was already Augustine's starting point: "omne signum etiam res aliqua est" (1826 [427]: 11), that is, "every sign is some thing." Augustine adds that the reverse is not true ("non autem omnis res etiam signum est," *ibid.*), but we shall see that such a distinction is inaccurate.

[2] My translation: "But when one takes an object as something which only represents another object, the idea one has of it is related to signification, and the first object is called *sign*."

detached methods of description (measured quantity) from the physical phenomenon itself (physical quantity) as clearly as the rationalists. With Galilei and Newton the sciences eventually took another direction which separated them from philosophically grounded empiricism: mathematics became, as Galilei had put it, the language of the (physical) nature. This made it possible not to admit any difference between a differential equation and the observable data.[3] The mathematical model upheld the strict division between the description and the described. In the twentieth century, however, physicists noticed that observations affect the behavior of energy and matter that predominate at the atomic scale. This led to the insight that some phenomena of reality must not be considered as independent from their examination. Physics thus demonstrated that neither the rationalist nor the early empiricist model of meaning suits all phenomena in the world.

With modern mechanics established, language was no longer essential for describing nature. The mathematical model grew more valuable than its verbal interpretation. In fact, this meant abandoning equating human reasoning with the human capacity to use language. Yet this "equation" has held almost throughout the history of Western philosophy, and it was boosted by rationalism and reaffirmed by the philosophy of language. It is now being defied by recent research on language. The latest studies that aim to explain the essential properties of human communication tend not to stress linguistic abilities. Tomasello (2003a, b) singles out the capacity of social sympathy as the faculty empowering humans to surpass simple conditioning in which many animals also succeed. He underscores the fact that complex communication can be achieved by means other than verbal. The most important example is sign language (think also of body language in general). It can attain the same complexity as spoken language. With regard to the sciences just mentioned, many hybrid devices are used, showing that verbal language is not powerful or functional enough to be used. One can think of diagrams – not only in the sciences, but also in everyday statistics (in newspapers or in the web, for instance); in many fields of social life, one uses tables and figures, arithmetic (including the use of banknotes and coins for a purchase), complex mathematical formulas and expressions, and so on.

12.1.2 Words Are Things (Signs Versus Ordinary Things)

I am now going to argue in favor of a non-dualist theory of communication as sketched out in the introduction. In view of the non-verbal communicative hybrids, I will try to figure out how signification emerges by considering the practical *use* of communicative tools. The theory will be usage-based in Tomasello's sense (2003a). It will ask what one can do with verbal and nonverbal entities and compare trees to

---

[3] Some still posit that the equation merely presents an interpretation.

"trees." This theoretical design will finally lead to an explanation of why language, as a special and extraordinary communicative tool, is so crucial in creating complex societies and therefore, in many fields, superior to other means of communication.

My starting point is the aforementioned observation that words and all kinds of signs are things that are used as other things are. When someone uses a thing, it can be a word or another kind of thing, but in both cases, she is engaged in communication – or at least some observer may believe she is. I will say *ordinary things* from now on to indicate things that are "ordinarily" not taken for signs (despite the apparent fact that signs are "an ordinary part" of everyday reality). The distinction between signs and ordinary things is blurry (though I will do my best to clarify it). When *all* things can be used in order to grant communicative options, both signs and ordinary things cannot be kept apart by saying that the former are used in communication and the latter not. If what I have said is right, every attempt to draw a sharp distinction between action and communication is futile because nonverbal action almost always has a communicative side-effect and communication cannot be produced without any kind of action.

Since these distinctions are so difficult to draw, I will speak of a *participant* when a person is assumed to be involved in communication in order to accentuate that a person can simply "participate" in a situation without any communicative intentions (from her point of view) and without speaking, but that this may be sufficient to call this participation a partaking in communication. The sketch presented here is phenomenological insofar as it only considers what informative material an observer of the world has (whether it be the participant herself or another observer of the situation). A participant attends to a situation which offers her so many cues that she reacts to them. With this phenomenological terminology I avoid the expressions *sender* and *receiver,* which silently assume that the one who sends a message knows about this effusion of information, and that the one who receives a signal interprets it as being sent. Although it is of course true that many participants understand some of their actions as successful or failed attempts to send a message, and although many participants plausibly identify sent messages as such, this labeling does not essentially characterize the communication taking place.[4]

A participant comes into contact with trees and "trees." I will discuss the difference between both in relation to how the participant *reacts* to either of them. She has her knowledge and her sensual data only, and the contact with both trees and "trees" is provided by her senses (by seeing or hearing either trees or "trees"). This is again seen from a phenomenological perspective. When a participant has learnt to identify certain things as distinct from others, and as belonging to

---

[4] Instead communication seems to be a basic behavior that many species on earth (for instance insects, see Hölldobler and Wilson 2009) employ to influence their fellows. It is not clear which the capacities are that enable humans to use such refined and complex means of communication (see Tomasello 2003a, Tomasello/Rakoczy 2003b). In the present paper, I present some characteristics that could contribute to these outstanding human abilities (abstract signs, for instance).

one class (say: trees), she has the choice of how to respond to being exposed to them. I propose to analyze the idea of "meaning" in terms of how many options this exposure offers and of which kind they are. When a participant sees a tree, what can she do with this sight? What can she do with a book, with a cooking knife, with a dishwasher? What can she do with a printed word?

The first problem is to say what a thing is, that is, what defines its unity (see Quine 1960). As for ordinary things, it is clear that the recognition of their unity depends on both acquired knowledge and physiological predisposition (see Peterson 2005 [2001]). But this is also true of signs, of course. Saussure tackled the question of what a communicative entity or unity is; he asked what a sign is and concluded that any combination of signs has the same qualities that its components have; the new sign is not simply a composition of two signs but a sign of its own. Without explicitly stating the consequence, he took every grammatical phrase, every sentence, and every speech for a sign. Things can be combined and become things of another nature (a colored cloth on a pole becomes a flag, syrup and champagne become Kir, and so on). Therefore, it is not so important if there are elementary entities: their combination does not say much about the result, and it is sufficient to recall the simple case of lexical composites to see the arbitrariness (why is a house-keeper not someone who owns a house?[5]). Certainly, the syntagmatic combination of elements does produce sense in a fairly predictable way, but, firstly, the predictability very much depends on the strength of the conditioning laid down in the elements, and, secondly, the regularities of syntagmatic combination add a specific sense of their own to the elements (see Langacker 2008). Syntax produces meaning. The result can be generalized: it is not clear and it cannot be clear what constitutes the unity of a sign or an ordinary thing. Every contact with reality requires an observer to analyze which entities there are.

This is why I stick to Langacker's notion of *thing*. He defines a thing as broadly as possible "as any product of grouping and reification" (2008, 105). This means that, for instance, a (reified) movement is a thing in Langacker's terminology. Reification produces many abstractions because it translates processes into compact entities, so "acceleration" and "tax increase" are signs that refer to *things* and to specific uses. Moreover, the way things relate to each other can be conveyed by means of specific combinations of signs (morphology and syntax in language). These structures can express movements, changes, and modifications of things. As Langacker points out throughout his book, they are rooted in basic processes of perception and structuring. However, they allow a participant to form abstract notions of things and processes, a point I am going to dwell upon in the next section of this paper.

While this indicates another similarity between ordinary things and signs, I would like to call attention to a simple but instructive difference: a sign is often a highly structured experience that would seem useless (without use!) if it were not

---

[5] This is an example Boris Gasparov gave in a lecture to illustrate de Saussure's concept of arbitrariness.

considered to *say* something. Since a participant has to decide what a distinct phenomenon is, printed or uttered words consist of recurring patterns that massively differ from other real-world sensations. This notion of sign is also very strongly connected to Tomasello's description of intention: to put a very structured thing before my eyes makes me think that I should draw my attention to it; if someone puts it there, I assume that it is her *intention* to influence my attention; if I do not see anyone placing it there, I tend to conclude that someone has had a specific intention in producing it. It is the central part of the secularization of Western thinking to admit that an intention is not the only explanation for highly structured objects, such as humans, plants, physical laws, or improbable coincidences. While pre-rationalistic models of signification accepted natural signs (which tacitly point to their author, God, or in polytheistic religions, to rival deities) alongside signs made by humans, rationalistic and modern semiotics only discusses "artificial" signs. However, attribution of intention (instead of, say, improbability) is a rather contingent option that tempts humans to assume wrong causalities but allow them at the same time to develop very complex communication, above all language. If this is right, the handicap of overestimating authorship is easily outbalanced by the capacity to communicate. But again, this dissimilarity does not explain very much. Many ordinary things are also highly structured (cars, for instance) without being considered signs in themselves. Some signs in everyday use (such as hand-waving) possess minimal structure. Even if signs seem to be often "different" from "ordinary" experience, this does not explain anything.

Despite the hybridity of communicational situations and despite the impossibility of separating "truly" communicative tools from "mere" things, it is evident that some kind of difference between "tree" and tree exists. Words provide specific and special features that they do not share with ordinary objects. To explain this difference, I will analyze three essential cases: 1° words which seem to identify an object (such as "tree"), 2° social speech, and 3° abstract concepts. These cases do not entail a complete typology; their division is even not systematic. But they are the most essential cases one has to cope with to describe communication.

12.1.3 Mental Signs

Some signs seem to stand for a specific ordinary object; they are used as their "representation." But the relation between things and "their" signs is by no means "natural," that is, it is arbitrary to compare suitcases with "suitcases" and to suggest that each ordinary thing has its counterpart sign. The rationalist and empiricist doctrines of the 17th century influenced the way in which reference would be understood. They replaced a model of signification, which included tense relationships between things and words by a model which made word-thing pairings the default case of sign use. (This is why spiritual uses of things suddenly became semiotically suspect and problematic; I only mention the famous case of the body of Christ and the bread as discussed in the *Logic of Port-Royal*, see

Arnauld and Nicole 1964 [1683], 124–128.) The new model had to ignore less clear uses of signs, and it had to dismiss all "rhetoric" devices because they no longer seemed to be useful means to evoke more specific ideas, but mere extravagant ornaments at best and manipulations at worst.

I am now going to contrast what a participant can do with an ordinary thing compared to a sign. The first task must be to investigate the seemingly simple relationship between a thing and "its" representing sign. These signs shall be called *object signs*. To equate sign and representation, that is, to reduce all signs to object signs, is a classic definition of signs and is usually credited to Augustine. Although, in fact, Augustine's definition is not restricted to object signs, it has been understood this way: for him a sign is "aliud aliquid ex se faciens in cogitationem venire" (1826 [427], 42), that is, something which makes something else come into one's mind. He discusses Christ's feet, which can invoke a specific idea, and includes natural signs as well as artificial signs. The major characteristic is an inner image popping up at the sight of a certain thing. Modern rationalist semiotics sharply divides natural and artificial signs (since the 17th century), resolving the former into a general notion of causality and shifting the latter into a mental insubstantial sphere. Semiotic models always imply theories of causality, to which they can be reduced. Until the 17th century, signs were the effects of some natural or artificial processes. The 17th century focused on the effects that are intended by a person and equated signification with deliberate reasoning. My proposal is to return to Augustine's idea and to understand semiotics by the effects things cause and in particular what distinguishes the effects of those things that are considered signs. Seen from the perspective of causality, the problem of Augustine's definition is that it encompasses simply everything. There is almost nothing that would not bring *anything* into one's mind. This is also the problem of pre-rationalist and rationalist models of signification: which effects of natural or artificial processes are or are not to be taken as signs remains contingent.

First of all, an object usually brings the idea of the object itself into mind (this is what Augustine hints at). This is a point which, for opaque reasons, is very often overlooked. When a participant is (more or less attentively) looking at a suitcase, this sight invokes the *idea* of a suitcase. Some objects would not call upon a specific idea, but such objects usually do not have a name the participant knows (for obvious reasons, I cannot give an example). To combine an object with a communicative label (such as a word) and to associate a specific idea with the sight are two events that usually concur at the same time and which in fact *imply* the very identification of the object.

Object signs have a very simple but far-reaching property. They are perceivable entities which can evoke some of the mental sensations associated with specific other things of the tangible reality ("a tree" makes me imagine a tree). Since it is difficult to define unities of ordinary things and to find exact matches of signs and ordinary things in all cases (what is a unicorn?), I will speak of *mental signs*. Mental signs are things that evoke sensual images or make me simulate a process or a situation mentally. This is how we shift the original idea of representation to another level.

It is now possible to compare the use of ordinary things to that of signs. Let me take the example of suitcases and "suitcases." One can put something inside an instance of suitcase, but not inside an instance of "suitcase." When a participant sees the word "suitcase" and compares the sight of the word "suitcase" with a suitcase, the major difference between both objects is not the mental idea both evoke, but the actions she can perform by using either. In this sense she can do *less* with "suitcases" than with suitcases. It is important to note that the sight of a suitcase always reminds a participant of what she can do with it; thus a suitcase always includes the potential use of a "suitcase," which does nothing more than make a participant think of a suitcase. In spite of that, signs possess qualities which outdo ordinary things. One among them is evident: it would be awkward if a participant had to show a suitcase whenever she wished to evoke its image. Signs are "easier at hand" than ordinary things. But since this advantageous quality pertains to all "lightweight" signs, not only to object signs, this discussion shall be postponed to one of the subsequent sections.

So what is wrong with considering mental signs as tools with which to represent ordinary things? Nothing. As I have stressed, semiotic models are nothing but models of causality. The rationalist and empiricist views of causality, based on logic, mathematics, experiments, and (from the 19th century on) statistics, were much better able to contribute to explanations of natural phenomena than precedent methods. This is why their partly subjacent, partly explicit idea of what a sign is could be so pervasive. It was accepted and spread widely. The logic of its success is easily explained as follows. If a sign can indeed be understood as a thing that, by being learnt, conditions certain modes of use, there is no reason why a participant would not have to learn to consider signs as tools of representation. There is no fault with this, and the present-day notion of what signs are is still grounded on this education. Yet it bars (and has done so until today) the view on the more complex interactions taking place in communication; it denies the equally important role of ordinary things in communication, and it degrades non-referential language (such poetic language or fiction) to exceptional or even parasitic cases. All this is misleading and encumbers the development of an adequate theory of language.

A final question remains with respect to mental signs: why could I not stick to the notion of signified and claim that the signified is the mental image of the possible actions, an image corresponding with the signifier, the thing that makes me associate these actions? In Saussure's definition of the sign, there is no thinkable separation of signifier and signified; there is no mental image of one without the other. Thus, he states that the coherent idea associated with a signifier only exists as long as there *is* a signifier. In fact, this supports the idea that a coherent reasoning is based on the use of language. However, I would argue that there is nothing which binds and collects the idea of possible actions; the mental image of a word is not directly linked with a set of actions. Of course, there can be strong conditions which would prohibit many inadequate responses, but the more frequent cases of weak and very weak conditions invite the participant to assemble the things around her in an ever new fashion that depends on her state of mind and on the particular experience in this moment.[6]

12.2 Social and Performative Signs

The word "suitcase" reminds a participant of a suitcase, but many words do not provide such material associations. While so-called abstract words such as "strength" and "resiliency" effect a material, senses-based meaning and can thus be taken as mental, it is very difficult to imagine a sensual experience associated with "nation," "taxes," or "methodology." These words are things offering options that are restricted to giving new options within communication itself. This is to say that their use is limited to diversifying further communicative actions, but they do not in the first place relate to ordinary things, sometimes not even remotely. I will call them *social signs*. Not all social signs are words: one can think of traffic signs, curbs, and gestures. It is very illuminating that these things are usually called *signs* in everyday and professional language. It seems to be clear that they somehow belong to the sphere of words. It is not because they have a communicative function and ordinary things do not (because every thing can have a communicative function), but because they have no uncommunicative function.[7]

Signs are by no means conventional in all cases – at least if one calls a meaning *conventional* only if it is defined by explicit contract or definition (for instance mathematical definitions, legal terms, etc.). Even traffic signs are not conventional but a matter of learning and custom. Only recently has judicial theory begun to realize that the awareness of norms does not originate in explication and proclamation, but in education. This is why a change of laws cannot easily change behavior, even if there is a wish to comply with the regulations (see Towfigh 2008). However, if the instruction is explicit, the object can become a conventional sign, that is, an object whose use is well known and accepted by mutual agreement. In such cases, the possible uses are sanctioned by the use of previous social signs; the "contract" is based on communication. An agreement is impossible without an explicit commitment to its content, and such a commitment can only be conveyed socially.

An agreement requires accepted signs of acquiescence. A participant *does* something by speaking. She then uses a *performative sign*. It is Austin's (1975 [1962]) initial idea to distinguish between constative and performative signs, a distinction he himself blurred for good reasons. (The constative sign is more or less

---

[6] This is no comment on the question of how much choice or free will a human being has. In fact, I am afraid that the question itself is only a philosophical artifact that cannot be rephrased in biological, physical, juridical, or even psychological terms without confusion.

[7] Of course, there is always the possibly of misuse. One can use a traffic sign as a weapon. In fact, one then uses the metal rather than the traffic sign, but the traffic sign is misused in any case.

equivalent to the mental sign in my terminology.) A performative sign differs from a constative sign in that the former cannot be replaced by a nonverbal object, and the behavioral options it allows are primarily verbal.[8] It is therefore a special case of the social sign, distinguished by the fact that the use of the sign is an act. An act is an event which is considered to change the state of the world. This in fact means that a performative sign is not so much characterized by general patterns of communication but by the delineation between act and receptive activity, a delineation that depends on concepts of free will, social responsibility, and so on, that is, on various complex social signs.

12.2.1 Abstract Signs and Sentences

Entire sentences do something quite different from social signs – they describe states and processes; they relate things to each other. All in all, they link communication to the human capacity of abstract reasoning and retrieving patterns of a higher order. I will speak of *abstract things* or *abstract signs* if things are combined to create a virtual experience and to evoke an idea that is only in part based on former experience. The combination of things in language is what allows a participant to do more with signs than with ordinary things. It is this very virtuality which empowers language so much. When a participant employs the abstract devices a language provides, she can evoke an idea that goes far beyond any idea an ordinary thing could suggest. The power of abstract combination originates from the human ability to imagine and to virtually analyze a situation, that is, from learning by experience and education the principles of possible real-world organization. However, it does not derive from the signs themselves. In fact, one has to acquire the knowledge of an effective use of language in order to combine signs in abstract thought. The advantage of abstract and sign-based combination is that the virtuality allows a participant to plan and evaluate a combination in her mind and to communicate it without much labor. The latter point is even more important. It allows a society to share new ideas of organization and leads to inventions and innovations.

It is an important insight from usage-based theory that not all sentences are built up with the use of variation and free combination (see Tomasello 2003a). To put it differently: not every sentence makes a new virtual experience emerge. A sentence is thus not automatically abstract only because it always relates two things to each other. Most of the sentences present a well known experience or idea, even if they

---

[8] An example: If I promise to give someone a gift, that means that she has the option to remind me of my obligation. It does not include handing out the gift. If a judge sentences me to five years in prison, the decision itself only communicates to policemen that they have the right to imprison me. The performative sign itself changes the behavioral options because the policemen could refer to the court decision when detaining me and would have to justify themselves if they let me go. That is, the court decision itself gives verbal options.

are expressed by the combination of signs which could be used in other contexts. For example: "I'm at home." This sentence relates me to a place and defocuses my activity; it does not say what I am doing at home. However, the expression is so fixed that its meaning does not derive from the combination of two things (me and my home), but becomes a sign of its own. To speak foreign languages often means to display one's ignorance of common expressions: even if one knows the "grammar," one makes collocation errors and does not speak "idiomatically." Common grammar is only a rough approach to describing a language.

In such a view, sentences ("propositions") can generally neither match nor mismatch with reality because they are signs which will be used themselves or just ignored. This is to say that signs can be used in specific situations as other things can, and they have no structural link with facts. Their validity ("truth") amounts to their usability only. The idea of correspondence with reality therefore only makes sense in an abstract epistemic structure that lays out strict rules determining when something is the case. Propositions expressed in a scientific language, for instance, can match or mismatch with reality. Such schemes (as scientific reasoning) include meta-rules which experience has shaped and which encapsulate knowledge about basic principles of causality and describability. Logic and applied mathematics are the most common and successful examples of such meta-rules. Coherence only applies to epistemic structures with well established meta-rules. An everyday description of reality, however, cannot be checked for coherence because in general the verbal description lacks a criterion or a pragmatic rule for clarity.

An apparent critique would contend that the sentence "she's not at home" can either be true or false. The problem is that such an analysis of the propositional content of the sentence misses the essential point of its use. The sentence evokes the impression of someone being at home; and the purpose of the sentence much depends on the situation. For example, it can be employed to prevent someone from visiting the aforementioned person. In this case, the sentence can either succeed or fail in influencing someone's action. The utterance, however, would not prompt a mental image totally disconnected from the person's location. It can of course make the participant assume that she has been lied to. Then she assumes that the aforementioned person *is* at home, but this does not mean to attribute a truth value to the proposition, but to ascribe to the speaker an abuse of the phrase. Mendacity exists, but it should not be analyzed in terms of truth values, but in terms of behavior and communicative manipulation.

Truth is important when the world is to be described independently from what a specific participant wishes to do. Abstract epistemic structures are often coherent even if none of them is complete. For example, mathematics, physics, and chemistry are coherent. But even though mathematics contains no apparent contradictions, it has actually shown that it cannot prove its own consistency, that is, the absence of any contradiction. In all other fields one has minor or major drawbacks that derogate consistency. Yet, there is coherence because the meta-rules governing these regimes of thought clearly set what a correct argument is and, hence, what a true and a false proposition must be (even if a particular decision cannot be made for given reasons). Coherence is a matter of construing a scientific or scholarly epistemic scheme which fulfills the rules it states. It can be more or less applicable to specifically delimited parts of the world (for example, physics for the measurable quantities). Since it includes knowledge about the construction of verities (such as logic), it can even allow a participant to draw conclusions about reality by mere reasoning and without any new contact with reality. Again, this is nothing that language enables her to do, but the capability of finding second-order and third-order patterns in the world.

12.3 The Supremacy of Language

12.3.1 Conditions and Modularization

If one tries to understand communication, it is, after what I have said, the wrong approach to single out language. Language provides some rather specific communicative possibilities, which are very relevant for complex societies but not characteristic of elementary communicative processes. All things, whether signs or ordinary things, have an impact on communication, and the role language plays is difficult to assess. After all, the purpose of language is *not* to represent ideas (neither socially nor mentally). And the mind does *not* work by means of language. Communication allows the conveyance of experience and control of human behavior. It produces very rich and powerful cultural and social institutions. But why and how can communication contribute to expansive social complexity and very eminent abstractions?

The first step in answering this is to look at the purpose of limiting selectable actions. (It turns out that such restrictions enhance social complexity.) First of all, fewer options, and above all more specific ones, increase the probability of controllable actions and reactions. To utter "go out now" makes a participant either go out or deny that request.[9] The connection of language tokens and actions allows the society to program complex institutions such as administration, science, and law.[10] Society can thus implement "systems" that control behavior beyond individual intention.

---

[9] An arm stretched out pointing to the door, however, can operate in quite the same way even if it can, in given contexts, say quite different things, such as "this is the door that must be repaired." By the way, there are only very few options which apply to *all* use of language (such as someone being out of acoustic reach, being deaf, playing a role on the stage, and so on), that is, which can be used at *any* time; but they invoke a different frame of communication by interrupting the flow of object-related reactions and switching to communication-related ones.

[10] Compared to other species, humans are not "reprogrammed" through genetic evolution but cultural evolution, which means that they are somewhat similar to von Neumann machines.

That a thing gives options means for a participant to have learnt *conditions* of its use. A participant learns that dealing with a thing allows her only a range of reactions. Thus, when I say *condition*, this is nothing but an abbreviation for *conditioning thing*. No condition can be thought of as detached from its material root. Absolutely crucial is the distinction between weak and strong conditions,[11] which is a gradual distinction, because the strength of conditions can be employed to adjust whether openness or a high probability of controlled events prevails. Weak conditions give a broad range of acceptable responses. They invite the participant to find her own way of using them or what they hint at. (To learn that the weather is going to be bad can make me stay at home, buy an umbrella, or just ignore the news.) Strong conditions clearly imply what can be done with them. Very strong conditions (in mathematics, for instance) enforce a clear distinction between a bad and a good use, between right and wrong, in radical cases even true and false. (To be asked the time only allows few adequate responses.)

Only if society finds a means to create "computable" and yet open behavior can a multifaceted culture evolve. This is because computability warrants a high probability of cultural reproduction, and openness allows for cultural adaptation. Computability requires granulation, that is, the emergence of digital entities which can be easily and safely copied and recombined (words, letters, and numbers, to mention only the most important ones). Without this granulation of probable and expectable structures, complex social and cultural accomplishments could not be achieved. Why does the restriction of options increase social and cultural complexity? A possible reason could be seen with the help of the difference between weak and strong conditions. Weak conditions implement an easy and fast use of a thing even in new situations, that is, immediate adaptation. Strong conditions, however, increase the probability of exact reproduction.

---

[11] Let me mention a difference which led philosophy to separate a signifying and a signified sphere. It is the difference between event-like speech acts and durable things. First of all there is in fact *no* apparent difference between words and things: words are as well in the world as are other things. Words are audible or visible. They have to materialize to exist. The difference, which became so important in semiotic models, lies beneath the received difference between words and things: it is the difference between ephemeral and persistent phenomena. *Ephemeral* phenomena have short life-spans, that is, they materialize for a brief period only (for instance, spoken words). *Persistent* phenomena, however, exist for a longer time and can be expected to be retrieved when the need arises (for instance, printed words). The difference between ephemeral and persistent entities is gradual, of course. Few things are considered eternal; some would even deny that there is anything that eternally exists. Ephemeral things have their span of life, too; it is only because they vanish soon from a human perspective that they are considered ephemeral. Human speech has been considered different from other things because it vanishes quickly; it is the logocentric tradition that Derrida famously analyzed. This tradition tends to ignore the fact that written language persists in time, and that spoken language, too, relies on persistent remnants (which Derrida calls "trace", 2002 [1967], 90). Words that are heard and read appear ephemerally, while the things they relate to are often persistent. Of course, this is far from being universally true or relevant. Printed words and recorded speech persist for a long time, and language often refers to short-lived events, such as explosions or sunsets.

But they also allow certain flexibility because the strictly conditioning entities can fit into complex systems. They are similar to Lego bricks (which are a product of serialized granulation). An exact reproduction is necessary if complex entities are to be built out of existing smaller entities, that is, if *modularization* should be possible. Modularization is the process that spawns many specializations (such as organs in animals or dedicated areas in the brain, modules and objects in coding, departments in organizations, and so on). It takes strong conditions for granted because it relies on the assumption that a higher level of a process can draw on a lower level without asking itself what the lower level does exactly. It leads to a division of tasks and to an abstraction of competence. As one knows from bulky bureaucracy, strong conditions can produce inflexibility, the inability to adapt to new situations. For many fields of human life, weak conditions are a counterbalance. Additionally, division and abstraction are not always functional. In many situations a fast and simple shift of attention, a phatic greeting, or a simple action is all that is needed. All specific information and all strong conditions would bind too much energy without any outcome. "Give me the spice over there" – to point a finger is all that is supposed to accompany the enunciation, and there is no need to specify which spice it is exactly, how it is supposed to be transported, and whom the speaker actually addresses. In most cases this is absolutely sufficient. It is not the default case that a word has a very specific meaning (or reference), but a highly improbable and complex case that requires a long cultural evolution.

Programmability does not mean that all human beings can be straightforwardly "manipulated" by "extern data." Of course, language can create much oppression. This is why totalitarian regimes always reprogram the language oppressed people use. The idea of programmable behavior, however, does not automatically imply a behaviorist view or the assumption that programmability entails coercion, tyranny, or at least a dull and uncreative cultural environment. To delimit potential actions does not necessarily mean to prescribe specific options. To propose a range of behavior need not exclude the possibility of risking an action unthought of before. Nonetheless, exactly this is done under authoritarian regimes. In fact, each time it becomes a challenge again for liberal societies to renegotiate the balance between order and chaos, both being equally necessary for a very adaptive cultural evolution.

Neither "a tree" nor a tree tells by itself what can be explicitly done with either. One has to find out. A usage-based theory of signification refutes the assumption that, as a universally valid rule, generalization applies to communication. In fact, one has to learn a lot of distinct knowledge about the use of words and ordinary things. This knowledge generally differs from participant to participant, and hence it would be futile to search the shared "definition of a word." This is why I believe that communication can be described by algorithms, but that these algorithms have always to be adaptive to new situations and must not store static information about "meaning."

However, generalizations occur, and they do so because of two antagonistic movements. On the one hand, one can try to use a thing (a word) in a new situation because the situation seems comparable or similar to other situations (a child may call any fruit *apple* as long as she does not learn that *apple* is more specific). On the other hand, particular generalizations become reusable patterns of their own; they become grammar or social norms. While the first movement is a natural and necessary consequence of the fuzziness of real phenomena, the second movement could be more human and comprise an inclination for abstractions (which Francis Bacon once stated, see 1990 [1620], I 114). It is this ability to predict the use of uses, this second-order use of things, that enables modularization.

12.3.2 Two Digressive Remarks

Let me make two side remarks. First, it is worth noting that the humanities lack a precise language and do not seem to have a need for it. Terminology often turns into mere jargon. The humanities tend to inflate the use of language and refrain from using diagrams, mathematical expressions, or other devices that refine conditions. So far, this is not a deficit, but their very feature. Their purpose is to find out which actions are or were selectable in a specific situation at a specific time. It would be difficult to limit acceptable responses by defining a strict terminology if the task is to describe the processes defining and resolving conditions. This could be why all important endeavors in the humanities are historical (especially archeological and etymological) and hermeneutic. All three styles of investigation help us trace the conditions given by things and words.

Second, Peirce's pragmaticism seems to be very close to the present proposal.[12] He famously defines pragmaticism by the following recipe, which would clear up what words mean:

> Consider what effects, that might conceivably have practical bearings, we conceive the objects of our conception to have. Then, our conception of those effects is the whole of our conception of the object. (Peirce 1998 [1878], 146.)

The central differences between my semantic and Peirce's pragmaticist approach lie in some emphases that place our explanations in direct opposition: generally, a participant cannot enumerate the effects an object has. She knows about its specific use in a specific situation, and this knowledge need not be explicit or even conscious.[13] Next, signs do not need interpretation, at least no more than ordinary things do. And, as we have seen, one should not oppose them to "their" objects in order to establish a relationship of representation (even though Peirce's

---

[12] I should discuss Wittgenstein's *Philosophical Investigations*, which are apparently highly important for my approach. But since his work requires a lengthy and detailed analysis, I do not fulfill my obligation in the present paper.

[13] Consider what Peirce posits (at least about symbols): "The entire intellectual purport of any symbol consists in the total of all general modes of rational conduct that, conditionally upon all the possible different circumstances and desires, would ensue upon the acceptance of the symbol" (1998 [1905], 282).

concept of interpretation is far from being static). As a final point, a participant can of course learn to enumerate effects and to analyze signs explicitly. But this is a highly developed way of abstract reasoning which, again, need not be targeted towards signs only.

Contrarily to my conviction, Peirce believes that language and reasoning are very much the same: "all thought whatsoever is a sign, and is mostly of the nature of language" (Peirce 1998 [1905], 270).[14] Therefore, he assumes that comprehension is an act very much related to (rational) reasoning. For him, one checks the validity or truth of an utterance by scrutinizing an action. In my view, however, one has to describe all actions human beings undertake in order to understand what *to understand* means. The actions of speaking and listening are not *categorically* different from other ways of acting and perceiving; there is no dualism. This is why, in everyday language, one is said to understand the functioning of a laser printer, a biological cell, or a friend's complaints.

But it is not clear whether Peirce's generalization of the concept of sign does not in fact have much in common with a cognitive or usage-based approach; I only wish to stress that I see more differences than similarities. A cognitive – I would perhaps rather say, *semantic* – approach degrades the very notion of sign to a perpetually heuristic concept.

12.4 Conclusions

To sum up, I propose to drop the distinction signifier/signified and give up the dualist tradition that took the distinction between mental and material processes (the body/soul difference) to be primordial. Instead of sharing these fundamental assumptions, I suggest examining how things are used and, among these things, how one finds words, which are not phenomena of a totally different order. Among all things there are those which are used preferably for mental purposes (i.e. to convey sensual experience) and those which are better suited to social ones; there are those which trigger narrowly defined reactions (strong condition) or permit a rather broad range of uses (weak condition). These distinctions do not simply replace the distinction signifier/signified, but they move our attention to the *specific* social programs taking place in society beyond representation. The idea of meaning is no longer considered a general category to describe "signs," but a sign is nothing but an object that comes with either rather weak or rather strong conditions that depend on learning and training.

The present sketch conciliates the constructivist and the realist view. It is constructivist in that it stresses the importance of conditions that are present even if they may be very weak; in the world there is no thing whose use does not at least

---

[14] When Peirce considers both thought and external entities as signs, he also attempts to undercut the dualist body/soul distinction.

in part depend on what one has learnt to attribute to it. Since a thing consists of its conditions from a participant's perspective, a thing is what the participant constructs. It is realist in that it departs from the existence of real entities that can be "manually" accessed and may teach us what can be done with them.

My sketch yields two simple conclusions. First, every ordinary thing can turn into a sign when it either increases or decreases communicative options, and conversely, every sign can lose its "significance." Second, communication cannot be understood if one looks at language only. The second point seems barely new since sociology and developmental psychology have, for many decades, stressed the importance of extralinguistic factors. Yet, semiotic theory still tends to consider fully developed language as specifically different from other real entities in its capacity to refer to things. My proposal, however, requests a more detailed look and a stronger attention paid to those communicative things which effectively rely on verbal language, that is, social (and abstract) things. Communicative situations in which someone states a fact about a concrete thing could be operated without the use of verbal language; whilst jurisdiction, for example, would be unthinkable. In order to understand verbal language one has to further analyze simple communicative situations where language plays no, or at most a minor, role on the one hand, and socially complex situations where language is indispensable on the other. Both endeavors have been being undertaken by developmental psychology (Tomasello 2000 [1999], 2003a) and by sociology (Luhmann 1999 [1997]). In exchange, a semiotic theory of its own is redundant.

The overall conclusion is that a semiotic theory which seeks to find a general pattern governing the relation between "signs" and "meanings" is entirely beyond reality. Semiotics as a discipline develops ideas about a phenomenon that in fact does not exist. To understand how meaning works is only possible in terms of sociology, archeology, and historical semantics – by examining what people were and are doing and what things they held and hold in their hands.

References

Arnauld, Antoine, and Pierre Nicole. (1683)1964. *Logique ou L'art de penser*. Paris: Despriz. Reprint, Lille: Giard.
Augustine. (427)1837. *S. Aur. Augustini Hipponensis Episcopi Opera Omnia*. Sermones 5.1. Paris: Apud-Gaume Fratres / Bibliopolas.
Austin, John L. (1962)1975. *How to Do Things With Words: The William James Lectures delivered at Harvard University in 1955*. Cambridge, Mass.: Harvard University Press.
Bacon, Francis. (1620)1990. *Neues Organon [New Organon, Novum Organum]*, 2 vols. Hamburg: Meiner.
Bennett, Maxwell R., and Peter M. S. Hacker. 2003. *Philosophical Foundations of Neuroscience*. Malden: Blackwell.
Bhabha, Homi K. (1994)2000. *The Location of Culture*. London: Routledge.
Derrida, Jacques. (1967)2002. *De la grammatologie*. Paris: Minuit.
Descartes, René. (1641)2005. *Meditationes de Prima Philosophia*. Stuttgart: Reclam.

Hölldobler, Bert, and Edward O. Wilson. 2009. *The Superorganism: The Beauty, Elegance, and Strangeness of Insect Societies*. New York: Norton.
Langacker, Ronald W. 2008. *Cognitive Grammar: A Basic Introduction*. New York: Oxford University Press.
Latour, Bruno. 2005. *Reassembling the Social: An Introduction to Actor-Network-Theory*. Oxford: Oxford University Press.
Latour, Bruno. (1991)2006. *Nous n'avons jamais été modernes: Essai d'anthropologie symétrique*. Paris: La Découverte.
Luhmann, Niklas. (1997)1999. *Die Gesellschaft der Gesellschaft*. Frankfurt am Main: Suhrkamp.
Peirce, Charles S. (1878)1998. "How to Make Our Ideas Clear." In *The Essential Writings*, edited by Charles S. Peirce, 137–157. Amherst: Prometheus.
Peirce, Charles S. (1905)1998. "What Pragmatism Is." In *The Essential Writings*, edited by Charles S. Peirce, 262–281. Amherst: Prometheus.
Peterson, Mary A. (2001)2005. "Object Perception." In *Blackwell Handbook of Sensation and Perception*, edited by E. Bruce Goldstein, 168–203. Malden: Blackwell.
Quine, Williard Van Orman. 1960. *Word and Object*. Cambridge, Mass.: MIT Press.
Quintilian. (~80)2001. *The Orator's Education*, 5 vols., translated by Donald A. Russell, Cambridge, Mass.: Harvard University Press.
Rancière, Jacques. (2003)2008. *Le destin des images*. Paris: Fabrique.
Saussure, Ferdinand de. (1916)2006. *Cours de linguistique générale*. Paris: Payot.
Tomasello, Michael. (1999)2000. *The Cultural Origins of Human Cognition*. Cambridge: Harvard University Press.
Tomasello, Michael. 2003a. *Constructing a Language: A Usage-Based Theory of Language Acquisition*. Cambridge: Harvard University Press.
Tomasello, Michael, and Hannes Rakoczy. 2003b. "What Makes Human Cognition Unique? From Individual to Shared to Collective Intentionality." *Mind & Language* 18.2: 121–147.
Towfigh, Emanuel Vahid. 2008. "Komplexität und Normenklarheit – oder: Gesetze sind für Juristen gemacht." *Preprints of the Max Planck Institute for Research on Collective Goods* 22.
Wellbery, David E. 1984. *Lessing's Laocoon: Semiotics and Aesthetics in the Age of Reason*. Cambridge: Cambridge University Press.